THE PARTY'S JUST BEGUN

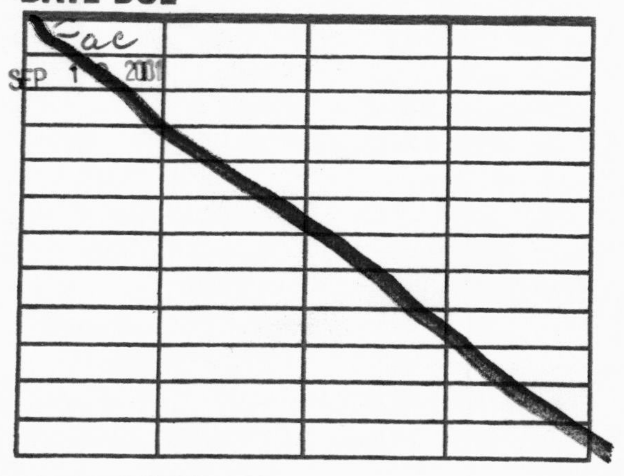

THE PARTY'S JUST BEGUN

• ☆ • ☆ •

Shaping Political Parties for America's Future

• ☆ • ☆ •

LARRY J. SABATO

University of Virginia

Scott, Foresman/Little, Brown College Division

Scott, Foresman and Company

GLENVIEW, ILLINOIS   BOSTON   LONDON

Library of Congress Cataloging-in-Publication Data

Sabato, Larry J.
The party's just begun.

Includes index.
1. Political parties—United States. 2. Voting—United States. I. Title.
JK2261.S22 1987 324.273 87-17141
ISBN 0-673-39746-7

1 2 3 4 5 6 7 8 9 10 - MPC - 93 92 91 90 89 88 87

Printed in the United States of America

• ☆ • ☆ •

Preface

THE "RUN UP" TO WRITING a book is not unlike the "run up" to an election. Timing, planning, and preparation determine a party's or a writer's success or failure. To get a good running start, an author needs plenty of help — and I received it in a thousand forms.

This study could never have been undertaken without the financial support given by the Earhart Foundation, the American Philosophical Society, and my own University of Virginia. I am most appreciative of their continued confidence in me.

At the heart of this study's findings are three public opinion polls taken for me by William R. Hamilton & Staff of Chevy Chase, Maryland (now Hamilton, Frederick & Schneiders of Washington, D.C.) and underwritten by the American Medical Association's political action committee, AMPAC. (See the Introduction for details.) The Hamilton firm and AMPAC share my concern for the health and well-being of the American political party system, and they allowed me complete freedom to ask anything and everything I wished to random samples of adult Americans. Their patience, professional assistance, and generosity were absolutely essential to my work, and I am deeply grateful to Peter Lauer, executive director of AMPAC, and William R. Hamilton, Keith Frederick, and Barbara Burbridge of the Hamilton organization.

At home in my own office were individuals who moved mountains for this project. My chief student assistant, Rebecca Hartley, is surely one of the best organized, most resourceful, and ever dependable human beings on the face of the earth. I am in her debt. My typists, Susan Carter and Diane Kyser, became adept at translating what passes for handwriting, and their energy and skill are remarkable. Also due the usual thanks for their valued support, counsel, and suggestions are colleagues and mentors Clifton McCleskey, H. G. Nicholas, and Mildred and Weldon Cooper. I also wish to acknowledge the help of my former departmental chairman, Robert H. Evans, and the director of the University's Miller Center, Kenneth W. Thompson, in securing university financial support, as well as the many very useful suggestions offered me by Professor John Bibby of The University of Wisconsin, Milwaukee; Professor Eric L. Davis of Middlebury College; Jeremy Gaunt, editor of *Campaign Practices Reports*; Professor Barbara Salmore of Drew University; my colleagues James Ceaser, Charles O. Jones, and Steven Finkel; and two other anonymous reviewers. The research assistance provided by University of Virginia students Steven Van Beek, Timothy Lidiak, Daniel Palazzolo, Russell Riley, Sarah Ryder, and Michael Refolo, the latter my able indexer and proofreader, was also essential to the completion of this project.

Last but hardly least in my list of credits are my editor, John S. Covell, whose understanding and careful work have contributed much to this volume; and Kathryn S. Daniel, who efficiently supervised the production of the project.

Surrounded by such competent people, and with no obvious scapegoats available, I must accept the customary responsibility for the errors that remain.

Larry J. Sabato
Charlottesville, Virginia

• ☆ • ☆ •

Contents

Tables and Figures

TABLES

FIGURES

THE PARTY'S JUST BEGUN

• ☆ • ☆ •

Introduction

IN A MUCH-PUBLICIZED BOOK more than a decade ago, noted political journalist David S. Broder declared that "The Party's Over," that political parties in the United States were on the decline, probably permanently, and that candidates and campaigns had become independent and even antiparty.[1] In the late 1980s it is becoming increasingly clear that, instead of facing oblivion, the two major political parties in America are stronger organizationally (at least at the national level) than at any other period in modern times. They provide considerable sums of money and an impressive range of services to their candidates, and they are becoming more influential in the electoral process with each passing year. Yet even so, the real crisis of the party decline correctly described by Broder remains unmet: how to regenerate partisan loyalty among a voting public that has become less responsive to partisan appeals. The underlying premise of this book is that, with the proper resolve and appropriate changes in law and practice, partisan loyalty *can* be regenerated and the parties *can* be significantly refurbished. The overriding purpose of this book is to propose realistic ways to accomplish this eminently desirable goal. I freely admit that I have crossed the line between analysis and advocacy in order that we may one day be able to say, "The Party's Just Begun."

The fundamental irony of the new American political constellation is simply this: voters are becoming increasingly independent of party identification at the same time as parties have become considerably enhanced organizationally. This independence, even disaffection, is hardly inconsequential, since it limits the parties' capacity to carry out many of their traditional functions and concentrates more power in the hands of party elites, especially those who control the technological resources. Without deeply rooted popular support, the parties can become superb service agencies for candidates, but cannot perform some of their critical functions in society nor assume a central role in our country's political life.

It is undeniable that few average citizens appear to care deeply about the political parties. Even among many relatively strong party identifiers, there is no love affair with their parties; at best, it is often a marriage of convenience. Yet a substantial majority of "political elites" — activists, ideologues, officeholders, opinion molders — do care, because they recognize the importance of the parties and appreciate the stability and order these organizations bring to American politics. More to the point of my undertaking, a large majority of mainstream political scientists in the field strongly support the party system and have become greatly concerned by signs of its decay.[2]

So there is a yawning gap between the perspective of those who study or practice politics and the view of the electorate at large. Why does that gap exist, and more importantly, what can be done to close it? If we believe that a healthy party system is necessary to a vital democracy — and the author is squarely in this camp and will use the first chapter to marshal arguments in support of this thesis — how can we reverse whatever party decline has taken place? In what ways might it be possible to tighten or reattach an individual's partisan ties when they have become loosened or severed? How can the parties as organizations realistically improve their capacities and play a more central role in the lives of everyday citizens?

These are the questions I hope to answer in this volume since I firmly believe that erosion of party loyalty and organization has weakened American democracy — and that regeneration is essential to meeting the political and governmental challenges that lie ahead. As E. E. Schattschneider proclaimed more than four decades ago, ". . . modern democracy is unthinkable save in terms of the parties. As a matter of fact, the condition of parties is the best possible evidence of the nature of any regime."[3] By Schattschneider's yardstick, the health of the American political system is not as robust as we would wish it to be.

Perhaps because so much public skepticism and cynicism about the political parties remain, I begin by making the case for parties in Chapter One. It is a defense as old as modern political science, but the collective failure of political scientists to convince a doubting electorate suggests that a retelling could do little harm and perhaps some good. What follows is a brief review of the history and evolution of the political parties in the United States, and a discussion of the "party in government" — the influence and operation of the parties in Congress, the presidency, the judiciary, and the states. Then the focus shifts to the modern transformation of party organization as a result of the new campaign technologies, revised campaign finance rules, and the needs of candidates. Next, the "party in the electorate" — the voters' ties to the parties — receives close scrutiny. The decline of partisan allegiance is documented, and the trends of realignment and dealignment are explained and analyzed. Finally, and perhaps most importantly, a detailed prescription for party revival that combines traditional and novel approaches is proposed in the two concluding chapters.

Throughout the book I draw data from three random-sample, national public opinion polls taken for this study by William R. Hamilton and Staff (now Hamilton, Frederick & Schneiders).[4] Two of the surveys, all of which were taken during 1986, had relatively large samples so that the views of key population subgroups could be accurately presented. Respondents were probed extensively about their party identifications, voting habits, and partisan activities; in all, 291 items were asked in the three surveys combined. As Chapters 6 and 7 will discuss, the results from these representative samplings of the electorate point the way toward purposeful reform and revival of the American party system.

Notes

1. David S. Broder, *The Party's Over: The Failure of Politics in America* (New York: Harper & Row, 1971).
2. There are some notable exceptions, of course, including M. Ostrogorski, Robert Dahl, and Theodore Lowi. See Ostrogorski, *Democracy and the Organization of Political Parties,* Vol. II (New York: Anchor, 1964); Robert Dahl, "On Removing Certain Impediments to Democracy in the United States" in Robert Horwitz, ed., *The Moral Foundations of the American Republic* (2nd ed.) (Charlottesville, Va.: The University Press of Virginia, 1982), 254; and Theodore Lowi, "Toward a More Responsible Three-Party System," *PS* 16 (Fall 1983): 705. Contrast their views, how-

ever, to the strongly pro-party perspectives of more representative political scientists such as David Adamany, James Ceaser, William Crotty, Samuel Eldersveld, Leon Epstein, Joel Fleishman, Malcolm Jewell, Clifton McCleskey, Nelson Polsby, Gerald Pomper, David Price, Austin Ranney, Frank Sorauf, and Martin Wattenberg, just to name a few, whose works are cited throughout this volume. As political theorist Carl J. Friedrich once wrote, "Parties are, it is now generally agreed, indispensable features of democracy." [From *Constitutional Government and Democracy* (4th ed.) (Waltham, Mass.: Blaisdell, 1968), 430.] Moreover, to judge from the bulk of published works in the last several decades, most American political scientists in the parties' subfield are supporters of two-party, rather than multiparty, competition.

3. E. E. Schattschneider, *Party Government* (New York: Rinehart, 1942), 1.
4. See Appendix, Public Opinion Survey Data.

CHAPTER ONE

• ☆ • ☆ •

The Case for Parties

THERE ARE NO MORE UNAPPRECIATED INSTITUTIONS in America than the two major political parties. Often maligned by citizens and politicians alike as the repositories of corrupt bosses and smoke-filled rooms, the parties nonetheless perform essential electoral functions for our society. Not only do they operate (in part) the machinery for nomination to most public offices, but the two parties serve as vital, umbrellalike, consensus-forming institutions that help counteract the powerful centrifugal forces in a country teeming with hundreds of racial, economic, social, religious, and political groups. The parties are often accused of dividing us; on the contrary, they assist in uniting us as few other institutions do. Just as important, they permit leaders to be successful by marshaling citizens and legislators around a common standard that elected executives can use to create and implement a public agenda.

The grand partnership of the Democratic and Republican parties has endured for thirty-two presidential elections, much longer than almost all the regimes around the world that existed when the association began. Yet the parties command precious little respect in some quarters. Many members of the press, especially those in television, frequently deride the parties and characterize them as archaic, undemocratic institutions. The judiciary has sometimes treated them as political outcasts and legal stepchildren. Presidents have frequently ignored them, choosing to run their election campaigns wholly apart from the party organization. Many congressional and gubernatorial contenders have run *against* the party, presenting themselves as worthy of public office precisely because they lacked party endorsement or experience. But the greatest scorn for parties — and the residual source of all the other indignities borne by the parties — has been expressed by the American electorate. Politics in general is held in low regard by the voters, and party politics lower still.[1] As Table 1.1 suggests, this disdain may even affect citizens' perceptions of elections. Voters in the 1986 United States Senate races rated a candidate's partisan affiliation as the least important factor of ten we included in a postelection survey. Just 34 percent said the candidate's party was very or fairly important in making their voting choice, compared to the 89 percent who

TABLE 1.1 Reasons for 1986 United States Senate Vote

QUESTION: "Thinking again about the U.S. Senate race in your state — I'd like to read you a list of reasons why some people have told us they chose particular candidates. For each, tell me how important each one was to you personally in making your choice for Senate. Here's the first one . . . was that a very important reason, fairly important, only slightly important, or not important at all in your choice?"

	PERCENT[a]	
RESPONSES[b]	VERY OR FAIRLY IMPORTANT	ONLY SLIGHTLY OR NOT IMPORTANT
How well my candidate had performed his job in the past.	89	8
To try to get something done about the weak U.S. economy.	83	14
To try to get something done about the poor farm economy.	77	22
The candidates' positions on President Reagan's Strategic Defense Initiative — the SDI.	64	28
The candidates' positions on trade legislation — protectionism vs. free trade.	57	38
Because the economy in my particular area is in bad shape and we needed some changes.	56	41

TABLE 1.1 *(continued)*

	PERCENT[a]	
RESPONSES[b]	VERY OR FAIRLY IMPORTANT	ONLY SLIGHTLY OR NOT IMPORTANT
I liked the candidate's style and personality.	49	49
Because during the campaign I heard or saw some negative things that I did not like about a candidate.	39	58
The need to give President Reagan the Republican majority he wants in the Senate.	38	59
Mainly because the candidate was of my political party.[c]	34	63

SOURCE: Poll 3 (see Appendix). These questions were only asked of the 797 respondents who lived in states with 1986 Senate races and who claimed to have voted.

[a]Totals do not add to 100 percent since "don't know" responses are not listed in table.

[b]Responses are listed in descending order of importance, as ranked by respondents. During the actual survey, the responses were rotated by the interviewers.

[c]It is possible that the qualifier "mainly" reduced the number of respondents willing to credit party affiliation as a reason for their vote choice. Yet as subsequent chapters will demonstrate, this response is part of a pattern: even though partisan affiliation is still an important voting cue (as measured objectively by political scientists), many citizens are unwilling to acknowledge party's influence upon them, preferring the more socially acceptable "independent" stance.

claimed the candidate's past job performance was vital to their decision, or the 64 percent who said the candidate's position on the Strategic Defense Initiative (SDI) influenced their vote. Yet political scientists have found repeatedly that an individual's party identification is perhaps the most crucial voting determinant of all.[2] Consider, too, that it is highly doubtful 89 percent of this representative sample had any real idea how their candidate had performed in the past, or that 64 percent even knew the candidates' positions on SDI, much less cared as greatly as they reported. The average voter's knowledge of political races is abysmally sparse. In this same poll, taken almost immediately after the 1986 Senate elections, 60 percent could not even *name* the two Senate candidates from their state — the same candidates whose records and positions on SDI so seemingly interested the respondents.[3]

Party as a Voting and Issue Cue

Whether most voters appreciate it or not, their partisan identification acts as an invaluable filter for information, a perceptual screen that affects how they digest the political news that manages to reach them. The party filter often is much more effective and encompassing than is realized, since it colors a wide range of voters' views on public issues and ideas. For instance, Table 1.2 presents the opinions of party identifiers on several topics. One would certainly expect a president's job approval rating to be a function of a citizen's party affiliation, and indeed it is: 93 percent of the Republicans gave President Reagan high marks in June 1986 while only 45 percent of the Democrats did so. But the party perceptual screen extends well beyond the evaluation of partisan officeholders to citizens' general outlooks on the past and future, and the degree of optimism or pessimism they express. Democrats, then, see the country moving on the wrong track by a decided margin, and they are harsh in their judgment of past economic performance and gloomy about future trends. By contrast, Republicans in the Reagan years are the picture of buoyancy: bullish on the economy and delighted about the country's direction. From vague, generalized feelings to specific views on controversial issues there is no better or more consistent indicator — and even predictor — of survey results than partisan affiliation.

Thus, party affiliation provides a useful cue for voters, particularly the least informed and interested, who can use party as a shortcut or substitute for interpreting issues and events they may little comprehend. But even better educated and more involved voters find party identification an assist. After all, no one has the time to study every issue carefully or to become fully knowledgeable about every candidate seeking public office.

Mobilizing Support and Aggregating Power

The effect of the party cue is enormously helpful to elected leaders. They can count on disproportionate support among their partisans in times of trouble, and in close judgment calls they have a home court advantage. The party perceptual screen even draws together ideologically diverse elements to the benefit of leaders; both conservatives and liberals within each party adjust their perceptions so that they see their chosen party as being in basic agreement with their beliefs (even if it's not true).[4] Thus the parties aid officeholders by giving them maneuvering room and by mobilizing support for their policies. Because there are only two major parties, pragmatic citizens who are interested in politics or public policy are mainly attracted to one or the other standard, creating natural majorities or near-majorities for party officeholders to command. The party creates a community of interest that bonds disparate groups together over time — eliminating the necessity of creating a coalition anew for every campaign or every issue. Imagine the chaos and mad scrambles for public support that would constantly ensue without the continuity provided by the parties.

Besides mobilizing Americans on a permanent basis, then, the parties convert the cacophony of hundreds of identifiable social and economic groups into a two-part (semi)harmony that is much more comprehensible, if not always on key and pleasing to the ears. The simplicity of two-party politics may be deceptive given the enormous variety in public policy choices, but a sensible system of representation in the American context might well be impossible without it. And those who would suffer most from its absence would not be the few who are individually or organizationally powerful — their voices would be heard under almost any system. As Walter Dean Burnham has pointed out, the losers would be the many individually powerless for whom the parties are the only effective devices yet created that can generate countervailing collective power on their behalf.[5]

A Force for Stability

This last argument may have the faint odor of revolution to it, but nothing could be further from the truth. As mechanisms for organizing and containing political change, the parties are a potent force for stability. They represent continuity in the wake of changing issues and personalities, anchoring the electorate as the storms that are churned by new political people and policies swirl around. Because of its unyielding, pragmatic desire to *win* elections (not just contest them), each party in a sense acts to moderate public opinion.

TABLE 1.2 Party Identification as an Interpretive Filter

QUESTIONS		PERCENT OF[a]		
		DEMOCRATS (N = 452)	INDEPENDENTS (N = 531)	REPUBLICANS (N = 386)
Reagan job approval[b]				
"Do you approve or disapprove of the way Ronald Reagan is handling his job as president?"				
	Approve	45	69	93
	Disapprove	47	25	4
Country's direction				
"Do you feel things in this country are generally going in the right direction or do you feel things have gotten pretty seriously off on the wrong track?"				
	Right direction	37	57	76
	Wrong track	55	34	17

Economy today				
"Compared to a year ago, do you think the national economy has gotten better, gotten worse, or stayed about the same?"				
	Better	23	39	49
	Worse	31	21	10
	Same	45	38	39
Economy next year				
"Looking ahead, do you think the economy of the United States will be better, about the same, or worse a year from today?"				
	Better	26	37	45
	Worse	34	23	10
	Same	34	32	37

SOURCE: Poll 1 (see Appendix).

[a]Totals do not add to 100 percent since "don't know" responses are not listed in table.

[b]This question was asked in June 1986, well before the Iran–contra scandal took its toll on Reagan's popularity. Even afterwards, however, a similar differential between partisans existed in Reagan's job approval ratings, to judge from public polls taken by the Gallup organization and CBS News/*The New York Times*, among others.

The party tames its own extreme elements by pulling them toward an ideological center in order to attract a majority of votes on election day. This is true even when relatively radical candidates win party nominations. The general election campaigns of Barry Goldwater in 1964 and George McGovern in 1972 stressed primarily mainstream issues and concerns, even though this may not coincide with our memories of them since they were never able to escape from torrid prenomination records and rhetoric. Yet even most Goldwater diehards in the GOP and passionate McGovernites among the Democrats understood the need for and approved the candidate's move to the moderate center. The election process itself, acting through the medium of the parties, "mainstreamed" many of the malcontents and firebrands.

This stabilizing process occurs with groups as well as individuals. The pragmatic nature of each American party sends it scurrying to attract each new politically active organization or element in the population. The newly enfranchised 18–21 year olds were fought over and assiduously courted in the early 1970s, with the Democrats winning the bulk of the new adherents thanks to their developing opposition to the Vietnam war.[6] Later in the same decade, fundamentalist Christians awakened politically. While first drawn to Democrat Jimmy Carter's "born again" personality, a substantial majority of the white evangelicals succumbed to Republican Ronald Reagan's charms in 1980 and 1984, partly on the basis of his party's conservative stands on defense and "family issues" (abortion, the Equal Rights Amendment, and the like).[7]

Another aspect of the stability the parties provide can be found in the nature of the coalitions they forge. There are inherent contradictions in these coalitions that, oddly enough, strengthen the nation even as they strain party unity. The Democratic New Deal majority, for example, included many blacks and most Southern whites — contradictory elements nonetheless joined in common political purpose. This party union of the two groups, as limited a context as it may have been, surely provided a framework for acceptance and reconciliation in the civil rights era. Nowhere can this be more clearly seen than in the South, where most state Democratic parties remained predominant after the mid-1960s by building on the ingrained Democratic voting habits of both whites and blacks to create new, moderate, generally integrated societies. A strikingly different modern coalition on the Republican side also illustrates the point. The anger and alienation of white fundamentalist Christians may be diffused somewhat by their involvement in GOP organizational and policy councils. While they frequently battle the establishment "Main Street" faction as well as the large contingent of libertarian young people who inhabit the Republican tent, the evangelicals also are forced to work *with* the others to accomplish their goals. Given the "family" orientation of fundamentalists, it may not be stretching reality too much to claim that political work within the Republican party integrates out-of-the-mainstream Christians into the nation's household, perhaps encouraging more tolerance and respect for the beliefs and traditions of their nonfundamentalist "family members" and party allies.

Unity, Linkage, Accountability

Parties provide the glue to hold together the disparate parts of the fragmented American governmental and political apparatus. The Founding Fathers designed a system that divides and subdivides power, making it possible to preserve individual liberty but difficult to coordinate and produce timely action. Parties help to compensate for this drawback by linking all the institutions and loci of power one to another. While rivalry between the executive and legislative branches of American government is inevitable, the partisan affiliations of the leaders of each branch constitute a common basis for cooperation, as any president and his fellow party members in Congress usually demonstrate daily. Even within each branch, there is intended fragmentation, and party once again helps to narrow the differences between the House of Representatives and the Senate, or between the president and his chiefs in the executive bureaucracy. Similarly, the federalist division of national, state, and local governments, while always an invitation to conflict, is made more workable and easily coordinated by the intersecting party relationships that exist among officeholders at all office levels. Party affiliation, in other words, is a sanctioned and universally recognized basis for mediation and negotiation laterally among the branches and vertically among the layers.

The party's linkage function does not end there, of course. Party identification and organization is a natural connector and vehicle for communication between the voter and the candidate as well as between the voter and the officeholder. The party connection is one means to ensure or increase accountability in election campaigns and in government. Candidates on the campaign trail and elected party leaders in office are required from time to time to account for their performance at party-sponsored forums and in party nominating primaries and conventions.

Political parties, too, can take some credit for unifying the nation by dampening sectionalism. Since parties must form national majorities to win the presidency, one region is guaranteed permanent minority status unless ties are established with other areas. The party label and philosophy is the bridge enabling regions to join forces, and in the process a national interest is created and served rather than a merely sectional one.

The Electioneering Function

The election, proclaimed H. G. Wells, is "democracy's ceremonial, its feast, its great function," and the political parties assist this ceremonial in essential ways. First, the parties funnel talented (and, granted, some not so able) individuals into politics and government. Hundreds of candidates are recruited each year by the two parties, and many of them are party-trained and briefed for their responsibilities on the hustings. Furthermore, many of their staff members — the ones who manage the campaigns and go on to serve in key governmental positions once the election is over — are also brought into politics by way of party involvement. Both parties are now providing "training schools" in campaign skills for staffers as well as candidates. Perhaps most importantly, the parties are directly contributing to their nominees' elections more than ever before in the modern era. As Chapter Three will discuss, the parties have become major providers of money and campaign services at all levels of politics.

Elections can only have meaning in a democracy if they are competitive, substantive, focused, and comprehensible to the average voter. These criteria probably could not be met in America without the parties. Even in the South, traditionally the least competitive American region, the parties today regularly produce reasonably vigorous contests at the state (and increasingly, the local) level. The rivalry between the parties promotes the competition necessary for the system's health even in basically homogeneous communities. Through national platforms and advertising campaigns, the parties assist in framing and defining the issues. Because they are a mechanism for accountability, they force their candidates to pay some attention to central party ideas and values. The simplicity of the labels themselves, and the voting cues they provide, keep elections somewhat understandable for the least involved citizens. In fact, the parties' duopoly in American politics assures simplicity by providing only two leading candidates for each office.

Policy Formulation and Promotion

Senator Huey Long of Louisiana, the premiere populist demagogue of this century, was usually able to capture the flavor of the average man's views about politics. Considering an Independent bid for president before his assassination in 1935, Long liked to compare the Democratic and Republican parties to the two patent medicines offered by a traveling salesman. Asked the difference between them, the salesman explained that the "High Populorum" tonic was made from the bark of the tree taken from the top down, while "Low Populorum" tonic was made from bark stripped from the root up. The analogous moral, according to Long, was this: "The only difference I've found in Congress between the Republican and Democratic leadership is that one of 'em is skinning us from the ankle up and the other from the ear down!"[8]

Long would certainly have insisted that his fable applied to the national party platforms, the most visible instrument by which parties formulate, convey, and promote public policy. Most citizens in our own era undoubtedly still believe that party platforms are relatively undifferentiated, a mixture of pablum and pussyfooting (as a more modern demagogue, George Wallace, might have phrased it in one of his presidential campaigns). Yet examine for a moment some excerpts from the 1984 Democratic and Republican national platforms, presented in Table 1.3. On a host of foreign and domestic issues, the two parties could not have taken more divergent substantive positions — and there is nothing mushy or tepid about the rhetoric employed, either.

The 1984 platforms were not exceptional in this regard. Gerald Pomper's study of party platforms from 1944 through 1976 demonstrated that each party's pledges were consistently and significantly different, a function in part of the varied groups in their coalitions.[9] Interestingly, some 69 percent of the specific platform positions were taken by one party but not the other. Such was also the case in 1984, when each side dwelt on some subjects that the other mostly or totally ignored. For Democrats these topics included pol-

TABLE 1.3 Comparison of the 1984 Democratic and Republican National Platforms on Selected Issues

DOMESTIC POLICY	
DEMOCRATIC	REPUBLICAN
Role of Government	
". . . the Reagan Administration has virtually wished away the role of government. When it comes to the economy, its view is that the government that governs best is one that governs not at all."	"By centralizing responsibility for social programs in Washington, liberal experimenters destroyed the sense of community that sustains local institutions. In many cases, they literally broke up neighborhoods and devastated rural communities. . . . We are the party of limited government."
Religion	
"The current Administration has consistently sought to reverse in the courts or overrule by constitutional amendment a long line of Supreme Court decisions that preserve our historic commitment to religious tolerance and church/state separation. The Democratic Party affirms its support of the principles of religious liberty, religious tolerance and church/state separation and of the Supreme Court decisions forbidding violation of these principles. We pledge to resist all efforts to weaken those decisions."	"We have enacted legislation to guarantee equal access to school facilities by student religious groups. Mindful of our religious diversity, we reaffirm our commitment to the freedoms of religion and speech guaranteed by the Constitution of the United States and firmly support the rights of students to openly practice the same, including the right to engage in voluntary prayer in schools."
Employment	
". . . the Democratic Party pledges a commitment to full employment. We believe the federal government must develop a major, comprehensive national jobs skills development policy targeted on the	"There are still federal statutes that keep Americans out of the work force. Arbitrary minimum wage rates, for example, have eliminated hundreds of thousands of jobs and with them, the opportunity for young

TABLE 1.3 *(continued)*

DOMESTIC POLICY	
DEMOCRATIC	REPUBLICAN
chronically unemployed and underemployed. We must launch special training programs for women who receive public assistance. We need to increase government procurement opportunities for small and minority firms . . ."	people to get productive skills, good work habits, and a weekly paycheck. We encourage the adoption of a youth opportunity wage to encourage employers to hire and train inexperienced workers."
Women's Rights	
"A top priority of a Democratic Administration will be ratification of the unamended Equal Rights Amendment."	"Our record of economic recovery and growth is an additional important accomplishment for women. It provides a stark contrast to the Carter–Mondale legacy to women: a shrinking economy, limited job opportunities and a declining standard of living."
Abortion	
"The Democratic Party recognizes reproductive freedom as a fundamental human right. We therefore oppose government interference in the reproductive decisions of Americans, especially government interference which denies poor Americans their right to privacy by funding or advocating one or a limited number of reproductive choices only."	"The unborn child has a fundamental right to life which cannot be infringed. We therefore reaffirm our support for a human life amendment to the Constitution, and we endorse legislation to make clear that the Fourteenth Amendment's protections apply to unborn children. We oppose the use of public revenues for abortion and will eliminate funding for organizations which advocate or support abortion."
Gun Control	
"We support tough restraints on the manufacture, transportation, and sale of snub-nosed handguns, which have no legitimate sporting use and are used in a	"Republicans will continue to defend the constitutional right to keep and bear arms . . . . Law-abiding citizens exercising their constitutional rights must not

(continued)

TABLE 1.3 *(continued)*

DOMESTIC POLICY	
DEMOCRATIC	REPUBLICAN
high proportion of violent crimes."	be blamed for crime. Republicans will continue to seek repeal of legislation that restrains innocent citizens more than violent criminals."

FOREIGN POLICY	
DEMOCRATIC	REPUBLICAN
Soviets and Communism	
"While not underestimating the Soviet threat, we can no longer afford simplistically to blame all of our troubles on a single 'focus of evil,' for the sources of international change run even deeper than the sources of superpower competition . . . we also recognize that the Soviets share a mutual interest in survival. They, too, have no defense against a nuclear war. Our security and their security can only be strengthened by negotiation and cooperation."	"We hold a sober view of the Soviet Union. Its globalist ideology and its leadership obsessed with military power make it a threat to freedom and peace on every continent. The Carter–Mondale illusion that the Soviet leaders share our ideals and aspirations is not only false but a profound danger to world peace."
Central America	
"We must terminate our support for the contras and other paramilitary groups fighting in Nicaragua. We must halt those U.S. military exercises in the region which are being conducted for no other real purpose than to intimidate or provoke the Nicaraguan government or which may be used as a pretext for deeper U.S. military involvement in the area."	"We support continued assistance to the democratic freedom fighters in Nicaragua. Nicaragua cannot be allowed to remain a communist sanctuary, exporting terror and arms throughout the region."

TABLE 1.3 *(continued)*

FOREIGN POLICY	
DEMOCRATIC	REPUBLICAN
Strategic Defense Initiative ("Star Wars")	
"His [Reagan's] Star Wars proposal would create a vulnerable and provocative 'shield' that would lull our nation into a false sense of security . . . this trillion-dollar program would provoke a dangerous offensive and defensive arms race."	"President Reagan has launched a bold new Strategic Defensive Initiative to defend against nuclear attack. We enthusiastically support the development of non-nuclear, space-based systems to protect the United States by destroying incoming missiles."

SOURCE: Official platforms of the 1984 Democratic and Republican national conventions.

icy on developing countries and civil rights for blacks, women, and gays. The Republican platform, by contrast, was more interested in judicial excesses, private property rights, and antipornography concerns.

Granted, then, that party platforms are quite distinctive. Does this elaborate party exercise in policy formulation mean anything? One could argue that the platform is valuable, if only as a clear presentation of a party's basic philosophy and a forum for activist opinion and public education. But platforms have much more impact than that. Cynics will be amazed to discover that about two-thirds of the promises in the victorious party's presidential platform have been completely or mostly implemented; even more astounding, one-half or more of the pledges of the *losing* party find their way into public policy (with the success rate depending on whether the party controls one, both, or neither house of Congress).[10] The party platform also has great influence on a new administration's legislative program and the president's State of the Union address. And while party affiliation is normally the single most important determinant of voting in Congress and in state legislatures,[11] the party–vote relationship is even stronger when party platform issues come up on the floor of Congress.[12] As Gerald Pomper concludes: "We should therefore take platforms seriously — because politicians appear to take them seriously."[13]

Promotion of Civic Virtue and Patriotism

In devising policy and platforms on the public stage, the parties assist in informing and educating the citizenry about vital issues. But the parties' promotion of civic virtue goes far beyond this. Because identification with a party is at the core of most Americans' political lives, the prism through which they see the world, many voters accept and adopt the parties' values and view of responsible citizenship. These values include involvement and participation; work for the "public good" in the "national interest" (as conceived in partisan terms, naturally); and patriotism and respect for American society's fundamental institutions and processes. The parties teach people to accept these values even if, as individual citizens, they fail to live up to them. For example, parties honor the act of voting as the irreducible minimum responsibility of a good citizen. Most citizens do not vote regularly, but because of political socialization by the parties, their families, and their schools, they know they *should* vote. Perhaps that is why, in each of our 1986 postelection surveys, 78 percent reported they had cast a ballot days earlier in November, when in fact a paltry 37 percent had actually gone to the polls![14]

At least people believe in voting in theory if not in practice. Party identification can also encourage belief and confidence in a society's institutions. Seymour Martin Lipset and William Schneider have found that Democratic and Republican identifiers have the highest confidence in American institutions while self-described Independents have the lowest, leading to their conclusion that "general confidence seems to be associated with partisanship *per se.*"[15]

A World Without Parties

If these are the roles parties play in American life, what would that life be like without a strong two-party system? Surely, even the parties' severest critics would agree that our politics will be the poorer for any further weakening of the party system. We have only to look at who and what gains as parties decline.

- *Special Interest Groups and PACs Gain.* Their money, labels, and organizational power can serve as a substitute for the parties' own. Yet instead of fealty to the national interest or a broad coalitional party platform, the candidates' loyalties would be pledged to narrow, special interest agendas instead. "Pressure groups may destroy party government but they cannot create a substitute for it," observed E. E. Schattschneider.[16]

- *Wealthy and Celebrity Candidates Gain.* Their financial resources or fame can provide name identification to replace party affiliation as a voting cue. Already at least a third of the United States Senate seats are filled by millionaires, and the number of inexperienced but successful candidates drawn from the entertainment and sports worlds seems to grow each year.
- *Incumbents Gain.* The value of incumbency increases where party labels are absent or less important, since the free exposure incumbents receive raises their name identification level. There would also be extra value for candidates endorsed by incumbents or those who run on slates with incumbents.
- *The News Media, Particularly Television News, Gains.* Party affiliation is one of the most powerful checks on the news media, not only because the voting cue of the party label is in itself a countervailing force but also because the "perceptual screen" erected by party identification filters media commentary. (People tend to hear, see, and remember the news items that reinforce their party attitudes and biases.)[17]
- *Political Consultants Gain.* The independent entrepreneurs of new campaign technologies (such as polling, television advertising, and direct mail) secure more influence in any system of party decline. Already they have become (along with some large PACs) the main institutional rivals of the parties, luring candidates away from their party moorings and using the campaign technologies to supplant parties as the intermediary between candidates and the voters.[18]

Many thoughtful citizens are deeply troubled by these prospects. Most Americans are concerned about the growth in single-issue politics and special interest financing of political campaigns,[19] and most want public office available to able citizens of modest means and those who are respected for knowledge more than fame. Few average voters, or anyone else, favor empowering the news media still further, and with good reason. The news industry's influence is already overweening and government conducted through the media inherently dangerous without the unifying and stabilizing influence of party identification. Moreover, is there anyone in or around politics who would not cringe at the assertion made by prominent Democratic political consultant Robert Squier, "The television set has become the political party of the future"?[20] The personality-cult politics encouraged by television is abhorrent; it is unaccountable, aloof from average voters, and prone to stylistic gimmickry. This disturbing development has been lovingly patterned by the very consultants who hail the medium of television and advance their interests at the parties' expense. The consultants' main alliance, of course, is with incumbent officeholders whose power they help preserve and who also electorally benefit in some ways from party woes. With 80 to 90 percent of incumbent officeholders at all levels regularly reelected, the last trend we ought to encourage is any weakening of party. Vigorous parties help to produce competition which, to judge from the ridiculously high incumbent reelection rates, our politics desperately needs.

There are many other unfortunate and debilitating side effects to party decline. Without the linkage provided by political parties, the Federalist division and the separation of powers in the American system leads to gridlock among the competing branches and layers of government. As Clifton McCleskey writes: "Dividing political power to prevent its abuse is the heart of constitutionalism, but it is as well an invitation to immobilism, endangering the capacity of government to act at all unless some bridging mechanism(s) can be found."[21] Only the political parties, says McCleskey, are "capable of generating political power from the people and transmitting it to public officials, so as to overcome the fragmentation within the government." The disturbingly frequent inability of our government to deal with seemingly intractable problems from massive budget deficits to the balance of trade may be due to a mismanaged presidency or an irresponsible Congress — but the ultimate cause can be found in what McCleskey believes is the inability of weakened political parties "to generate sufficient political power to turn the constitutional mill."[22]

With atrophied parties, public officials have more difficulty developing popular support for their programs, and they have to expend more energy to do it. The most vital connection they have to voters and to other officeholders is devalued. Compromise becomes more elusive, both in government and among political groups in elections. Consensus is forged less easily, and effective action to combat whatever problems are plaguing society cannot be taken. If serious inadequacies persist for too long, dissatisfaction and instability would inevitably grow, perhaps producing the volatility and divisive fragmentation of a multiparty system that features transient, emotional issues and colorful personalities but little hope of competent, successful government.

Citizens lose mightily under such conditions, and in fact suffer whenever parties are incapacitated to any great degree, since they cannot use the parties as a tool to influence officeholders. Accountability without parties is impossible in a system as multifaceted as America's. After all, under the separation of powers arrangement, no one — not even the president — can individually be held responsible for fixing a major problem because no one alone has the power to do so. Collective responsibility by means of a common party label is the only way for voters to ensure that officials are held accountable for the performance of the government.

Any diminution of party strength is also likely to lead to a further decline in voter turnout, something the United States can hardly afford since it already has one of the lowest voter participation rates in the democratic world. The parties currently provide the organizational stimulus for the volunteer involvement of millions. Additionally, their get-out-the-vote efforts on election day increase turnout by at least several percent in most cases,[23] amounting to several million extra voters in national contests. Without the parties' work, many fewer citizens would cast a ballot and take an interest in politics. Those who did would be more easily swept up by the political tides of the moment, and a necessary element of stability would be removed from the electoral system.

Already, as party ties weaken, increasing volatility can be observed in the electorate. Voters are making their voting choices later and later in the campaign season. Whereas in elections in the 1950s a majority of the voters had already chosen their candidates *before* the general election began, by the 1980s a large majority was delaying making a decision until September or later. In at least two recent elections (1980 and 1986), 9 percent of the voters waited until election day itself to make a choice.[24] At times, these later deciders vote heavily in one direction, depending on last-minute events and the final twists of a campaign.[25] It can be dangerous when important elections hinge on one or two developments in a campaign's waning hours; the vote should be based on a broad evaluation of individual and national interest, coupled with retrospective judgment of a party's performance in office and speculation on the promise of party candidates. Strong party identification once prevented this pronounced volatility by anchoring a voter during late-developing political storms.

Forces of Decline and Revival

If these are the increasingly visible results of party decline, what forces arrayed against the parties have produced the deterioration? Perhaps the problem stems from the individualism that is so much a part of the American character. This "don't fence me in" attitude held by most voters is supplemented by a natural suspicion of aggregated power in big organizations. In one of our polls, we asked respondents how they viewed the "many large institutions such as government, labor unions, corporations, and utilities in America today." Only 24 percent agreed with the statement "Being big is *good* because it allows these institutions to work better and get more done," while 58 percent chose the alternate position, "Big is *bad* because these institutions are wasteful and have too much power."[26]

Many social, political, technological, and governmental changes (which will be discussed more thoroughly in the concluding chapters) have also contributed to party woes. Historically, the government's assumption of important functions previously performed by the parties, such as printing ballots, conducting elections, and providing social welfare services, had a major impact. In the large cities, particularly, party organizations once were a central element of life for millions, sponsoring community events and entertainment, helping new immigrants to settle in, giving food and temporary housing to those in immediate need — all in exchange for votes, of course. But as these social services began to be seen as a right of citizenship rather than a privilege extended in exchange for a person's support of a party, and as the flow of immigrants slowed dramatically in the 1920s, party organizations gradually withered in most places.

Simultaneously, the Progressive-inspired direct primary usurped the power of nomination from party leaders and workers, giving it instead to a much broader and more independent electorate and thus loosening the tie between the party nominee and the party organization. Progressive civil service laws also removed much of the patronage used by the parties to reward their loyal followers.

In the post–World War II era, extensive social changes fed the movement away from strong parties. Broad-based education emancipated many voters from complete reliance on the cue of party label. Education also fed the growing issue-oriented politics, which tends to cut across party lines and encourage the party-straying habit of ticket-splitting.[27] At the same time, millions of people began to move out of the cities, which are easily organizable because of population density, and into the sprawling suburbs, where a sense of privacy and detachment can often deter the most energetic of organizers. Electorally, as we have already reviewed, the trends were almost all antiparty: the preeminence of television and the personality politics it brings, the rise of political consultants, the growth of PACs and interest groups, and the development of a cadre of independent-minded candidates and officeholders who had reached their posts without the help of their parties and wanted to remain as free as possible of party restraints.

Fortunately for those who see the compelling need for stronger parties, there are also winds at the parties' backs today, forces that are helping to reverse decades of decline. None may be more important than the growing realization of the worth of political parties by many journalists and officeholders, as well as the continued advocacy of party-building reforms by many academics and political practitioners. The resolve of recent national party leaders, such as Republican National Committee Chairmen William Brock and Frank Fahrenkopf and Democratic party leaders Paul Kirk (Democratic National Committee chairman) and Tony Coelho (chairman until 1987 of the Democratic Congressional Campaign Committee), has been of paramount significance to the ongoing revival of political party organizational and financial might.[28] Additionally, the application of new campaign technologies to help *parties* (not just individual candidates) raise money, advertise, and contact supporters has been a healthful if insufficient tonic, with potential for even greater good, as later chapters will suggest and propose.

The Definitions of Party

So far I have avoided defining the object of my attentions, and with good reason. Political scientists and other observers differ significantly in their precise descriptions of the term "political party." In 1770 the great British parliamentarian Edmund Burke began to develop the classic model of the responsible, centralized, disciplined, and issue-oriented political party when he called it "a body of men united, for promoting by their joint endeavors the national interest, upon some particular principle in which they are all agreed."[29] It was really Burke's conception that was expanded upon in the late 1940s by the Committee on Political Parties of the American Political Science Association in their landmark report, *Toward a More Responsible Two-Party System.*[30] The APSA Committee urged the American parties to be more concerned with policies and issues by offering the voters a clear ideological choice and following up to ensure that their successful candidates enacted those policies once in office. The APSA Committee-preferred model, of course, is far removed from both the traditional American party "machine," which was highly disciplined but deemphasized issue politics, and the conventional modern state and national party, which is relatively decentralized, permeable, centrist, and without much authority to enforce election mandates.[31] As we have seen, though, the party platforms are more sharply issue-defined and divergent than is commonly believed, and find their way into law to a surprising extent. The parties have become more "responsible" than many reformers would have dreamed possible at the turn of the century.

Other political scientists, such as Joseph Schlesinger, have chosen to focus in recent years on the pragmatic essence of parties by defining the party as "a group organized to gain control of government in the name of the group by winning election to public office."[32] This model concentrates exclusively on office-seekers, and excludes both their non-office-seeking supporters and the voters who elect them and who may identify with the group.

My own definition is at once pragmatic — how could it be otherwise in the American mold? — and inclusive: *A political party is a group of officeholders, candidates, activists, and voters who identify with a group label and seek to elect individuals to public office who run under that label.* My model is not a disciplined, "responsible party" one, but neither should it imply that parties are unprincipled. Pragmatism does *not* require the abandonment of principle; it demands merely that the validity of all concepts be tested by their practical results. While pragmatic in this sense, the American parties have adopted discernibly distinctive philosophies and have taken generally different approaches to governing, especially in recent times. My definition also emphasizes the *raison d'être* of American parties (contesting elections), as well as the trinity of groups necessary to produce a true political party rather than simply an interest group: the party in office or seeking office, the party activists who comprise the organization, and the party in the electorate (voters who, to varying degrees, identify with the party label).

In this volume, I am particularly concerned with the party in the electorate. There will always be plenty of ambitious individuals to seek office under a major party's standard. There will likely always be an adequate (though perhaps not ample) number of activists attracted by specific issues and personalities to hold the key positions in the party organization. What is no longer certain, though, is whether there will be sufficient support for, and loyalty to, the major parties among the uninvolved pool of voters to prevent fragmentation and sustain the current political arrangement that so clearly benefits this nation. Some modern definitions of party, while useful for certain kinds of analysis, are deficient precisely because they exclude the essential band of party identifiers found in the general electorate. Political parties without people, without a firm and extensive foundation of support drawn from the ranks of average voters, are lifeless shells incapable of performing some of their indispensable functions. That is too often an apt description of many Democratic and Republican state and local organizations today. As this chapter has tried to make clear, the country's future depends upon vibrant parties, and developing vibrant parties calls for strengthening the tie between party and voter and for bringing the organizations to life with a broader base of committed individuals rather than just more money and dazzling technologies.

Later on, in Chapters Four and Five, we will explore at length the perceptions of party that voters currently possess, with an eye to using that information to build the party in the electorate. Before that, however, we need to sketch the history of party development in the United States and to examine the substantial changes that have occurred in both the party in office and the party organization.

Notes

1. See Frank Sorauf *Party Politics in America* (5th ed.) (Boston: Little, Brown and Co., 1984), 26; and Jack Dennis, "Trends in Support for the American Party System," *British Journal of Political Science* 5 (April 1975): 229.

2. See, for example, Angus Campbell et al., *The American Voter* (New York: Wiley, 1960); and Norman H. Nie, Sidney Verba, and John R. Petrocik, *The Changing American Voter* (Cambridge, Mass.: Harvard University Press, 1976).
3. The question called for unprompted recall of both candidates' names: "Do you happen to recall the names of the two major candidates who ran for the U.S. Senate this year from your state?" Any reasonable facsimile of the names was accepted. Undoubtedly, recall would have been greater if voters had been permitted to choose names from a list, but the contention that many voters know relatively little about candidates and elections is certainly valid. In our June survey (Poll 1), respondents were asked this basic question: "Do you happen to know which party — the Democrats or the Republicans — controls the U.S. Senate?" After almost six consecutive years of a GOP Senate majority, and at a time when the focus of most political stories centered on the fate of Senate control in the upcoming elections, 53 percent said either the Democrats were in charge (26 percent) or they wouldn't even wager a guess when their chances were 50–50 to guess correctly (27 percent).
4. See Richard A. Brody and Benjamin I. Page, "Comment: The Assessment of Policy Voting," *American Political Science Review* 66 (1972): 450–458; and Gregory B. Markus and Philip E. Converse, "A Dynamic Simultaneous Model of Electoral Choice," *American Political Science Review* 73 (1979): 406–423.
5. Walter Dean Burnham, *Critical Elections and the Mainsprings of American Politics* (New York: Norton, 1970), 132–133.
6. Actually, most of the 18–21 year olds never even registered to vote, but of those who did, George McGovern won a narrow majority of them in his 1972 presidential bid — the only age group he carried in his landslide loss.
7. Fundamentalist party identification trends are discussed in Chapters Four and Five.
8. As quoted in Ken Bode, "Hero or Demagogue?" *The New Republic* 195 (March 3, 1986): 28.
9. Gerald M. Pomper with Susan Lederman, *Elections in America* (2nd ed.) (New York: Longman, 1980), 145–150, 167–173.
10. See David E. Price, *Bringing Back the Parties* (Washington, D.C.: Congressional Quarterly Press, 1984), 284–288.
11. See, for example, Sarah McCally Morehouse, "Legislatures and Political Parties," *State Government* 59: 1 (1976): 23.
12. Pomper, *Elections in America.*
13. Ibid.
14. Polls 2 and 3. This overreporting of voting participation is standard, alas. And in both survey questions, respondents were made to feel less guilty because "a lot of people weren't able to vote":

    Poll 2: "Talking about the recent election, we find that a lot of people were not able to vote. In checking the list of voters in your precinct, would we find that you did or did not vote on Tuesday, November 4th?"

Poll 3: "A lot of people weren't able to vote in the elections earlier this month because of one reason or the other. How about you — did you get a chance to actually vote earlier this month or not?"

15. Seymour Martin Lipset and William Schneider, *The Confidence Gap* (New York: The Free Press, 1983), 103–104.
16. E. E. Schattschneider, *Party Government* (New York: Rinehart, 1942), 208–209.
17. See, for example, Doris A. Graber, *Mass Media and American Politics* (2nd ed.) (Washington, D.C.: Congressional Quarterly Press, 1984), 135–176.
18. See Sabato, *The Rise of Political Consultants: New Ways of Winning Elections* (New York: Basic Books, 1981).
19. I do not completely share this concern, and believe that the "threat" posed by PACs has been greatly exaggerated. Nonetheless, the current system of campaign finance leaves much to be desired. See Sabato, *PAC POWER: Inside the World of Political Action Committees* (New York: W. W. Norton, 1984); see also Chapters Six and Seven.
20. As quoted in the *Washington Post*, November 10, 1986, Al.
21. Clifton McCleskey, "Democratic Representation and the Constitution: Where Do Political Parties Fit In?" *University of Virginia Newsletter* 60 (July 1984): 61–64, at 61.
22. Ibid., 63.
23. Sabato, *The Rise of Political Consultants*, 197–198.
24. Poll 3; Campbell et al., *The American Voter*, 78; and Martin P. Wattenberg, *The Decline of American Political Parties, 1952–1980* (Cambridge, Mass.: Harvard University Press, 1984), 130–131. In 1952 and 1956 half or more of the voters made a presidential choice before the start of the general election campaign, but in 1980 half decided during the general election and 9 percent on election day itself (compared to just 2 percent on election day in both 1952 and 1956). In 1986 our second postelection survey asked respondents when they had "finally made up" their minds on how they "were going to vote for U.S. Congress this year." Thirty-seven percent claimed to have decided before September, and 59 percent in September or later, including 14 percent during the last week of the election and 9 percent on election day itself.
25. See Wattenberg, ibid., who cites the case of the 1980 presidential election. One recent gubernatorial election in Virginia provides another case study of last-minute voting influences. See Larry Sabato, *Virginia Votes, 1979–1982* (Charlottesville: Institute of Government, University of Virginia, 1983), 83–85.
26. Poll 1. Ten percent volunteered that "it depends" and 8 percent had no opinion.
27. Nie, Verba, and Petrocik, *The Changing American Voter.*
28. Brock, a former United States Senator from Tennessee, was RNC chairman from 1977 to 1981, and later special trade representative and Secretary of Labor in the Reagan administration. Fahrenkopf became RNC chairman in 1983, and Kirk won the DNC post in 1985. Coelho, a Cal-

ifornia congressman, left his DCCC position in 1987 when he was elected House Majority Whip.

29. From Burke's *Thoughts on the Cause of the Present Discontents.* See also the splendid discussion in Giovanni Sartori, *Parties and Party Systems: A Framework for Analysis,* Vol. 1 (New York: Cambridge, University Press, 1976), 1–29.
30. The report was published by Rinehart of New York in 1950.
31. See Price, *Bringing Back the Parties,* 107–109.
32. Joseph A. Schlesinger, "The New American Political Party," *American Political Science Review* 79 (1985): 1153.

CHAPTER TWO

• ☆ • ☆ •

The Evolving Party

DESPITE THE ABSENCE of any constitutional sanction for political parties, and the open hostility of many of the nation's early leaders toward the emerging political parties in the 1790s, parties have been a remarkable constant of American political life over more than a century and a half. But while the institutions have symbolized continuity, their form and substance have changed radically with the passage of time, reflecting the conditions of politics and government in each age. Like the Constitution itself, political parties have proven to be pragmatic and flexible, altering their identities, structures, and operations to suit the needs of the contemporary electorate in every era. Particular parties have come and gone; even the enduring Democratic and Republican parties have been utterly transformed several times in all but name. Parties have based themselves in small caucuses of elites, mass movements generated by geography and issues, big-city machines of service delivery and feudal loyalties, and most recently the technological innovations of modern communications. For all of these diverse manifestations, the essence of the party idea has remained the same, even as the functions performed by the parties have changed. In this chapter we will first sketch the evolution of the party — idea and reality — as it has developed in the United States. Then we will concentrate on how political parties influence and define the government at state and national levels and on how the parties are, in turn, shaped by their interaction with the fundamental processes and institutions of American government.

The Inevitability of Party

Many of the Republic's leading statesmen in the late eighteenth century feared that parties would upset the delicate consensus that existed in the new nation. To their great credit, they were unwilling to sacrifice individual liberty to prevent the formation of parties. At the same time, they were convinced that the American system would effectively strangle the influence of parties by dividing power in an intricate and elaborate fashion, frustrating any party's attempt to dominate and control the government.[1] Thus, while liberty would give rise to parties, the parties' subsequent failures would cause them to wither away, reasoned James Madison and others. But as Schattschneider surmised:

> The scheme, in spite of its subtlety, involved a miscalculation. Political parties refused to be content with the role assigned to them. The vigor and enterprise of the parties have therefore made American political history the story of the unhappy marriage of the parties and the Constitution, a remarkable variation of the case of the irresistible force and the immovable object, which in this instance have been compelled to live together in a permanent partnership.[2]

Thanks to the nearly universal support and admiration for George Washington, the nation's first years were marked by relative harmony and the absence of any clearly defined organizational factions, though the early clashes between Alexander Hamilton and Thomas Jefferson (and their respective supporters) portended the partisan divisions to come. For his part, Washington made warnings about the evils of parties a centerpiece of his Farewell Address in 1796:

> Let me now . . . warn you in the most solemn manner against the baneful effects of the spirit of party generally . . .
>
> It exists under different shapes in all governments, more or less stifled, controlled, or repressed; but in those of the popular form it is seen in its greatest rankness and is truly their worst enemy . . .
>
> It serves always to distract the public councils and enfeeble the public administration. It agitates the community with ill-founded jealousies and false alarms; kindles the animosity of one part against another; foments occasionally riot and insurrection. It opens the door to foreign influence and corruption . . .
>
> There is an opinion that parties in free countries are useful checks

> upon the administration of the government, and serve to keep alive the spirit of liberty. This within certain limits is probably true; and in governments of a monarchical cast patriotism may look with indulgence, if not with favor, upon the spirit of party. But in those of the popular character, in governments purely elective, it is a spirit not to be encouraged.[3]

Ironically, though, Washington's personal farewell also marked the departure of partyless politics in the United States.[4] By the presidential election of 1800, two congressional party caucuses composed of like-minded members had organized around the competing standards of Hamilton — the Federalists, supporters of strong central government — and Jefferson and Madison — the Republicans, who preferred empowering states rather than the federal government. The caucuses nominated presidential candidates, and the Republicans' Jefferson defeated incumbent President John Adams, who had become identified with the Federalists. Jefferson, then, became the first president elected as the nominee of a political party. (Readers will, I hope, indulge an author from the University of Virginia in his belief that this fact alone provides a high recommendation for the nascent party system.) At about the same time, the legislative caucuses began communications with supporters in the states, and "committees of correspondence" formed sporadically as the first manifestations of local party organization.

Resistance to the party system was still great, however. Even the congressional caucus leaders viewed their activities as merely a necessary evil, required by the subversion and maneuvering taking place on the other side. This discomfort eventually resulted in the virtual disintegration of the presidential caucus system. The Federalists were repeatedly unsuccessful in their presidential efforts, and by 1816 they ceased to nominate a candidate. From 1816 to 1824 during James Monroe's presidency, America experienced a relatively party-free period at the national level, the so-called Era of Good Feelings, when personalities, not party, held sway. (The television age is not the first candidate-centered era in our country's history!)

The absence of party conflict proved brief and unnatural, though. Even during Monroe's tenure, many state party organizations thrived, and inevitably, new national factions formed, fueled in part by the enormous increase in the electorate that took place between 1820 and 1840, when property requirements as a condition of suffrage were abolished in most states. Also, by the 1820s all the states save for South Carolina that had selected presidential electors indirectly (by vote of the state legislature) shifted to popular election of Electoral College slates, thus transforming presidential politics. Caucus nominations, criticized as elitist and antidemocratic, gave way to selection at large party conventions. The new Democratic party, formed around the charismatic populist President Andrew Jackson, combined much of the old Republican party and most newly enfranchised voters. It held the country's first major national presidential nominating convention in 1832.[5] Jackson's strong personality helped to polarize politics, and opposition to the president coalesced into the Whig party, whose early leaders included Henry Clay. The incumbent Jackson defeated Clay in the 1832 presidential contest, and became the first chief executive nominated and elected by a truly national, popularly based political party.

The Whigs and the Democrats continued to strengthen after 1832, establishing state and local organizations almost everywhere. Their competition was usually fierce and closely matched, and they brought the United States the first broadly supported two-party system in the Western world.[6] Unfortunately for the Whigs, the issue of slavery sharpened many already present and divisive internal party tensions, and these led to its gradual dissolution and replacement by the Republican party. Formed in 1854, the Republican party set its sights on the abolition (or at least the containment) of slavery, and it was able to assemble enough support from the Whigs, antislavery Northern Democrats, and others to win the presidency for Abraham Lincoln in a fragmented 1860 vote.

From that election to this day, the same two great parties — the Republicans and the Democrats — have dominated American elections. Control of an electoral majority has seesawed back and forth between the two parties. The dominance of the Republicans in the Reconstruction era eventually gave way to a highly competitive system from 1876 to 1896. In the latter year, however, the GOP skillfully capitalized on fears of the growing agrarian populist sentiment in the Democratic party to fashion a dominant and enduring majority of voters that essentially lasted until the early 1930s, when the Great Depression created the conditions for a Democratic resurgence. Franklin Roosevelt's New Deal coalition of 1932 (the South, ethnics, organized labor, farmers, liberals, and big city machines) basically characterized both the Democratic party and the prevailing national majority until at least the late 1960s. The period since 1970 has seen neither party clearly dominant, as more and more voters have seemed to view their partisan attachments as less important. (This development will be a major subject of discussion in Chapter Five.)

The modern era seems very distant from the "Golden Age" of parties from the 1870s to the 1920s. Immigration from Europe (particularly Ireland, Italy, and Germany) fueled the development of big-city party organizations that ruled with an iron hand in their domains. Party and government were virtually interchangeable in those instances. The parties were the providers of needed services, entertainment, and employment. The devotion they engendered among their supporters, voters, and officeholders helped to produce startlingly high voter turnout — 75 percent or better in all presidential elections from 1876 to 1900 compared to less than 55 percent today[7] — as well as the greatest legislative discipline ever achieved among party contingents in Congress and many state legislatures.[8]

As we reviewed in Chapter One the heyday of the party — at least a certain *kind* of party — has passed. The reduction in patronage, the direct primary, the spread of nonpartisan elections, the substitution of the Australian (or secret) ballot for the party-sponsored ballot,[9] the cutoff of immigration in the 1920s by Congress, and the growth of the social welfare state — where services became governmental rights and not party privileges — all took a toll. This decline can be exaggerated, though, and it often is. Viewing parties in the broad sweep of American history, it becomes clear that first, while political parties have evolved considerably and changed form from time to time, usually they have been reliable vehicles for mass participation in a representative democracy. In fact, the gradual but steady expansion of suffrage itself was orchestrated by the parties. Just as Schattschneider insisted, "In the search for new segments of the populace that might be exploited profitably, the parties have kept the movement to liberalize the franchise well ahead of the demand. . . . The enlargement of the practicing electorate has been one of the principal labors of the parties, a truly notable achievement for which the parties have never been properly credited."[10] Second, the parties' journey through American history has been characterized by the same redoubtable ability to adapt to prevailing conditions that is often cited as the genius of the Constitution. Flexibility and pragmatism mark both, and help to ensure both their survival and the success of the society they serve. Third, despite massive changes in political conditions and frequent dramatic shifts in the electorate's moods, the two major parties have not only achieved remarkable longevity, they have almost consistently provided strong competition for one another and the voters at the national level. Of the twenty-six presidential elections in the century from 1884 to 1984, for instance, the Republicans won fourteen and the Democrats twelve. Even when calamity has struck the parties — the Great Depression or Watergate for the Republicans, the Civil War or McGovernism for the Democrats — they have proven tremendously resilient, sometimes bouncing back from landslide defeats to win the next election. Perhaps most of all, history teaches us that the development of parties in the United States was an inevitability. Human nature alone guarantees conflict in any society; in a free state, the question is simply how to contain and channel conflict productively without infringing on individual liberties. The Founding Fathers' utopian hopes for the avoidance of faction have given way to an appreciation of the parties' constructive contribution to conflict definition and resolution during the years of the American republic.

A Note on One-Partyism and Third-Partyism

The two-party system has not gone unchallenged, of course. At the state level two-party competition was once severely limited or nonexistent in much of the country.[11] Especially in the one-party Democratic states of the Deep South and the rock-ribbed Republican states of Maine, New Hampshire, and Vermont, the dominant party's primary nomination was considered tantamount to election, and the only real contest was an unsatisfying intraparty one where factions were fluid and the multiplicity of candidacies proved confusing to voters.[12] Even in most two-party states there existed dozens of cities and counties that had a massive majority of voters aligned with one or the other party, and thus were effectively one-party in local elections. Obviously, historical, cultural, and sectional forces primarily accounted for the concentration of one party's supporters in certain areas. The Civil War's divisions, for instance, were mirrored for the better part of a century in the Democratic predisposition of the South and the Republican proclivities of the Yankee northern states. Whatever the combination of factors producing one-partyism, the condition has certainly declined precipitously in the last quarter-century.[13]

The spread of two-party competition, while still uneven in some respects, is one of the most significant political trends of recent times, and virtually no one-party states are left. There are no purely Republican states anymore, and the heavily Democratic contingent has been reduced to, at most, Alabama, Georgia, Louisiana, Mississippi, Arkansas, and Maryland. (Note, though, that in each of these states one or more Republicans have been elected to the governorship or United States Senate in the last decade.) Ironically, as Chapters Four and Five will explore, the growth of two-party competition has been spurred less by the developing strength of the main parties than by party weakness, illustrated by the decline in partisan loyalty among the voters. In other words, citizens are somewhat more inclined to cross party lines to support an appealing candidate regardless of party affiliation, thus making a victory for the minority party possible whether or not it has earned the win through its own organizational hard work. It should also be noted that the elimination of pockets of one-party strength adds an element of instability to the system, since even in lean times of national electoral disaster each party was once assured of a regional base from which a comeback could be staged.[14] Nonetheless, the increase in party competitiveness can be viewed positively, since it eliminates the odious effects of one-partyism and guarantees a comprehensible and credible partisan choice to a larger segment of the electorate than ever before.

Third-partyism has proven more durable than one-partyism, though its nature is sporadic and intermittent, and its effects on the political system less weighty on the whole. Given all the controversy and coverage third parties generate, one could be excused for thinking they were extraordinarily important on the American scene. But as Frank Sorauf has concluded, third parties in fact "have not assumed the importance that all the attention lavished on them suggests."[15] Not a single minor party has ever come close to winning the presidency, and only seven minor parties have won so much as a single state's Electoral College votes.[16] Just four third parties (the Populists in 1892, Theodore Roosevelt's Bull Moose party in 1912, the Progressives in 1924, and George Wallace's American Independent party in 1968) have garnered more than 10 percent of the popular vote for president.[17]

Third parties find their roots in sectionalism (as did the South's Dixiecrats in 1948), in specific issues (such as the agrarian revolt that fueled the Populists), and in appealing charismatic personalities (Theodore Roosevelt is perhaps the best example). Many of the minor parties have drawn strength from a combination of these sources. The American Independent party enjoyed a measure of success because of a dynamic, demagogic leader (George Wallace), a firm geographic base (the South), and an emotional issue (civil rights). Above all, third parties make electoral progress in direct proportion to the failure of the two major parties to incorporate new ideas or alienated groups, or to nominate attractive candidates as their standard-bearers. Certainly in the media age, this latter qualification has grown in importance. John Anderson's 1980 Independent presidential bid was spurred not by geography or specific issues or Anderson's persona but by intense dissatisfaction among some voters with the major party nominees (Jimmy Carter and Ronald Reagan).[18]

Third parties, then, are akin to shooting stars that may appear briefly and brilliantly but do not long remain visible in the political constellation. The United States is the only major Western nation that does not have at least one significant, enduring third party, and there are a number of explanations for this. Unlike many European countries that use proportional representation and guarantee parliamentary seats to any faction securing even as little as 5 percent of the vote, the United States has a "single member, plurality" electoral system that requires a party to get one more vote than any other party in a legislative constituency or in a state's presidential election in order to win. To paraphrase Vince Lombardi, finishing first is not everything, it is the only thing in American politics; placing second, even by a smidgen, doesn't count, and this condition obviously encourages the aggregation of interests into as few parties as possible (the democratic minimum being two).

Other institutional factors undergird the two-party system as well. The laws in most states make it difficult for third parties to secure a place on the ballot, while the Democratic and Republican parties are often granted automatic access. Democrats and Republicans in the state legislatures may have little in common, but one shared objective is to make sure the political pie is cut into only two sizeable pieces, not three or more smaller slices. The public funding of campaigns, where it exists, is far more generous for the two major parties. At the national level, for instance, third-party presidential candidates receive money only *after* the general election *if* they have garnered more than 5 percent of the vote, and *only* in proportion to their total vote; the major-party candidates, by contrast, get large, full general election grants immediately upon their summer nominations. The news media, too, are biased — legitimately so — against minor parties, which are given relatively little coverage compared to major-party nominees. The media are only reflecting political reality, of course, and it would be absurd to expect them to offer equal time to all comers. Still, it is a vicious cycle for the minor candidates: a lack of broad-based support produces slight coverage, which minimizes their chances of attracting more adherents.

Beyond the institutional explanations are historical, cultural, and social theories of two-partyism in America.[19] The dualist approach, frequently criticized as overly simplistic, suggests that there has always been an underlying binary nature to United States politics. Whether it was the early conflict between eastern financial interests and western frontiersmen, the sectional division of North and South, the more current urban versus rural or urban versus suburban clashes, or even the natural tensions of democratic institutions (the government against the opposition, for instance), dualists see the processes and interests of politics inevitably reducing the players into two great camps. Others emphasize the basic social consensus existing in American life. Whatever their ideological leanings and despite great diversity in heritage, the vast majority of Americans accept without serious question the fundamental structures of our system: the Constitution, the governmental setup, a lightly controlled free enterprise economy, and so on. This consensus, when allied with certain American cultural characteristics developed over time (pragmatism, acceptance of the need for compromise, a lack of divisive social class consciousness), produces the conditions necessary for a relatively nonideological, centrist politics that can naturally support two moderate alternative parties that offer change when it is wanted but continuity even then. This suggests again the extra-Constitutional genius of the two-party system, and the secret of the two parties' success in shutting out third parties before they establish a long-term beachhead. The essential pragmatism, centrism, and flexibility of the major parties allows them to absorb the acceptable, reasonable elements and issues of prominent minor parties, quickly depriving third parties of their *raison d'être.* The passion for power and victory that drives both Democrats and Republicans overrides ideology and prevents rigidity. Unless a kind of rigor mortis takes hold in the future in one or both major parties — with, say, the capture of party machinery by unyielding extremists of right or left — it is difficult to imagine any third party becoming a major, permanent force in American politics. The corollary of this axiom, though, is that the major parties must be eternally vigilant to avoid such ideologically inspired takeovers, and the best preventative medicine is to expand participation in party activities to as broad-based a group of voters as possible. Neither party is doing a particularly good job of this at present — a subject to which I will return in the last two chapters.

For the foreseeable future, though, third parties likely will continue to play useful supporting roles similar to their historically sanctioned ones. They can popularize ideas that might not receive a hearing otherwise. They can serve as vehicles of popular discontent with the major parties and thereby induce change in major-party behavior and platforms. They may well presage and assist future party realignments as they have sometimes done in the past. In a few states third parties will also continue to take a unique part in political life, as the Conservative and Liberal parties of New York do.[20] But in an open, permeable two-party system that is supplemented by generous means of expressing dissent and registering political opposition in other ways (court challenges, interest group organizing, and even — sadly — the all too well-accepted practice of nonvoting), third parties will continue to have a limited future in the United States.

The Basic Structure of American Political Parties

Third parties may be insubstantial, but the structure of the two major parties is not elaborate either. The first national party committees were skeletal and formed some years after the creation of the presidential nominating conventions in the 1830s.[21] First the Democrats in 1848 and then the Republicans in 1856 established national governing bodies (the Democratic National Committee, or DNC, and the Republican National Committee, or RNC) to make arrangements for the quadrennial conventions and to coordinate the subsequent presidential campaigns. The DNC and RNC were each composed of one representative from each state — expanded to two in the 1920s after the post of state committeewoman was established — and the states had complete control over the selection of their representatives. In addition, the congressional party caucuses in both houses organized their own national committees, loosely allied with the DNC and RNC. First, the National Republican Congressional Committee (NRCC) was started in 1866 when the congressional GOP was feuding with Abraham Lincoln's successor, President Andrew Johnson, and wanted a counterweight to his control of the RNC. At the same time House and Senate Democrats set up a similar committee. After the popular election of United States senators was initiated in 1913 with the ratification of the Seventeenth Amendment to the Constitution, both parties organized separate Senate campaign committees. Interestingly, this tripartite arrangement of national committee, House committee, and Senate committee[22] has persisted in both parties until the present day, and each party's committees are housed together in Washington. Generally, the relationship among the three committees in each party is cooperative, although some rivalry and competition are understandably apparent from time to time in these siblings.

The memberships of both the RNC and DNC have grown considerably in size over the decades, but the DNC's expansion has been much greater, and it is now more than twice the size of the RNC—390 DNC members to just 165 for the RNC as of 1987. (Democrats ruefully note that while the DNC is double the RNC's membership, the RNC is much larger where it counts: staff, money, and organization.) Since 1972 the Democrats have also abandoned the principle of equal DNC representation for all states, and have assigned the number of committeepersons on the basis of each state's population and its past voter support for the party's candidates. While the national conventions formally ratify all national committee members, the real choices are still made in the states, with selection methods varying widely (from election at state party conventions — the most common means — to primary election, selection by state central committees or designation by the party delegation to the national presidential convention).

The key national party official is the chairperson of the DNC or RNC. While the chair is formally elected by the national committee, he or she is usually selected by the sitting president or newly nominated presidential candidate, who is accorded the right to name the individual for at least the duration of his or her campaign. Only the postcampaign out-of-power party committee actually has the authority to appoint a chairperson independently. Oddly enough, it is those committee-crowned chairpersons who generally have the greatest impact, because they come to the post at times of crisis when a leadership vacuum exists. (A defeated presidential candidate is technically the head of the national party until the next nominating convention, but the reality is naturally otherwise as a party attempts to shake off a losing image.) The chair often becomes the prime spokesperson and arbitrator for the party during the interregnum, and he or she is called upon to damp down factionalism, negotiate candidate disputes, raise money, and prepare the machinery for the next presidential election. Balancing the interests of all potential White House contenders is a particularly difficult job, and strict neutrality is normally expected from the chair. In recent times both parties have benefited from adept leadership while out of power. RNC Chairman William Brock during the Carter presidency and DNC Chairman Paul Kirk during the second Reagan term both skillfully used their positions to strengthen their parties organizationally and to polish the party images. By contrast, party chairpersons selected by incumbent presidents and presidential candidates tend to be close allies of the presidents or candidates and often subordinate the good of the party to the needs of the campaign or White House. During the Carter presidency, for example, DNC Chairmen Kenneth Curtis and John White were creatures of the White House who acted as cheerleaders for their chief executive but did little to keep the Democratic party competitive with the then-strengthening GOP organization. Because of their command of presidential patronage and influence, a few national party chairpersons selected by presidents have become powerful and well known, such as Republican Mark Hanna during the McKinley presidency and Democrat James Farley under President Franklin Roosevelt. Most presidentially appointed chairs, however, have been relatively obscure; the chance for a chairperson to make a difference and cut a memorable figure generally comes when there is no competition from a White House nominee or occupant.

Much of any party chairperson's efforts are directed at planning the presidential nominating convention, the most publicized and vital event on the party's calendar. Until 1984, gavel-to-gavel coverage had been standard practice on all national television networks, and even after the recent cutbacks on some channels, a substantial block of time is still devoted to the conventions. The nomination of the presidential ticket naturally receives the lion's share of attention, but the convention is also the ultimate governing body for the party itself. The rules adopted and the platform passed at the quadrennial conclave are durable guideposts that steer the party for years after the final gavel has been brought down. Most of the recent party chairpersons, in cooperation with the incumbent president or likely nominee, have tried to orchestrate carefully every minute of the conventions in order to project just the right image to voters at home. By and large, they have succeeded, though at the price of draining some spontaneity and excitement from the process.

From 1974 to 1982 the Democratic party also held a midterm convention (also called a *mini-convention*).[23] Designed to provide party activists a chance to express themselves on policy and presidential performance (whether the chief executive was a Democrat or a Republican), the midterm convention instead mainly generated worry among the party leadership and elected officials about the factional infighting and ideological posturing that might be on display before a national audience. While none of the midterm gatherings was a disaster (and none a roaring success, either), by 1986 the Democrats had decided to avoid potential divisiveness and save the $2 million necessary to hold the convention, and it was canceled.

A less expensive programmatic alternative, the policy council, has been used extensively by both parties during their out-of-power years in recent decades.[24] The councils generally have been composed of elected officials (particularly members of Congress) and party leaders, with the councils divided into task forces and study groups in key issue areas. Critiques of administration policies have been released with some regularity, though the reports have usually been longer on criticisms than proposals of specific alternatives. The two most famous and successful of these programmatic bodies were the National Democratic Advisory Council, which operated during some of the Eisenhower years (1956–1961) under the direction of DNC Chairman Paul Butler, and the Republican Coordinating Committee of RNC Chairman Ray Bliss during Lyndon Johnson's administration (1965–1968). These policy groups were not always well received, especially by party congressional leaders who believed that the councils encroached on their territory and prerogatives. A useful model of an inoffensive yet productive council has been provided by the most recent out-of-power party attempt to provide policy research and direction to its organization. DNC Chairman Paul Kirk's creation in 1985 of a Democratic Policy Commission as a noncontinuing study group with a fixed mandate — to provide a mainstream, moderate policy foundation for Democratic presidential candidates to use in 1988 — was a welcome innovation. The commission, chaired by former Utah Governor Scott Matheson, held open public hearings and debates for a year around the country before writing and publishing a thoughtful report in 1986.[25] (This prototype of party policy formulation will be discussed further in Chapter Six.)

While *national* committee activities of all kinds attract most of the media attention, the party is structurally based not in Washington but in the *states and localities.* Except for the campaign finance arena, virtually all governmental regulation of political parties is left to the states, for example, and most elected officials give their fealty to the local party divisions they know best. Most importantly, the vast majority of party leadership positions are filled at subnational levels. The pyramidal arrangement of party committees at least theoretically provides for a broad base of support. The smallest voting unit, the precinct, is also the fundamental building block of the party, and each of the more than 100,000 precincts in the United States potentially has a committeeman or woman to represent it in each party's councils. (Sadly, the reality is that many of these posts go unfilled or unenergetically pursued.) The precinct committeepersons are the key foot soldiers of any party, and their efforts are supplemented by party committees above them in the wards, cities, counties, towns, villages, and congressional districts. The state governing body supervising this welter of local party organizations is usually called the state central (or executive) committee, and it comprises representatives from all major geographic units, as determined by and selected under state law. Generally, state parties are free to act within the limits set by their state legislatures without interference from the national party except in the selection and seating of presidential convention delegates. National Democrats have been particularly inclined to regulate this aspect of party life.[26]

The formal structure of party organization is supplemented by numerous official, semiofficial, and unaffiliated groups that combine and clash with the parties in countless ways. Both the DNC and RNC have affiliated organizations of state and local party women (the National Federation of Democratic Women and the National Federation of Republican Women), and there are youth divisions as well (the Young Democrats of America and the Young Republicans National Federation), which have a generous definition of "young" — up to and including age 35. The state governors in each party have their own party associations, too. Just outside the party orbit are the supportive interest groups and associations that often provide money, manpower, or other forms of assistance to the parties. Labor unions, progressive political action committees, teachers, black and liberal women's groups, and the Americans for Democratic Action comprise some of the Democratic party's organizational cohorts, while business PACs, the United States Chamber of Commerce, fundamentalist Christian organizations, and some antiabortion agencies work closely with the Republicans.

Each party also has several institutionalized sources of policy ideas. Though unconnected to the parties in any official sense, these so-called think tanks are quite influential. During the Reagan administration, for instance, the right-wing, well-funded Heritage Foundation placed many dozens of its conservatives in important governmental positions and its issue studies on subjects from tax reform to South Africa carried considerable weight with policymakers.[27] The more moderate and bipartisan American Enterprise Institute also supplied the Reagan team with people and ideas. On the Democratic side, liberal think tanks proliferated during that party's Reagan-induced exile.[28] More than a half dozen policy institutes formed after 1980 in an attempt to nurse the Democrats back to political health. The Center for National Policy (formerly the Center for Democratic Policy), for instance, has sponsored several conferences and published a number of papers on Democratic policy alternatives.

Finally, there are extraparty organizations that form for a wide variety of purposes, including "reforming" a party or moving it ideologically to the right or left. There is a long history of these groups; among the better-known efforts are some in Wisconsin, California, and New York.[29] In the latter case, for example, Democratic reform clubs were originally established to fight the Tammany Hall machine, and about seventy clubs still prosper by attracting well-educated activists committed to various liberal causes. More recently, both national parties have been favored (or bedevilled) by the formation of new extraparty outfits. The Democrats are being pushed by both halves of the ideological continuum. The Democratic Leadership Conference (DLC) was launched in 1985 by moderate-conservative Democrats concerned about what they perceived as the leftward drift of their party and its image as the captive of liberal special interest groups.[30] Composed of over 100 current and former Democratic officeholders (such as Senator Sam Nunn of Georgia, former Governor Charles Robb of Virginia, and United States Representative Richard Gephardt of Missouri), the DLC has a staff of four, an annual budget of $400,000, and an office across the street from the DNC in Washington. Understandably, the DLC is not popular with the national party leadership, which views it as a redundant rival and a potentially divisive and money-draining forum.[31] Party leaders have been equally concerned about a left-leaning force organizing from within the partisan ranks, Jesse Jackson's National Rainbow Coalition. With a staff of eleven and headquarters in Washington, the Coalition is obviously a vehicle for Jackson's presidential ambitions, but beyond that, its goals of mass membership (at $25 annual dues), hundreds of state and local charter affiliates, and endorsements of Independent candidates when Democratic nominees are found to be "unacceptable," present a clear challenge to party hegemony in the eyes of at least some party officials. Republicans have their extraparty problems too, the most prominent of which is North Carolina Senator Jesse Helms's Congressional Club, one of the largest political action committees in the United States. The Club has 118,000 official members and millions of direct mail contributors, and has raised a phenomenal $27 million just in the 1980s.[32] Mirroring the philosophy of its founder and patron saint, the Club is fiercely conservative and dedicated to "purifying" the Republican party ideologically. Much like Jesse Jackson and the Rainbow Coalition at the opposite end of the political spectrum, Helms and the Club will maneuver within or without the party as circumstances dictate. "It's a third force," Helms once said of his handiwork. "The Club will work with anybody, Republicans or Democrats, wherever we can help the conservative cause."[33]

The Party in Government

THE CONGRESSIONAL PARTY

The structure of political parties we have reviewed so far has been electoral, self contained, and apart from governing institutions. Another dimension of party exists — and, to a great degree, thrives — *within* government, as a critical, essential mechanism of all its branches and layers.

In no segment of American government is the party more visible or vital than in the Congress. In this century the political parties have dramatically increased the sophistication and impact of their internal congressional organizations. Prior to the beginning of every session each party in both houses of Congress caucuses separately to select party leaders (House speaker or minority leader, Senate majority and minority leaders, whips, and so on) and to arrange for the appointment of members to each chamber's committees. In effect, then, the parties organize and operate the Congress. Their management systems have grown quite elaborate; the web of deputy and assistant whips for House Democrats now extends to about one-fourth of the party's entire membership.[34] Although not invulnerable to pressure from the minority, the majority party in each house generally holds sway, even fixing the size of its majority on all committees — a proportion frequently in excess of the percentage of seats it holds in the house as a whole.

Party leaders have some substantial tools at their disposal to enforce a degree of discipline in their troops. While seniority usually determines most committee assignments, an occasional choice plum may be given to the loyal and withheld from the rebellious. A member's bills can be lovingly caressed through the legislative process, or given the shad treatment and summarily dismissed without so much as a hearing. Pork barrel — government projects yielding rich patronage benefits that are the sustenance of many a legislator's electoral survival — may be included or deleted in the appropriations process. Small favors and perquisites (such as the allocation of desirable office space or the scheduling of floor votes for the convenience of a member) can also be useful levers. Then, too, there are the campaign aids at the command of the leadership: money from party sources or the leader's personal political action committee,[35] endorsements, appearances in the district or at fundraising events, and so on. On rare occasions, in extreme cases, the leaders and their allies in the party caucus may even impose sanctions of various sorts (such as the stripping of seniority rights or prized committee berths) to punish recalcitrant lawmakers.[36]

In spite of all these weapons in the leadership's arsenal, the congressional parties lack the cohesion that characterizes parliamentary legislatures. This is not surprising, since the costs of bolting the party are far less in the United States than in, say, Great Britain. A disloyal English parliamentarian might very well be replaced as a party candidate at the next election; in America, it is more likely that the independent-minded member of Congress would be electorally rewarded — hailed as a free spirit, a man of the people who can stand up to the party bosses. Moreover, defections from the ruling party in a parliamentary system bring a threat of the government's collapse and with it, early elections under possibly unfavorable conditions; fixed unchangeable election dates in the

United States mean the consequences of defection are much less dire. Also, a centralized, unicameral parliament with executive and legislative branches effectively fused permits relatively easy hierarchical, programmatic control by party leaders. The separate executive, the bicameral power-sharing, and the extraordinary decentralization of Congress's work are all institutional obstacles that limit the effectiveness of coordinated party action. Finally, party discipline is hurt by the individualistic nature of American politics: campaigns that are candidate centered rather than party oriented; the diversity of electoral constituencies to which members of Congress must understandably be responsive; the largely private system of election financing that indebts legislators to wealthy individuals and nonparty interest groups more than to their parties; and the importance to lawmakers of attracting the news media's attention — often more easily done by showmanship than by quiet, effective labor within the party system.

These are formidable barriers indeed to the operation of responsible, potent legislative parties. Therefore, it is impressive to discover that party labels consistently have been the most powerful predictor of congressional roll call voting, and in the last few years even more votes have been closely following the partisan divide. While not invariably predictive, as in strong parliamentary systems, a member's party affiliation has proven to be the indicator of his or her votes more than 70 percent of the time in recent years; that is, the average representative or senator votes with his or her party on about 70 percent of the votes that divide a majority of Democrats from a majority of Republicans. (See Table 2.1 and Figure 2.1.) In recent years more than half of the roll call votes in the House and Senate also find majorities of Democrats and Republicans on opposite sides. (See Table 2.2 and Figure 2.2.) High levels of party cohesion are especially likely to be seen when votes are taken in several areas. The votes that organize the legislative chambers (such as the election of a Speaker), set up the election machinery and campaign laws, and seat challenged members command nearly unanimous support on behalf of the party's basic interests. Those votes involving key parts of the president's program also frequently divide the parties. Finally, certain policy issues (such as social security, welfare state programs, and union–management relations) as well as party platform issues that directly and manifestly affect the party's image or its key constituencies produce substantial party voting.[37]

Until the decade of the 1980s there had been a substantial decline in party voting in Congress. At the turn of the century almost three-quarters of all the recorded votes saw a majority of one party voting against a majority of the other party, and astoundingly a third or more of a session's roll calls would pit at least 90 percent of one party against 90 percent or more of the other party. This was at a time when two Speakers of the House (Republicans Thomas B. Reed and Joseph G. Cannon) possessed almost dictatorial authority and therefore could enforce strict voting discipline.[38] But the Speaker's powers were curtailed drastically between 1909 and 1911, a development that combined with the internal GOP strains and splits produced by Progressivism to reduce party harmony and unity in congressional voting. The Democrats of the New Deal coalition also had their own fractures and contradictions (blacks versus whites, northern liberals versus southern conservatives, urban areas versus rural locales, and so forth). The effect of these tensions and the other antiparty trends discussed in Chapter One was to leave party majorities opposing each other on only about 40 percent of recorded votes through the latter 1960s and the 1970s. In the last several years, however, party voting has increased noticeably. (See again Tables 2.1 and 2.2 and Figures 2.1 and 2.2.) The 99th Congress, which held office in 1985 and 1986, produced the greatest partisan divide in more than three decades.[39] A majority of Democrats opposed a majority of Republicans on 55 percent of all recorded votes. (No other Congress has exceeded 50 percent since these figures were first compiled by the Congressional Quarterly in 1954.) The average Democratic member voted with his or her party (on votes dividing party majorities) about 76 percent of the time, while the average Republican did so in over 74 percent of the cases.

There are many reasons for the recent growth of party unity and cohesion. Some are the result of long-term political factors. Both congressional parties, for instance, have gradually become more ideologically homogeneous and internally consistent. Southern Democrats today are more moderate and far closer philosophically to their northern counterparts than the South's legislative barons of old ever were; similarly, there are few liberal Republicans left in either chamber of Congress, and GOP representatives from all regions of the country — with a few exceptions — are moderately to very conservative. At the same time, strong two-party competition has come to almost all areas of the nation, and the electoral insecurity produced by vigorous competition seems to encourage party unity and cooperation in a legislature (perhaps as a kind of "circling the wag-

TABLE 2.1 "Party Unity" Scores in the House and Senate (Average Individual Support for Party on Votes Dividing Party Majorities), 1959–1986

		HOUSE		SENATE		ALL CONGRESS AVERAGE	
YEAR	CONGRESS	D (%)	R (%)	D (%)	R (%)	D (%)	R (%)
1986	99	79	70	72	76	75.5	73.0
1985	99	80	75	75	76	77.5	75.5
1984	98	74	73	70	76	72.0	74.5
1983	98	76	74	71	74	73.5	74.0
1982	97	72	69	72	76	72.0	72.5
1981	97	69	74	71	81	70.0	77.5
1980	96	69	71	64	65	66.5	68.0
1979	96	69	73	68	66	68.5	69.5
1978	95	63	69	66	59	64.5	64.0
1977	95	68	71	63	66	65.5	68.5
1976	94	66	67	62	61	64.0	64.0
1975	94	69	72	68	64	68.5	68.0
1974	93	62	63	63	59	62.5	61.0
1973	93	68	68	69	64	68.5	66.0
1972	92	58	66	57	61	57.5	63.5
1971	92	61	67	64	63	62.5	65.0
1970	91	58	60	55	56	56.5	58.0
1969	91	61	62	63	63	62.0	62.5
1968	90	59	64	51	60	55.0	62.0
1967	90	67	74	61	60	64.0	67.0
1966	89	62	68	57	63	59.5	65.5
1965	89	70	71	63	68	66.5	69.5
1964	88	69	71	61	65	65.0	68.0
1963	88	73	74	66	67	69.5	70.5
1962	87	70	70	65	64	67.5	67.0
1961	87	77	73	74	68	75.5	70.5
1960	86	65	65	60	66	62.5	65.5
1959	86	79	79	67	72	73.0	75.5

SOURCE: *Congressional Quarterly Almanacs* (Washington, D.C.: Congressional Quarterly, Inc.).

D = Democrats

R = Republicans

FIGURE 2.1 "Party Unity"* Scores, 1959–1986

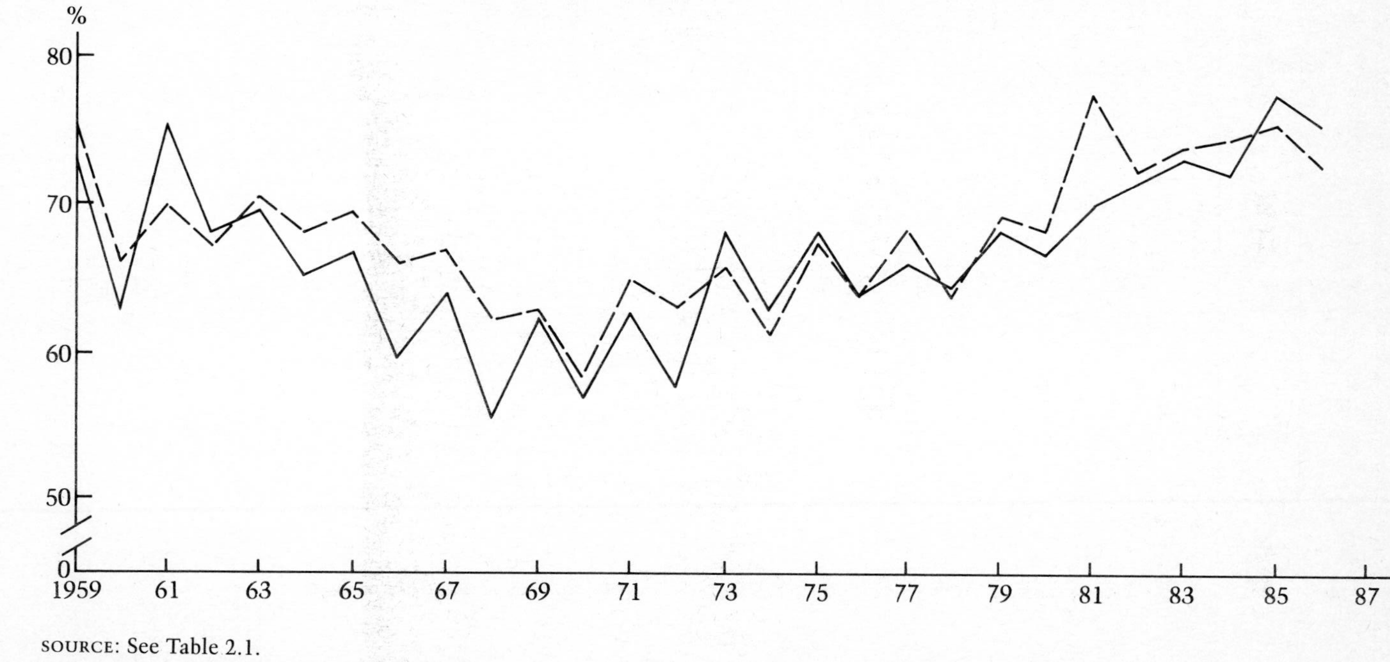

SOURCE: See Table 2.1.

*All Congress average.

Republicans — — — —

Democrats ————

TABLE 2.2 Party Voting in the House and Senate (Percent of Votes Finding Majorities of Democrats and Republicans on Opposite Sides), 1954–1986

YEAR	CONGRESS	HOUSE (%)	SENATE (%)	ALL CONGRESS AVERAGE
1986	99	57	52	54.5
1985	99	61	50	55.5
1984	98	47	40	43.5
1983	98	56	44	50.0
1982	97	36	43	39.5
1981	97	37	48	43.5
1980	96	38	46	42.0
1979	96	47	47	47.0
1978	95	33	45	39.0
1977	95	42	42	42.0
1976	94	36	37	36.5
1975	94	48	48	48.0
1974	93	29	44	36.5
1973	93	42	40	41.0
1972	92	27	36	31.5
1971	92	38	42	40.0
1970	91	27	35	31.0
1969	91	31	36	33.5
1968	90	35	32	33.5
1967	90	36	35	35.5
1966	89	41	50	45.5
1965	89	52	42	47.0
1964	88	55	36	45.5
1963	88	49	47	48.0
1962	87	46	41	43.5
1961	87	50	62	56.0
1960	86	53	37	45.0
1959	86	55	48	51.5
1958	85	40	44	42.0
1957	85	47	36	41.5
1956	84	50	53	51.5
1955	84	41	30	35.5
1954	83	38	47	42.5

SOURCE: *Congressional Quarterly Almanacs* (Washington, D.C.: Congressional Quarterly, Inc.).

FIGURE 2.2 Party Voting in the House and Senate, 1954–1986

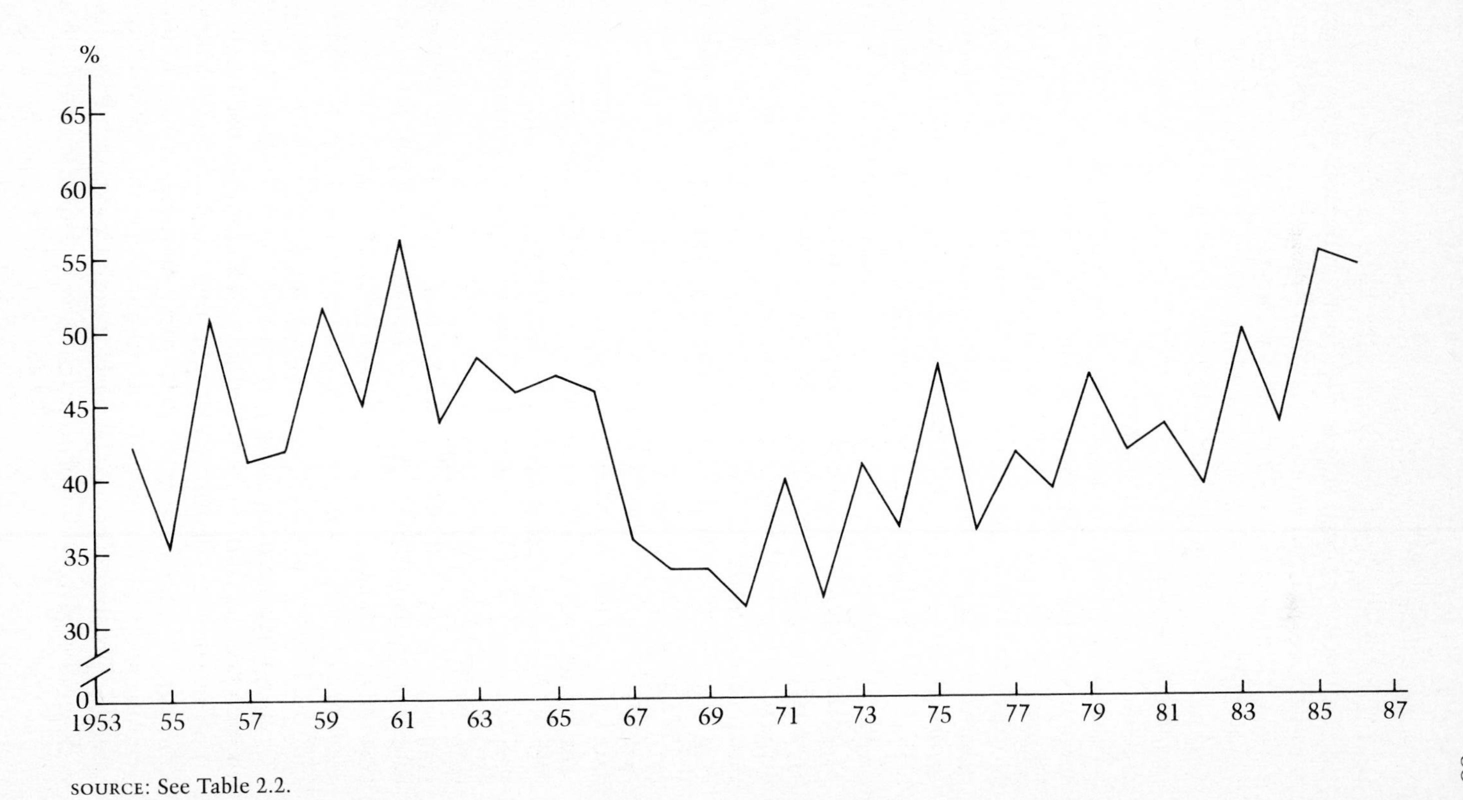

SOURCE: See Table 2.2.

ons" effect).[40] The circumstances of contemporary politics are also producing greater legislative cohesion. There is growing dissatisfaction on the Republican side of the House aisle with their seemingly semipermanent minority status, and the increased militancy of some GOP members of Congress has raised the partisan hackles of many Democrats, polarizing the House a bit more along party lines. On the other side of the Capitol, the looming partisan struggle over control of the Senate in 1985 and 1986 appeared to increase the party consciousness of both groups of senators.

One of the least recognized but most enduring effects of the Watergate scandal was to stimulate the strengthening of the congressional parties long after Richard Nixon had departed the White House. The Watergate-spawned election of seventy-five reform-minded freshman Democrats in 1974 led to a revolt against the seniority system in early 1975. Three senior, unresponsive chairmen were deposed, the power of the committee system was diminished, and a crucial barrier to the influence of party thus fell. When a rigid seniority system could be guaranteed to protect members who consistently bucked their party, committee chairs' support of party positions in recorded votes was quite low. After the 1975 display of party caucus muscle, though, chairpersons dramatically increased their solidarity with the party majority, scoring even higher than backbenchers on party unity scales.[41] This chair–caucus harmony has continued for more than a decade after the revolt, enabling almost all committee chairs to prevent any effort to remove them. The occasional rebellion, such as the one directed against House Armed Services Committee Chairman Les Aspin in early 1987, serves to remind other committee leaders of the importance of staying within party norms.[42]

The House Democratic Caucus (the group of all Democratic House members) has taken on life and new responsibilities beyond challenging chairpersons, and this development has assisted the furtherance of party cohesion.[43] Closed caucus meetings to discuss upcoming bills, to plan general strategy, to air complaints about the actions (or inaction) of party leaders and committees, and to direct that certain legislation be taken up or killed have been held with some frequency. If nothing else, the meetings provide leaders and chairpersons with a clear sense of party opinion. In addition to the revitalization of the caucus, a number of other post-Watergate changes has strengthened the party role in Congress.[44] Party leaders were given greater control over the flow of House business in 1975 through the Speaker's power to nominate the chair and the majority party members of the Rules Committee; once obstructionist, the committee has now been transformed into a reliable ally of the leadership. Additionally, the assignment of members to committees and the nomination of committee chairs has been placed more firmly in the control of party leaders (though their choices are still occasionally rejected by the party caucus). The recent centralization of the budget-making process has also given the leadership more influence,[45] and their reach has been extended still further by a substantial increase in staffing and support services for the Speaker, majority leader, and party whips.[46] Not by any measure have all the new reforms built up party power; some, such as the proliferation of subcommittees, have been detrimental, making Congress more difficult to manage and mobilize. But on the whole, conditions are becoming more supportive of party unity and conducive to purposive party leadership than at any time in recent years. This is particularly true in the House of Representatives, where the majority Democrats have been willing to use the rules to give their party key advantages (such as firm control of the Rules Committee and proportional overrepresentation on most committees).

Lastly, it should be noted that the extra-congressional party organizations have played a role in the renewed cohesiveness observed within Congress. As we will discuss at length in the next chapter, each national party committee has been recruiting and training House and Senate candidates as never before, and devising common themes for all nominees in election seasons — work that may help to produce a consensual legislative agenda for each party. The carrot and stick of party money and campaign services, such as media advertising production and polling, is also being used to convert independent candidates into party team players. Clearly, the more important the party organization can be to a legislator's election and reelection, the more attention a legislator is likely to pay to his or her party.

THE PRESIDENTIAL PARTY

Political parties may well be more integral to the operation of the legislative branch than the executive branch, but it is the presidential party that captures the public imagination and shapes the electorate's opinion of the two parties. In our very personalized politics, voters' perceptions of the incumbent president and the presidential candidates determine to a great degree how citizens perceive the parties.

A chief executive's successes are his or her party's successes; the president's failures are borne by the party as much as the individual. The image projected by a losing presidential candidate is incorporated into the party's contemporary portrait, whether wanted or not. As the only independently elected candidate of the national party, the president today naturally assumes the role of party leader (as does the White House nominee of the other party), though this was not the intention of the nation's founders. They had hoped for a nonpartisan presidency, a great unifier and elected monarch. George Washington fit the preconceived notion perfectly, but his was a brief tradition. From 1800 onwards (with the lone exception provided by James Monroe's White House tenure) presidents were identified with party groupings, and beginning with Andrew Jackson were formally the nominees of full-fledged national parties.

The juggling of contradictory roles is not always easy for a president. Expected not only to bring the country together as ceremonial chief of state and to forge a ruling consensus as head of government, the president must also be an effective commander of a sometimes divisive partisan subgroup. Along with the inevitable headaches party leadership brings, though, there are clear and compelling advantages that accompany it (as suggested in Chapter One). Foremost among them is a party's ability to mobilize support among voters for a president's program, especially among its own partisans. Also, the executive's legislative agenda might be derailed more quickly without the common tie of party label between the chief executive and many members of Congress; all presidents appeal for some congressional support on the basis of shared party affiliation, and they generally receive it. In recent decades, as Table 2.3 and Figure 2.3 indicate, the average legislator of the president's party has backed the chief executive two-thirds to three-quarters of the time, whereas the average member of the opposition has done so only one-third to one-half the time. There is considerable variance among presidents, of course, since circumstances and executive skill differ. Ronald Reagan's support among GOP senators has been exceptionally high, for instance, while Jimmy Carter and Dwight Eisenhower (in his second term) had more than the usual degree of trouble with their House partisans. Finally in this listing of presidential party assets, it is worth noting that a president's own election to office would be nearly impossible without the volunteer work and organizational aid provided to the nominee by the party.

TABLE 2.3 Average "Support Scores" for Members of Congress on Votes Related to the President's Program, 1953–1986

		SENATE		HOUSE		ALL CONGRESS AVERAGE	
YEAR	PARTY OF PRESIDENT	D (%)	R (%)	D (%)	R (%)	D (%)	R (%)
1953	Republican	46	68	49	74	47.5	71.0
1954	Republican	38	73	44	71	41.0	72.0
1955	Republican	56	72	53	60	54.5	66.0
1956	Republican	39	72	52	72	45.5	72.0
1957	Republican	51	69	49	54	50.0	61.5
1958	Republican	44	67	55	58	49.5	62.5
1959	Republican	38	72	40	68	39.0	70.0
1960	Republican	43	66	44	59	43.5	62.5
1961	Democrat	65	36	73	37	69.0	36.5
1962	Democrat	63	39	72	42	67.5	40.5
1963	Democrat	63	44	72	32	67.5	38.0
1964	Democrat	61	45	74	38	67.5	41.5
1965	Democrat	64	48	74	41	69.0	44.5
1966	Democrat	57	43	63	37	60.0	40.0
1967	Democrat	61	53	69	46	65.0	49.5
1968	Democrat	48	47	64	51	57.0	49.0
1969	Republican	47	66	48	57	47.5	61.5
1970	Republican	45	60	53	66	49.0	63.0
1971	Republican	40	64	47	72	43.5	68.0
1972	Republican	44	66	47	64	45.5	65.0
1973	Republican	37	61	35	62	36.0	61.5
1974	Republican	39	56	44	58	41.5	57.0
1975	Republican	47	68	38	63	42.5	65.5
1976	Republican	39	62	32	63	35.5	62.5
1977	Democrat	70	52	63	42	66.5	47.0
1978	Democrat	66	41	60	36	63.0	38.5
1979	Democrat	68	47	64	34	66.0	40.5
1980	Democrat	62	45	63	40	62.5	42.5
1981	Republican	49	80	42	68	45.5	74.0
1982	Republican	43	74	39	64	41.0	69.0
1983	Republican	42	73	28	70	35.0	71.5
1984	Republican	41	76	34	60	37.5	68.0
1985	Republican	35	75	30	67	32.5	71.0
1986	Republican	38	79	25	66	31.5	72.5

SOURCE: *Congressional Quarterly Almanacs* (Washington, D.C.: Congressional Quarterly, Inc.).

NOTE: Scores represent the percentage of recorded votes on which members voted in agreement with the president's announced position.

D = Democrats

R = Republicans

FIGURE 2.3 Average "Support Scores" for Members of Congress on Votes Related to the President's Program, 1953–1986

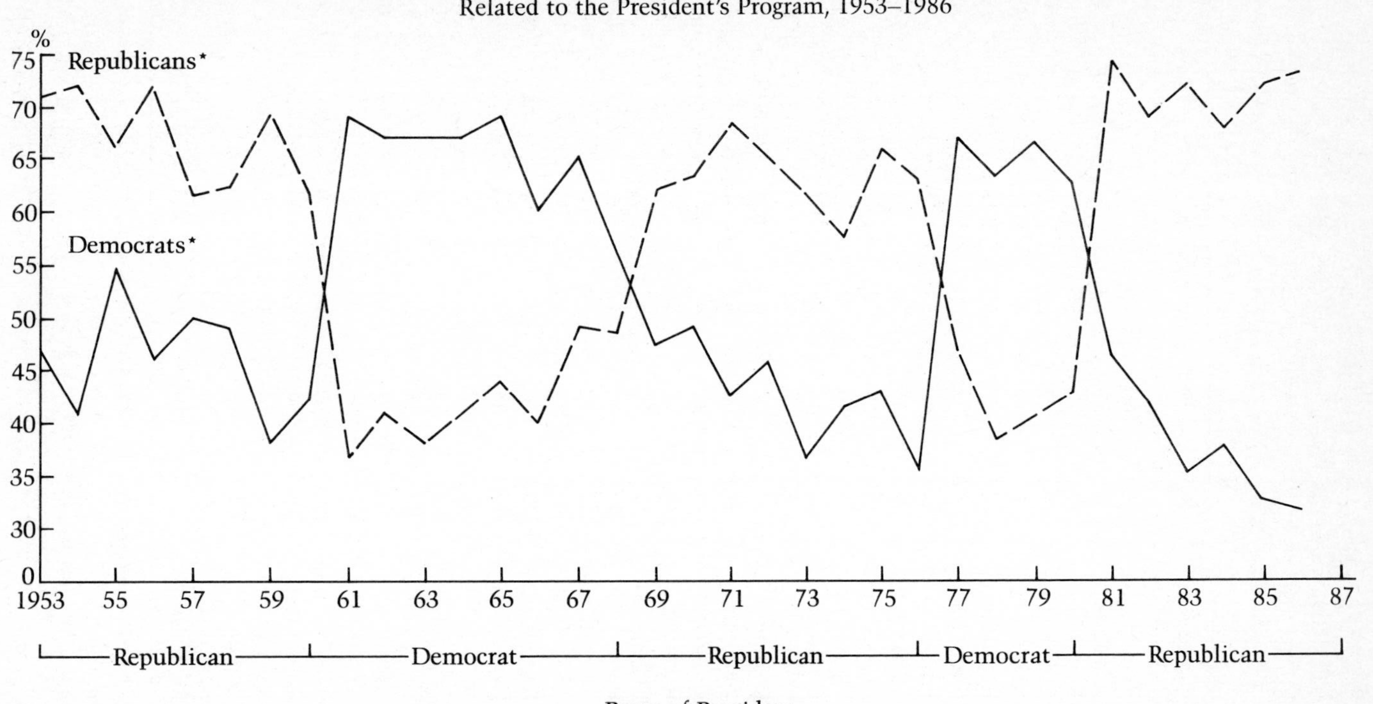

SOURCE: See Table 2.3.

*All Congress average

These party gifts to the president are reciprocated in other ways. In addition to compiling a record for the party and giving substance to its image, presidents appoint many activists to office, recruit candidates, raise money for the party treasury, campaign extensively for party nominees during election seasons, and occasionally provide some "coattail" help to fellow office-seekers who are on the ballot in presidential election years.

Some presidents take their party responsibilities more seriously than others. In this century Democrats Woodrow Wilson and Franklin Roosevelt were exceptionally party oriented and dedicated to building their party electorally and governmentally. In his first term Wilson worked closely with Democratic congressional leaders to fashion a progressive and successful party program, and Roosevelt was responsible for constructing the enduring New Deal coalition for his party and breathing life into a previously moribund Democratic National Committee. Republican Gerald Ford, during his brief tenure in the 1970s, also achieved a reputation as a party builder, and he was willing to undertake campaign and organizational chores for the GOP (especially in fundraising and barnstorming for nominees) that most other presidents minimized or shunned.

Sadly, most modern chief executives have been in an entirely different mold. Dwight Eisenhower elevated nonpartisanship to an art form, and while it may have preserved his personal popularity,[47] it proved a disaster for his party. Despite a full two-term occupancy of the White House, the Republican party remained mired in minority status. Eisenhower never really attempted to transfer his high ratings to the party, and in 1958 even implied that he would not mind if some of his GOP critics were defeated for reelection.[48] And his impolitic vetoing of an important bill sponsored by Maine's Republican Senator Frederick G. Payne just two days before the 1958 election contributed to Payne's loss.[49] Lyndon Johnson kept the DNC busy with such important tasks as answering wedding invitations sent to the First Family,[50] and when many of the Democratic senators and representatives elected on his presidential coattails were endangered in the 1966 midterm election, LBJ canceled a major campaign trip on their behalf lest his policies get tied too closely to their possible defeats. Democrats lost forty-seven House seats, three Senate seats, and eight governorships in a 1966 debacle Johnson did little to prevent. Probably no other president's attitude toward his party was ever as contemptuous as Richard Nixon's. He discouraged the GOP from nominating candidates against conservative southern

Democrats in order to improve his own electoral and congressional position, and subordinated the party's agenda almost wholly to his own reelection in 1972. Shunting aside the Republican National Committee, Nixon formed the infamous Committee to Re-elect the President, known by the most appropriate acronym of our time: CREEP. So ignorant of CREEP's abuses were party leaders that the Republican party organization itself was essentially exonerated during the Watergate investigations. (Unfortunately for GOP candidates in 1974, the public failed to make this fine distinction.) Jimmy Carter showed little interest in his national party either. Elected as an outsider in 1976, Carter and his top aides at first viewed the party as another extension of the Washington establishment they had pledged to ignore. Carter and his DNC chairmen failed to develop the Democratic party organizationally and financially to keep it competitive during a critical period, while the Republicans were undergoing a dramatic revitalization. Later, during his fateful 1980 reelection campaign, Carter was properly criticized for diverting DNC personnel and resources to his presidential needs rather than permitting them to pursue essential partywide electoral tasks.

Fortunately, modern chief executives now have an alternative model well worth emulating. Ronald Reagan has been the most party-oriented president of recent times. "As one who often has been critical of other aspects of Reagan's stewardship," wrote the journalist David Broder, "I want to salute the man who, more than any other president I have ever covered, pays his dues and unselfishly aids the growth of his political party."[51] In 1983 and 1984 during his own reelection effort, Reagan made more than two dozen campaign and fundraising appearances for all branches of the party organization and candidates at every level. More than 300 television advertisement endorsements were taped as well, including one for an obscure Honolulu city council contest.[52] Reagan has even shown a willingness to get involved in the nitty-gritty of candidate recruitment, frequently calling in strong potential candidates to urge them to run.[53] During the pitched and ultimately losing battle to retain control of the Senate for the Republicans in 1986, Reagan played the good soldier, visiting twenty-two key states repeatedly and raising $33 million for the party and its candidates.[54] Unlike Eisenhower, Reagan has been willing to attempt a popularity transfer to his party and to campaign for Republicans whether they are strongly loyal to him personally or not;[55] unlike Johnson, Reagan has been willing to put his prestige and policies to the test on the hustings; unlike

Nixon, Reagan spent time and effort helping underdogs and long-shot candidates, not just likely winners;[56] unlike Carter, Reagan has signed more than seventy fundraising appeals for party committees and has taken a personal interest in the further strengthening of the GOP's organizational capacity.

However, even Reagan has been unsuccessful in providing much coattail help to his party's nominees lower down on the ballot.[57] His initial victory in 1980 was one factor in the election of a Republican Senate, but his landslide reelection in 1984 (like Nixon's in 1972) had almost no impact on his party's congressional representation.[58] There is little question that the coattail effect has diminished sharply compared to a generation ago, as a number of studies have shown.[59] Partly, the decreased competitiveness of congressional elections has been produced by artful redistricting and the growing value of incumbency.[60] But voters are also less willing to think and cast ballots in purely partisan terms — a worrisome development that limits presidential leadership and hurts party development. We will be returning to this subject in subsequent chapters.

THE PARTIES AND THE JUDICIARY

Americans view the judiciary as "above politics" and certainly non-partisan. Many judges are quick to agree. Yet not only do justices follow the election returns and allow themselves to be influenced by popular opinion, they are also products of their party identification and possess the very same partisan perceptual screens as all other politically aware citizens.

While legislators are far more partisan than judges, it is wrong to assume that judges reach decisions wholly independent of partisan values. First of all, judges are creatures of the political process, and their posts are considered patronage plums. They are selected by presidents or governors for their abilities but also as members of the executive's party and sometimes as representatives of a certain philosophy or approach to government. In this century every president has appointed judges overwhelmingly from his own party; Jimmy Carter and Ronald Reagan, for instance, drew 95 percent or more of their judicial choices from their respective parties.[61] Furthermore, Democratic executives are naturally inclined to choose liberal individuals for the bench, who may be friendly to the welfare state or critical of some business practices. Republican executives generally lean toward conservatives for judicial posts, hoping they will be tough on criminal defendants and restrained in the use of court power. Research has long indicated that party affiliation is in fact a moderately good predictor of judicial decisions, at least in some areas.[62] In other words, party matters in the judiciary just as it does in the other two branches, though it certainly matters less on the bench than in the legislature and the executive.

Many of the judges appointed to office have long careers in politics as loyal party workers or legislators. Some jurists are even more overtly political, since they are elected to office. In a majority of states at least some judicial positions are filled by election, and seventeen states hold outright partisan elections, with both parties nominating opposing candidates and running hard-hitting campaigns.[63] In some rural counties across America, local judges are not merely partisanly elected figures; they are the key public officials, controlling many patronage jobs and the party machinery itself. Obviously, therefore, in many places in the United States, judges by necessity and by tradition are not above politics, but in the thick of it. While election of the judiciary is a questionable practice in light of its specially sanctioned role as impartial arbiter, partisan influence exerted both by jurists' party loyalties and by the appointment (or election) process is useful in retaining some degree of accountability in a branch often accused of being arrogant and aloof.

Party affiliation affects judges, then, but their decisions in cases involving political parties have had a profound effect on the health of party organizations as well. The judicial record on party has been very mixed. On one hand, the courts historically have had a hands-off approach to parties, generally refusing to involve themselves in their internal, political affairs.[64] On the other hand, the courts have sometimes made extensive and damaging intrusions into party affairs. Few would argue with some Supreme Court decisions invalidating party rules and nomination procedures that violated basic constitutional rights, such as *Smith v. Allwright* in 1944[65] when the Texas Democratic party was prohibited from permitting only whites to vote in its primary. But the Court has been far too insistent on the "right" of third-party and Independent candidates to easy access to the ballot, ignoring both the essential stability a two-party system brings and society's right to shore up that system.[66] And in the area of patronage, the Court has devastated the parties. In two separate decisions in 1976 and 1980,[67] appointment to government jobs on the basis of party affiliation — a time-honored practice that gives the parties vital rewards and incentives to use in building their organizations — was severely limited. While patronage will be the subject of further commentary in the concluding chapter, it may suffice for now to cite Supreme Court Justice Lewis Powell, who dissented in both of the Court's ill-considered patronage rulings: "Patronage — the right to select key personnel and to reward the party 'faithful' — serves the public interest by facilitating the implementation of policies endorsed by the electorate."[68]

In another legal sphere, however, the recent judicial news for parties has been good. Twice (in 1975 and 1981) the Supreme Court has held that when national party rules for presidential delegate selection conflict with state law, the party rules take precedence.[69] In both cases, the national Democratic party's specifications overrode conflicting Illinois and Wisconsin statutes on the basis of a party's constitutionally protected "freedom of political association." This associational right was taken a giant step further in 1986 in *Tashjian v. Republican Party of Connecticut,*[70] when the Court ruled that a state could not require a political party to hold "closed" primary elections, where only registered party members may vote, if the party preferred another system. A party's First Amendment associational rights, said the Court, guaranteed the party, not the state, the choice of nominating conditions. The broad implications of this ruling for state regulation of the parties will be discussed in Chapter Seven.

THE PARTIES AND STATE GOVERNMENTS

Most of the conclusions just reached about the party's relationship to the legislature, the executive, and the judiciary apply as well to the state level. The national parties, after all, are organized around state units, and the basic structural arrangement of party and government is much the same in Washington and the state capitals. Remarkably, too, the major national parties are the dominant political forces in all fifty states. This has been true consistently; unlike Great Britain or Canada, the United States has no regional or state parties that displace one or both of the national parties in local contests. Occasionally in American history a third party has proven locally potent, as did Minnesota's Farmer–Labor party and Wisconsin's Progressives, both of which elected governors and state legislative majorities earlier in this century. But over time none have survived,[71] and every state's two-party system mirrors national party dualism, at least as far as labels are concerned.

There are some party-oriented differences at the state level, though. Governors in many states tend to possess even greater influence over their parties' organizations and legislators than do presidents.[72] Many governors have far more patronage positions at their command than does a president, and these material rewards and incentives give governors added clout with activists and officeholders. In addition, tradition in some states permits the governor to take a role in selecting the legislature's committee chairs and party floor leaders, and some state executives even attend and help direct the party legislative caucuses — activities no president would ever undertake. Moreover, forty-three governors possess the item veto denied the national executive.[73] The item veto permits the governor to veto single items (such as individual pork barrel projects) in appropriations bills. Whereas a president must often accept objectionable measures as part of a bill too urgent or important to be vetoed, a governor gains enormous leverage with legislators by means of the item veto.

Just as the party relationship between the executive and the legislature tends to be stronger at the state level than in Washington, so also is the party role in the legislature itself more high-profile and effective. Most state legislatures surpass the United States Congress in partisan unity and cohesion.[74] While only 43 percent of congressional roll calls from 1954 to 1986 have produced majorities of the two parties on opposite sides, a number of state legislatures (including Massachusetts, New York, Ohio, and Pennsylvania) have achieved party voting levels of 70 percent or better in some years.[75] Not all states display party cohesion of this magnitude, of course. Nebraska has an officially nonpartisan legislature, and the lack of two-party competition in the South has left essentially one-party legislatures split into factions, regional groupings, or personal cliques. As real intraparty competition reaches the legislative level in southern states, however, party cohesion in the legislatures is likely to increase.

One other party distinction is notable in many state legislatures. Compared to the Congress, state legislative leaders have much more authority and power, and this is one reason why party unity is higher in the state capitols.[76] The strict seniority system that usually controls committee assignments in Congress is less absolute in most states, and legislative leaders often have considerable discretion in appointing the committee chairs and members. The party caucuses, too, are usually more active and influential in state legislatures than in their Washington counterparts. In some legislatures, the caucuses meet weekly or even daily to work out strategy and count votes, and nearly one-fourth of the caucuses bind all the party members to support the group's decisions on key issues (such as appropriations measures, tax issues, and procedural questions).[77] Not just the leaders and caucuses but the party organizations as well have more influence over legislators at the state level. State legislators are far more dependent than their congressional counterparts on their state and local parties for election assistance. While members of Congress have large government-provided staffs and lavish perquisites to assist (directly or indirectly) their reelection efforts, state legislative candidates need party workers and, increasingly, the party's financial support and technological resources at election time.

The party in government has changed in important ways in recent decades, as we have just reviewed. But its modifications have been evolutionary compared to the revolution in party organization that has taken place in the matter of a few years. This transformation in party machinery — its dimensions and implications — is the focus of the next chapter.

Notes

1. E. E. Schattschneider, *Party Government* (New York: Rinehart, 1942), 6–8.
2. Ibid., 8.
3. George Washington, "Farewell Address," in *Writings* (Washington, D.C.: U.S. Government Printing Office, 1940), vol. 35, 223–228.
4. See, generally, William Nisbet Chambers, *Political Parties in a New Nation: The American Experience, 1776–1809* (New York: Oxford University Press, 1963); Chambers and Walter Dean Burnham, eds., *The American Party Systems: Stages of Political Development* (New York: Oxford University Press, 1967); Richard Hofstadter, *The Idea of a Party System: The Rise of Legitimate Opposition in the United States, 1780–1840* (Berkeley: University of California Press, 1970); Richard P. McCormick, *The Second American Party System: Party Formation in the Jacksonian Era* (Chapel Hill: University of North Carolina Press, 1966); Roy F. Nichols, *The Invention of the American Political Parties* (New York: Macmillan, 1967); and Clifton McCleskey, "Democratic Representation and the Constitution: Where Do Political Parties Fit In?" *University of Virginia Newsletter* 60 (July 1984): 61–64, at 62–63.

5. The National Republicans (one forerunner of the Whig party) and the Anti-Masonic parties each had held more limited conventions in 1831.
6. Great Britain, by contrast, did not develop truly modern parties until the 1870s, once the electorate had been broadened by the Reform Acts of 1832 and 1867.
7. Voter turnout in presidential elections from 1876 to 1900 ranged from 75 to 82 percent of the potential (male) electorate, compared with 53 to 55 percent in contemporary elections. See *Historical Statistics of the United States: Colonial Times to 1970,* Part 2, Series Y-27-28 (Washington: Government Printing Office, 1975), based on unpublished data prepared by Walter Dean Burnham.
8. Frank Sorauf, *Party Politics in America* (5th ed.)(Boston: Little, Brown & Co., 1984), 22.
9. This topic will be discussed in Chapter Seven.
10. Schattschneider, *Party Government*, 48.
11. See V. O. Key, Jr., *American State Politics: An Introduction* (New York: Knopf, 1956).
12. See V. O. Key, Jr., *Southern Politics in State and Nation* (New York: Knopf, 1949).
13. See John F. Bibby, Cornelius P. Cotter, James L. Gibson, and Robert J. Huckshorn, "Parties in State Politics," in Virginia Gray, Herbert Jacob, and Kenneth Vines, eds., *Politics in the American States* (4th ed.) (Boston: Little, Brown, 1983), 66, Table 3.3; also Larry Sabato, *Goodbye to Good-Time Charlie: The American Governorship Transformed* (2nd ed.) (Washington, D.C.: Congressional Quarterly Press, 1983), 116–138.
14. Sorauf, *Party Politics in America,* 61.
15. Ibid., 51.
16. The seven are: Anti-Masonic party (1832 — 7 electoral votes), American (Know-Nothing) party (1856 — 8 electoral votes), People's (Populist) party (1892 — 22 electoral votes), Progressive (Bull Moose) party (1912 — 88 electoral votes), Progressive party (1924 — 13 electoral votes), States Rights (Dixiecrat) party (1948 — 39 electoral votes), and American Independent party (1968 — 46 electoral votes).
17. Roosevelt's 1912 effort was the most successful; the Bull Moose party won 30 percent of the popular vote for president (though only 17 percent of the Electoral College votes). Roosevelt's is also the only third party to run ahead of one of the two major parties (the Republicans).
18. Anderson only received 7 percent of the vote in the end, though at points in the contest polls had shown him well above 20 percent.
19. Sorauf, *Party Politics in America,* 40–43.
20. New York election law makes the Conservatives and Liberals (and, more recently, the Right to Life antiabortion party) potential power brokers since as an alternative to placing their own adherents on the ballot they can nominate the candidates of a major party to run under their labels instead, thus encouraging the major parties and their nominees to court them assiduously.
21. David E. Price, *Bringing Back the Parties* (Washington, D.C.: Congressional Quarterly Press, 1984), 36–38.

22. The precise current party committee names are: the Democratic Congressional Campaign Committee, the National Republican Congressional Committee, the Democratic Senatorial Campaign Committee, and the National Republican Senatorial Committee.
23. Price, *Bringing Back the Parties,* 275–279.
24. Ibid., 264–290.
25. Democratic Policy Commission, "New Choices in a Changing America" (Washington, D.C.: Democratic National Committee, September 1986).
26. Price, *Bringing Back the Parties,* 38–40.
27. Sidney Blumenthal, "Outside Foundation Recruited the Inside Troops," *Washington Post,* September 24, 1985, A1, A10.
28. Robert Kuttner, "What's the Big Idea?", *The New Republic* 194 (November 18, 1985): 23–26.
29. Sorauf, *Party Politics in America,* 79–81.
30. Richard E. Cohen, "Democratic Leadership Council sees Party void and is ready to fill it," *National Journal* 18 (February 1, 1986): 267.
31. Dom Bonafede, "Kirk at the DNC's Helm," *National Journal* 18 (March 22, 1986): 703–707.
32. See Larry Sabato, *PAC POWER: Inside the World of Political Action Committees* (New York: W. W. Norton, 1984), 104, 116, 151; and Irwin B. Arieff, Nadine Cohodes, and Richard Whittle, "Senator Helms Builds a Machine of Interlinked Organizations to Shape Both Politics, Policy," *Congressional Quarterly Weekly* 40 (March 4, 1982): 479–505.
33. As quoted in *Virginian-Pilot and Ledger Star,* May 11, 1986, C1.
34. See *Congressional Quarterly Weekly* 43 (February 9, 1985): 283.
35. See Sabato, *PAC POWER,* 116.
36. Such cases are few, but a deterrent nonetheless. Several United States senators were expelled from the Republican caucus in 1925 for having supported the Progressive candidate for president the previous year. In 1965 two southern House Democrats lost all their committee seniority because of their 1964 endorsement of GOP presidential nominee Barry Goldwater, as did another southerner in 1968 for his backing of George Wallace's third-party candidacy. In early 1983 the House Democratic caucus removed Texas Congressman Phil Gramm from his Budget Committee seat because of his disloyalty in working more closely with Republican Committee members than his own party leaders. (Gramm resigned his seat, was reelected to it as a Republican, and used the controversy to propel himself into the United States Senate in 1984.)
37. See Julius Turner (with Edward V. Schneier, Jr.), *Party and Constituency: Pressures on Congress* (Baltimore: Johns Hopkins Press, 1970), 33–39.
38. Price, *Bringing Back the Parties,* 51–53.
39. See *Congressional Quarterly Weekly* 44 (November 15, 1986): 2901.
40. Joseph A. Schlesinger, "The New American Political Party," *American Political Science Review* 79 (1985): 1168.
41. Sara Brandes Crook and John R. Hibbing, "Congressional Reform and Party Discipline: The Effects of Change in the Seniority System on

Party Loyalty in the U.S. House of Representatives," *British Journal of Political Science* 15 (April 1985): 207–226.

42. Aspin survived the challenge to his power, but only after a bitter struggle in the Democratic Caucus.
43. Timothy E. Cook, "The Electoral Connection in the 99th Congress," *PS* 19 (Winter 1986): 19–20.
44. Price, *Bringing Back the Parties,* 64–69.
45. Allen Schick, *Reconciliation and the Congressional Budget Process* (Washington, D.C.: American Enterprise Institute for Public Policy Research, 1981).
46. Price, *Bringing Back the Parties,* 67.
47. See Fred I. Greenstein, *The Hidden-Hand Presidency* (New York: Basic Books, 1982).
48. *National Journal* 18 (October 11, 1986): 2397.
49. Ibid.
50. Rhodes Cook, "Reagan Nurtures His Adopted Party to Strength," *Congressional Quarterly Weekly* 43 (September 28, 1985): 1927–1930.
51. David S. Broder, "A Party's Soldier," *Washington Post,* October 20, 1985, C7.
52. Ibid.
53. Cook, "Reagan Nurtures His Adopted Party," 1927–1928.
54. *Washington Post,* November 3, 1986, A10, and November 5, 1986, A21.
55. Broder, "A Party's Soldier." Broder cites the case of Oregon GOP United States Senator Robert Packwood, often a caustic critic of Reagan's, who asked for and received the first presidential media reelection endorsement of the 1986 campaign season.
56. Cook, "Reagan Nurtures His Adopted Party," 1930.
57. Ibid.
58. The GOP picked up just fifteen House seats and lost two Senate seats in 1984; in 1972 the tally was similar, with a gain of twelve House seats and a loss of two Senate berths.
59. George C. Edwards III, *Presidential Influence in Congress* (San Francisco: Freeman, 1980); and Herbert M. Kritzer and Robert B. Eubank, "Presidential Coattails Revisited: Partisanship and Incumbency Effects," *American Journal of Political Science* 23 (1979): 615–626.
60. Lyn Ragsdale, "The Fiction of Congressional Elections as Presidential Events," *American Politics Quarterly* 8 (1980): 375–398; and Thomas E. Mann and Raymond E. Wolfinger, "Candidates and Parties in Congressional Elections," *American Political Science Review* 74 (1980): 617–632.
61. Figures provided by my colleague, Henry J. Abraham.
62. See Sidney Ulmer, "The Political Party Variable on the Michigan Supreme Court," *Journal of Public Law* 11 (1962): 352–362; Stuart Nagel, "Political Party Affiliation and Judges' Decisions," *American Political Science Review* 55 (1961): 843–850); David W. Adamany, "The Party Variable in Judges' Voting: Conceptual Notes and a Case Study," *American Political Science Review* 63 (1969): 57–73; Sheldon Goldman, "Voting Behavior on the United States Courts of Appeals, 1961–1964,"

American Political Science Review 60 (1966): 374–383; and Robert A. Carp and C. K. Rowland, *Policymaking and Politics in the Federal District Courts* (Knoxville: University of Tennessee Press, 1983).

63. Sorauf, *Party Politics in America,* 382–387.
64. Jerome Mileur, "Federal Constitutional Challenges to State Party Regulation," a paper prepared for the annual meeting of the American Political Science Association, Washington, D.C., August 30–September 2, 1986, 35–36.
65. 321 U.S. 649 (1944).
66. See the Ohio cases involving George Wallace [*Williams v. Rhodes,* 393 U.S. 23 (1968)] and John Anderson [*Anderson v. Celebreeze,* 103 S. Ct. 1564 (1983)]. The Court essentially ruled that Ohio and the other states could not discriminate against third party and Independent presidential candidacies by placing burdensome restrictions on them (early deadlines, substantial signature-gathering requirements, and the like).
67. *Elrod v. Burns,* 427 U.S. 347 (1976) and *Branti v. Finkel,* 445 U.S. 507 (1980). See also Clifton McCleskey, "Parties at the Bar: Equal Protection, Freedom of Association, and the Rights of Political Organizations," *Journal of Politics* 46 (1984): 346–368.
68. *Branti v. Finkel,* ibid., at 526–529.
69. *Cousins v. Wigoda,* 419 U.S. 477 (1975) and *Democratic Party v. La Follette,* 450 U.S. 107 (1981). The former is the Illinois case; the latter is the Wisconsin case.
70. 107 S. Ct. 544 (1986). See Elder Witt and Jeremy Gaunt, "Closed Primary Laws Barred by 5–4 Supreme Court Ruling," *Congressional Quarterly Weekly* 16 (December 13, 1986): 3064–3065.
71. The Farmer–Labor party did survive in a sense; having endured a series of defeats, it merged in 1944 with the Democrats, and Democratic candidates still officially bear the standard of the Democratic–Farmer–Labor (DFL) party. At about the same time, also having suffered severe electoral reversals, the Progressives stopped nominating candidates in Wisconsin. The party's members either returned to the Republican party, from which it had split off early in the century, or became Democrats.
72. Sorauf, *Party Politics in America,* 378.
73. Larry Sabato, *Goodbye to Good-Time Charlie: The American Governorship Transformed* (2nd ed.) (Washington, D.C.: Congressional Quarterly, 1983), 76–77.
74. Price, *Bringing Back the Parties,* 83–84.
75. Ibid.
76. Sarah McCally Morehouse, "Legislatures and Political Parties," *State Government* 59: 1 (1976): 19–24.
77. Ibid. The most active legislative caucuses include those of Colorado, Idaho, and New York. On the other hand, five states besides nonpartisan Nebraska have no party caucuses at all: Alabama, Arkansas, Louisiana, Mississippi, and Texas.

CHAPTER THREE

• ☆ • ☆ •

The Modern Transformation of Party Organization

THE GREAT IRONY OF MODERN POLITICAL PARTIES is that as more and more commentators have bemoaned their decline, both party organizations have grown increasingly mightier. There is really no mystery to this superficially puzzling paradox, for the contending elements of the parties' contradictory rise and fall are partly cause and effect. It is the *party-in-the-electorate,* the voters' sense of partisan identification and loyalty, that has seemed to diminish, and this perceived threat to the parties' political hegemony has been one major stimulus to their self-initiated organizational regeneration.

The usually prescient political consultant Joseph Napolitan had it exactly wrong when he declared, "the new [campaign] technologies make parties, if not obsolete, then certainly obsolescent."[1] The very technologies that once enabled candidates to run independently of their parties are creating immense opportunities for the parties to bring candidates and voters back to their moorings. Candidates are being supplied with party funds and election services unparalleled in sophistication and quality.[2] And voters today are being contacted by party workers at more than double the rate of the 1950s — an era when party loyalties were considerably more pronounced.[3]

Following a short sketch of the parties' place in the prevailing structure of campaign finance, this chapter's investigation of the new organizational parties will begin with the story of the GOP, since Republicans nationally and in many of the states have led the way. Long depicted in New Deal mythology as a stodgy collection wedded to the status quo, the Republican party has in fact become the vehicle of revolutionary change in party activity and organization. For many years the complacent Democrats let their lingering majority in the electorate and GOP presidential mistakes produce their election victories. But after landslide national defeats in 1980 and 1984, they have undertaken a party reconstruction in earnest, using the Republicans as their model. While still far from parity with the GOP, the Democrats are well on their way to becoming more structurally comparable and electorally competitive again. The tumult at the top has had dramatic repercussions for state and local parties, too, and the state of party "federalism" as well as the broader implications of organizational renewal for American democracy will also be discussed in this chapter.

The Parties and the New Campaign Finance Laws

A brief review of the existing campaign finance framework will set the stage for our dissection of the parties' resurgence, for an understanding of how these laws have affected the parties is a necessary precondition to comprehending the changes in party activity that have occurred. A thorough discussion of the massive overhaul in campaign finance from 1971 to 1979 is beyond our scope here,[4] but it is worth noting that the reformers in and out of Congress who spearheaded the changes did not purposely set out to harm the parties — but neither was party building one of their goals. In the rush to correct the abuses apparent during the Watergate scandals, the political parties were often treated as part of the problem, and the parties have had to adapt as best they could to a system not of their own making.

As it has evolved, the parties have overcome many obstacles in the campaign finance statutes and taken advantage of every opportunity offered by them, expanding and extending the law in ways only dimly foreseen (if at all) by the bill's original backers. For example, in restricting individuals to $20,000 annually in party donations, the new law dried up a valuable source of cash for both parties. But the parties initiated broad-based direct mail programs instead, producing a financial empire of millions of small contributors instead of a relative handful of financial angels. In this way, then, the new law unintentionally did the parties a sizeable favor. Another example of party adaptation and aggrandizement can be found in the provisions regarding contributions to candidates. Political party committees are treated in the law the same as political action committees (PACs) in one crucial respect: they are limited to direct gifts of $5,000 per candidate per election (with the primary and general election counted separately).[5] But in House races these party contributions are being multiplied, since the national party committee, the state party committee, and the national party's congressional campaign committee are usually each eligible to give the $5,000 maximum. Thus, as much as $30,000 ($5,000 × 2 elections [primary and general][6] × 3 separate party committees) can be directly contributed to every party nominee for the United States House. In Senate elections, the national party committee and the senatorial campaign committee may give a combined maximum of $17,500 to each candidate, and another $10,000 can be added from the state party committee for a total of $27,500 in direct gifts.

These contribution limits are not generous, given the enormous costs of competitive election campaigns today. Most Senate candidates, even in small states, spend well over a million dollars, and it is the rare House candidate in a marginal district who spends less than a quarter of a million dollars. Fortunately for the parties, direct contributions can be significantly augmented with coordinated expenditures — party-paid general election campaign expenditures (for television advertising, polling, etc.) made in consultation and coordination with the candidate.[7] The coordinated expenditure limits are set surprisingly high. In the case of presidential candidates, the national party committees can spend up to two cents times the nations' voting age population (plus an adjustment for inflation[8]); in 1984 this amounted to about $6.9 million.[9] For House candidates the national and state parties may each spend $10,000 plus an inflation adjustment; the party committees together could thereby spend $43,620 in 1986 on behalf of each House nominee.[10] Senate candidates are the beneficiaries of even higher limits on coordinated expenditures. The national and state parties can each spend $20,000 (plus an inflation factor) or two cents times the state's voting age population (plus inflation), whichever is greater. In 1986 the party expenditure limits amounted to $87,240 in the eight smallest states to over $1.7 million in California — or a national total maximum of about $12 million for each party in the thirty-four Senate con-

tests. Importantly, the national party committee is permitted to act as the state party committee's *spending agent;* that is, with the state party's agreement, the national committee can assume the state party's permitted portion of the coordinated expenditures.[11] This privilege centralizes power in the national committees, and unburdens weaker state party committees that otherwise might not be able to contribute the maximum.

Other aspects of the new campaign finance laws have proven far less beneficial to political parties. Perhaps no unintended consequence of the reforms has worked a greater hardship than the elaborate reporting requirements and complicated rules and regulations accompanying the statutes. Even many campaign attorneys are thoroughly confused by the intricate interpretations issued by the Federal Election Commission,[12] and a substantial number of state party chairs claim the laws hinder their activities.[13] At the least, the regulations force state and local committees to separate their federal campaign efforts from campaigns at other levels (which do not come under the iron hand of federal law). This can be both administratively unwieldy and financially costly. Even worse, the campaign laws can have a chilling effect on state and local parties, discouraging them from participating at all in federal contests for fear of the legal, organizational, and budgetary consequences.

The reporting requirements have not slowed the growth of political action committees, of course; their formation was dramatically spurred by the new campaign laws,[14] and PACs are clearly institutional rivals for the donations of politically active voters as well as the affections of candidate-recipients.[15] Additionally, the parties have been especially hamstrung in presidential contests.[16] Public financing subsidies flow not through the parties but directly to presidential candidates, and the parties have no role even in certifying candidates for funding eligibility. The public financing law also contains a provision for the funding of third-party and Independent presidential candidates, which can be viewed as encouraging political fragmentation and undermining the two-party system.[17] And the fact that each major-party presidential candidate is limited to an overall general election expenditure ceiling probably encourages more spending on the "efficient" communication medium of television and less on more invisible (but possibly more effective) organizational work by the parties.[18] Finally, in 1976, when the Supreme Court allowed absolutely unlimited *independent expenditures* — money spent by an individual or group on behalf of a candidate without any consultation with him or her[19] — it unleashed yet another party rival, for while parties are restricted in their spending, the sky's the limit for Independent individuals and groups.

Partially because the antiparty effects of the campaign finance laws became increasingly apparent, Congress passed two pieces of ameliorating and welcome legislation. First, in 1978 it extended to political parties the same low postage rate available to nonprofit and educational groups, a move which further stimulated direct mail fundraising by the parties. Second, and more importantly, Congress amended the finance law in 1979 to authorize state and local parties to make unlimited expenditures to conduct voter registration and get-out-the-vote drives for presidential tickets, and to produce unlimited quantities of election paraphernalia (buttons, bumper stickers, etc.) for all federal candidates.[20] Not only have many state and local parties used the provision extensively, but the two national parties have organized expansive funding programs for some of these activities since the money raised — called "soft money" — often does not have to be fully disclosed as does the "hard money" given to, or spent specifically for, federal candidates. Soft money gifts can also sometimes be accepted from otherwise prohibited sources (union and corporate treasuries, for instance).[21] Because soft money is not always disclosed and since the *national* parties are frequently taking centralized command of privileges meant for *state and local* parties, soft money is controversial. Nevertheless, the parties have, in the words of one observer, driven "a Brink's truck through this provision in the law."[22] The Republicans alone raised and spent $10 to $15 million in soft money in 1980, and both parties together probably exceeded $20 million in soft money expenditures during the 1984 presidential election.[23]

The soft money programs emphasize yet again that the parties have been energetic and ingenious in applying — and maneuvering around — the new campaign finance laws. Before these laws took full effect, the parties had supplied about 17 percent of the war chests of 1972 congressional candidates.[24] The impact of the statutes was dramatic at first, and the parties fell to about 7 percent of the total by 1978. But by 1986, when direct contributions, coordinated expenditures, soft money, and special cut-rate party services to candidates[25] are included, the proportion of campaign money provided to congressional candidates appears to be once again in the 15 to 17 percent range — a complete recovery of prominence engineered by the parties themselves with the aid of the 1978 and 1979 modifications in the campaign finance laws. This party proportion is often underestimated because soft money and cut-rate services are improperly left out of the calculation. If individual and PAC contributions that were solicited by the parties and steered directly to the candidates (and thus not technically counted as party gifts) were also included, the proportion of congressional candidates' war chests traceable to the parties would be even higher.[26]

Republicans: The Party of Prosperity

We have so far treated the parties alike in assessing the impact of the campaign finance statutes, but the reality is quite different. The Republican party has thoroughly outclassed its Democratic rival in almost every category of campaign service and fundraising. Since Herbert Hoover's day, the GOP has suffered from the stigma of economic hard times, but the Republican party organization now has become the mirror-image model of prosperity.

Perhaps it has always been this way. The Republicans were the first to staff their national party in 1918, and in 1936 they created the first full-time salaried national chairman.[27] Their attention to the details of party organization and their level of party financing has usually been greater than that of the Democrats, at least since the 1950s.[28] There are a number of explanations for the disparity between the two major parties. Until 1980 the Republicans were almost perennially disappointed underdogs, especially in congressional contests, and they therefore felt the need to give an extra effort. The GOP had the willingness, and enough electoral frustrations, to experiment with new campaign technologies that might hold the key to elusive victories. Also, since Democrats held most of the congressional offices and thus had most of the incumbency perquisites and staff, Republican nominees were forced to rely more on their party to offset built-in Democratic advantages. The party staff, in other words, compensated for the Democratic congressional staff, and perhaps also for organized labor's divisions of election troops, which were usually at the beck and call of Democratic candidates. Then, too, one could argue that the business and middle-class base of the modern GOP has a natural managerial and entrepreneurial flair possessed and demonstrated by the party officers drawn from that talented pool of people.[29]

Whatever the causes, the contemporary Republican party has organizational strength unparalleled in American history and unrivaled by the Democrats. As Table 3.1 shows, the Republicans have outraised the Democrats by enormous margins in all recent election cycles, never by less than 2½ to 1 and usually by a considerably higher ratio.[30] Democrats must struggle to secure enough money to meet the basic needs of most of their candidates, while in the words of a past chairman of the Democratic Senatorial Campaign Committee, "The single biggest problem the Republicans have is how to legally spend the money they have."[31] This GOP fundraising edge inevitably enhances the aid provided party nominees, as Table 3.1 also demonstrates. The Republicans have been able to give nearly the legal maximum gift (both in direct contributions and coordinated expenditures) to every reasonably competitive Senate and House candidate, and frequently the money is given "up front," immediately after a primary when a nominee's war chest is depleted and the need is greatest. Within days after winning their respective GOP United States Senate nominations in 1986, for example, Linda Chavez had received $305,000 from the National Republican Senatorial Committee, and Ed Zschau of California was on the air courtesy of the NRSC with a $700,000 media blitz directed against his opponent, Democratic Senator Alan Cranston. The candidate contribution totals presented in Table 3.1 actually understate by a considerable margin the Republican party's lead. Because the GOP so

TABLE 3.1 Political Party Finances, 1976–1986[a]

	TOTAL RECEIPTS (IN $ MILLIONS)		TOTAL CONTRIBUTIONS TO AND EXPENDITURES FOR PARTY CANDIDATES[b] (IN $ MILLIONS)	
YEAR	DEMOCRATS	REPUBLICANS	DEMOCRATS	REPUBLICANS
1976	18.2	45.7	3.9	6.3
1978	26.4	84.5	2.3	8.9
1980	37.2	169.5	6.6	17.0
1982	39.3	215.0	5.1	19.9
1984	98.5	297.9	11.6	25.0
1986	61.8	252.4	8.0	17.8

SOURCE: Federal Election Commission.

[a]Includes total for the national senatorial and congressional committees as well as all other reported national and state/local spending.

[b]All presidential, Senate, and House candidates are included.

frequently bumps up against the allowable ceiling on contributions and expenditures, it sends additional aid through back channels: soft money, individuals' donations solicited and collected for specific candidates by the party (and thus counted as individual gifts despite the party's role), and cut-rate party in-kind services for media, polling, and consultants. One journalist estimated that the GOP had at least a $30 million advantage just in the closest 1986 Senate races when money from all sources was taken into account.[32]

Not only congressional candidates but office hopefuls at all levels benefit from the party largesse. Republican gubernatorial nominees in 1986 received about $2.4 million from the Republican National Committee and its affiliated Republican Governors Association.[33] Even state legislative candidates are collecting millions of dollars each election cycle from the national party and some associated political committees.[34]

Most of the Republican money is raised through a phenomenally successful direct mail program, which was begun in the early 1960s and accelerated in the mid-1970s when postage and production costs were relatively low.[35] From a base of just 24,000 names in 1975, for example, the national Republican party had expanded its direct mail list of proven donors to over 2.1 million by 1984. For all major national divisions of the Republican party combined, direct mail produces about three-quarters of total revenue, and it does so, amazingly, with an average contribution of under $35. Direct mail can be said to have broadened the committed base of the party, since contributing money usually strengthens the tie between a voter and any organization. Most of the rest of the GOP's funds come from larger donors who secure membership and the accompanying privileges in various Republican contributor groups. For instance, the Republican National Committee designates any $10,000 annual giver an "Eagle," and those under the age of 35 who give $5,000 as "Junior Eagles" (the yuppie division). In return, receptions, meetings, and access to policymakers are held for and delivered to the 950-plus donors at frequent intervals.

The Republican cash is used to support a dazzling variety of party activities and campaign services, including:[36]

- *Party Staff:* Several hundred operatives are employed by the three major GOP committees (RNC, NRCC, NRSC) in election years, and even in the off years, well over 150 hold full-time positions. There is great emphasis on *field staff,* i.e., staff members sent to and stationed in key districts and states who maintain close communication between local and national party offices. The congressional committee alone had a field contingent of 35 in 1986.

- *Voter Contact:* In 1982, 1984, and 1986 the Republicans conducted massive telephone canvassing operations to identify likely Republican voters and to get them to the polls on election day. In 1986, for instance, the GOP used paid callers in seventeen phone centers across the country to reach 10.5 million prospective voters in twenty-five states (all but two of them with Senate races) during the general election campaign. Nearly 5.5 million previously identified Republicans were re-called just before election day, many of whom heard an automated message from the president: "This is Ronald Reagan and I want to remind you to go out and vote on Tuesday . . ." In addition, 12 million pieces of "persuasive" (nonfundraising) direct mail were sent to households in the last two weeks of the campaign — many letters sent to the same homes receiving telephone calls in the hope that multiple messages would be more effective.
- *Polling:* The national Republican committees spend about $90,000 a month for national, state, and local public opinion surveys, and they have accumulated an enormous storehouse of data on American attitudes generally and marginal districts in particular. Many of the surveys are provided to GOP nominees at a cut-rate cost.[37] In important contests the party will frequently commission *tracking polls* — continuous surveys that enable a campaign to chart its daily rise or fall.[38] The information provided in such polls is invaluable in the tense concluding days of an election, and party tracking surveys have been cited by a number of GOP campaign managers as crucial in the election of their candidates.
- *Media Advertising:* The national Republican party operates a sophisticated in-house media division that specializes in the design and production of television advertisements for party nominees at all levels. About 70 to 100 candidates are helped in an election cycle. Not only do they obtain expert and technically superior media commercials, but the party offers its wares for a minimal fee, often including the actual time-buying — that is, the purchase of specific time slots on television shows for broadcasting the spots. The candidates thus save the substantial com-

missions and fees usually charged by independent political consultants for the same services.

Perhaps of greater significance than *candidate* commercial production is the GOP's *party* institutional advertising. Since 1978 the Republicans have aired spots designed to support not specific candidates but the generic party label. Beginning with the 1980 election, the GOP used institutional advertising to establish basic election themes. "Vote Republican — for a Change" spots attacked the Democratic Congress in 1980. Then-House Speaker Tip O'Neill was lampooned by an actor who ignored all warning signs and drove a car until it ran out of fuel. ("The Democrats are out of gas," surmised the narrator as "Tip" futilely kicked the automobile's tire.) Another ad starred a "real-life" unemployed factory worker from Baltimore, a lifelong Democrat who plaintively asked, "If the Democrats are so good for working people, then how come so many people aren't working?" In the 1982 midterm congressional election the defensive focus of a $15 million institutional campaign was "give the guy [Reagan] a chance" and "stay the course" with the president in the midst of a deep recession and high unemployment. For instance, a white-haired mailman was seen delivering social security checks fattened with a cost of living increase, reminding elderly voters that Reagan had kept his promise, and urging, "for gosh sake, let's give the guy a chance." The spot was highly rated by viewers, like the earlier 1980 ads, and while some moderate Republican candidates resisted being tied to Reagan during one of the most unpopular periods of his presidency, pre- and postelection surveys suggested that the GOP-sponsored media campaign was, on the whole, helpful to the party and to individual candidates.[39] From time to time, the Republicans have also aired generic institutional spots in noncampaign seasons, such as a $1 million series in March 1983 supporting Reagan's economic policies.

□ *Candidate Recruitment and Staff Training:* All the major national committees of the Republican party are heavily involved in identifying and recruiting potentially strong candidates. The congressional committee was credited with helping persuade about 100 House candidates to run in 1980, for instance.[40] Simultaneously, the party seeks to train the political volunteers and paid operatives who will manage the candidates' campaigns. Since 1976 the Republicans have held annually about a half dozen week-long "Campaign Management Colleges" for staffers, and in 1986 the party launched an ambitious million-dollar "Congressional Campaign Academy," which offers ten-week, all-expenses-paid training courses for about 140 prospective campaign managers, finance directors, and press relations staff.

- *Research and Data Sharing:* Early in each election cycle the national party staff prepares voluminous research reports on Democratic opponents, analyzing their public statements, votes, and attendance records. These reports are made available to GOP candidates and their aides. So are party compilations of likely individual and PAC contributors for each Republican candidate. The national party will even produce direct mailings for campaigns and prepare issue papers and briefing materials for candidates (yet another way that the national party can influence the themes struck and positions taken by its nominees).[41] The RNC also encourages state party committees to tap into its extensive computer data files, which include survey, electoral, and issue information of all types. The computer tie-ins are provided for small fees, and subscribers gain entry to a sophisticated data processing network called "Repnet" that contains five major programs for financial accounting and reporting, political targeting and survey processing, mailing list maintenance, donor preservation and information, and correspondence and word processing. The RNC has also developed its own campaign software package for use by state party organizations on minicomputers.
- *Party Communications and Outreach:* The Republican party produces a slick monthly magazine called *First Monday,* a local party and volunteer-oriented publication called *County Line,* and periodic briefing papers on current issues. The circulation of each is in the tens of thousands, and none of them, it should be noted, incorporates any kind of fundraising appeal. Party communication extends well beyond publications. The GOP has its own ten-minute videotape, "The Republican Party: Building a Strong America," a glossy promotional designed to motivate and inspire volunteers. The party has also frequently tried to cast its net more widely by communicating with groups outside the inner party circle. The $300,000 "Project Adelante!" ("Come in and move forward!") was aimed at Hispanic voters in 1986, and utilized media advertising and a widely distributed calendar of Hispanic events to attract the attention of the target group. A Republican party desire to attract more working women — a sector of the elector-

ate that disproportionately favors Democrats — led to the convening of ten party-sponsored "Alliance for Opportunity" conferences in cities around the country in 1985 and 1986. The meetings featured not just political pitches and issue briefings but also seminars on career and personal development. Finally, the Republicans have tried to capitalize on their newfound appeal to young people by airing radio and television spots on youth concerns, and by conducting voter registration drives and distributing absentee ballot applications on the nation's campuses. A comparison of the College Republicans with their Democratic counterparts is some measure of the GOP's commitment: the College Republicans have a full-time Washington staff and an annual budget of $250,000, compared to the College Democrats' paltry $2,000 budget and lack of any central office or staff.[42]

The GOP's Trouble in Paradise

Despite an overwhelming financial edge and service sophistication, all is not well in the Republican organizational paradise. Success has bred self-satisfaction and complacency, encouraged waste, and caused the party to place too much reliance on money and technology and not enough on the foundation of any party movement — people. As former United States Senator Paul Laxalt (R-Nevada), outgoing general chairman of the national Republican party, was forced to admit in 1987: "We've got way too much money, we've got way too many political operatives, we've got far too few volunteers . . . We are substituting contributions and high technology for volunteers in the field. I've gone the sophisticate route, I've gone the television route, and there is no substitute for the volunteer route."[43]

In the two concluding chapters, we will return to this real and significant problem, correctly pinpointed by Laxalt, that plagues both parties today. But the difficulty is currently more severe on the GOP side, ironically because it is so wealthy. While the Democrats are forced to recruit grassroots volunteers since they cannot afford the alternative, the Republicans have taken the easy road by hiring professionals. This latter route is superficially efficient, of course, because it avoids continual training expenses and amateurism, but it is far more costly in the long run. Slickness can replace sincerity and apathy can wither a party's do-or-die volunteer corps, whose sheer dedication often delivers electoral victory.

The GOP discovered this anew, to their chagrin, in 1986. Despite their huge spending and technology lead over the Democrats, the Republicans lost control of the Senate with a substantial eight-seat turnover. But almost as stunning as the margin of defeat was the GOP's loss of nine of the eleven closest Senate contests. In 1980, 1982, and 1984 combined the Republicans had won seventeen of the twenty-one cliffhangers, a record that had been attributed in good part to superior party services and resources. Actually, this explanation was always a simplistic one; Reagan's coattails in 1980 (and to a much lesser degree in 1984) and the strength of individual GOP candidates in 1982 had as much or more to do with the final election returns. Except in the most extreme cases when the gap between the two parties is yawning, technology and money can probably only add two or three percent to a candidate's margin. The rest is determined by the nominee's quality and positions, the general electoral tide prevailing in any given year, and the energy of party troops in the field. GOP cash and services may have rescued a couple of Republican senators in 1986,[44] but far more were probably lost because they were inept candidates and the party lacked depth and commitment at the grassroots level. Particularly in a midterm election when the party's presidential candidate does not appear on the ballot to lead and unify his slate, state and local nominees rise or fall mainly on their own merits, and the impact a national party can have on the results of most races is more limited than press reports sometimes suggest.

Moreover, the national GOP has fallen prey to an expertise overload that has made it top-heavy with political consultants promoting their elaborate, often error-prone technological schemes at the expense of plain, effective volunteer party building. In 1985 alone the three Washington-based Republican party committees spent about $5.8 million for consultant contracts, and 39 separate consultants raked in more than $50,000 each.[45] This bonanza has led to an unseeemly rush by GOP consultants to ride the gravy train, and some apparently deliver little in return for the largesse.[46] James Rosebush, the former chief of staff to First Lady Nancy Reagan, received $12,000 from the RNC to help with its "volunteerism" effort in 1986, though only a few months later he reported, "I can't remember the name of the program." Another consultant enjoying a particularly lucrative arrangement with the RNC confided in an off-the-record remark, "Most of the consultants hired by the RNC do hardly anything to earn their fees and they get picked up because they know someone."[47] Republican leaders finally recognized as much, and with revenues and fortunes sagging during the Iran-contra scandal, the RNC terminated or sharply cut back contracts with over two dozen consultants in mid-1987.[48]

Its "old boy" network of campaign operatives did enable the Republican party to buy friends, maintain a stable business for helpful consultants, and draw some of the operatives closer to the party instead of just to individual candidates. The price of keeping these consultants on the party reservation was high, however. Beyond the cost of their own hefty fees, consultants can encourage wasteful and sometimes harmful use of party resources. Many of the GOP's "in-house" consultants claimed that the 1986 congressional electorate was focusing on purely local issues. While that may have been true — and is quite naturally the case in most years when war, recession, and national scandal are absent — the GOP had skillfully devised unifying themes in 1980, 1982, and 1984 (some of these institutional appeals were discussed earlier). The decision to forgo a national advertising program in favor of themelessness in 1986 allowed the Democrats to avoid divisive, ideological issues that were framed in terms favorable to the GOP and to run their campaigns emphasizing more agreeable local concerns. Many analysts credited the Republican midterm election losses in part to this crucial strategic error.[49] Substituting for the lost lure of hot issues was the cool methodology of paid telephone-bank canvassing. Consultants had recommended this option in order to "kick our turnout up 10 percent."[50] Nationwide turnout in 1986 instead fell to a record low 37.3 percent of eligible voters.[51]

Poor judgment by consultants and party staffers also directly contributed to the defeat of a once-favored GOP Senate candidate in 1986. The RNC, in cooperation with the Louisiana state Republican party, hired a Chicago-based firm, Ballot Security, Inc., to conduct a drive aimed at purging individuals who had moved, died, or did not exist from the voter registration rolls in order to prevent voter fraud.[52] The drive was conducted solely in precincts that had produced less than 20 percent of the vote for President Reagan in 1984 — a group of voting districts overwhelmingly populated by blacks. The Republicans mailed letters to all registered voters in these precincts, and about 31,000 were returned as undeliverable. But these elusive voters were never removed from the rolls as the GOP had intended. Instead, a state judge ruled the program illegal as a violation of the Voting Rights Act, and the DNC filed a federal court suit to stop the effort.[53] Reaction in the black community was understandably harsh, and as a result black turnout was probably boosted and solidified for the Democratic candidate, United States Representative John Breaux. Moreover, the controversy grabbed the headlines and made it difficult for the previously frontrunning GOP nominee, Representative Henson Moore, to maintain any momentum. When Breaux won, he made a special point "to thank, most of all, the state and national Republican parties for making this possible."[54] To make matters worse, the GOP had also planned to employ the same purging process in other states, opening the party up to severe criticism around the country in the 1986 campaign's final days. The Democrats made the most of their opportunity, airing radio spots on black stations and announcing an Election Day telephone hotline to hear any complaints of voter intimidation at the polls.[55]

The ballot security program has been only one of several wasteful, counterproductive, or oversold fiascos dotting the Republican party record in recent years. With great fanfare in 1985, the RNC launched a plan to convert 100,000 Democrats in Florida, Louisiana, North Carolina, and Pennsylvania, but despite strenuous efforts the goal was not met within the unwisely set, self-imposed deadline of one hundred days. Democrats were thus able gleefully to pronounce an otherwise impressive performance to be a failure.[56] Also, the National Republican Senatorial Committee was forced to withdraw radio ads targeted to appeal to evangelical Christians because of the strong offense taken by some Jewish organizations.[57] (The spots asked, "Ever think about what's important to you? It's probably simple: a steady job, a healthy family, and a personal relationship with Christ.") The Republican party's off-year direct mail and television campaigns seeking to "soften up" incumbent Democratic members of Congress for later defeat have occasionally backfired as well, alienating potential congressional allies just before crucial votes on Reagan administration-backed proposals.[58] Excess money itself has been the root of some evils. For several election cycles the NRSC has operated a generous slush fund to pay various "office expenses" (such as television tapings and transmission, photographs, etc.) of United States senators.[59] This scheme allowed the committee to funnel almost $1.4 million to the party's senators in 1983 and 1984, for example, and while these contributions are valuable and do not count against the limits on party gifts to its candidates, they have been much criticized for skirting the election law and traditional practice. Finally, no party expenditure of funds has been more ridiculed and resented than the great bonus caper of 1986, when approximately $257,000 in bonuses was awarded to some eighty-seven employees by the NRSC on the day after the Republicans lost control of the United States Senate.[60] The victorious Democratic party handed out no bonuses, by the way; to the victors belong the spoils, and to the losers, apparently, go the bonus checks.

This problem may well be self-correcting, both because the GOP's large donors became incensed when the bonus awards were made public (and as a consequence, the practice will almost certainly be limited or discontinued in the future) and because Republican fund-raising is also reaching its upper limits. Already, oversolicitation of party donors is in evidence; direct mail prospecting for new contributors is yielding smaller gains; and the overall party war chest, as Table 3.1 indicates, declined in 1986 from the previous election cycle for the first time since the modern GOP era began. (This decline continued into 1987, fueled by the Iran-contra arms deal disclosures, and the RNC was forced to fire forty of its staff members in July 1987.) It may simply be that most possible Republican contributors have already been identified over a decade of intense prospecting, and that all the party can reasonably hope to do now is find enough new donors to replace those who cease giving each year. No one believes that a financial bust is approaching for the Republicans, but the boom times fueled by direct mail are over for the moment. Absent new sources of money to be proposed in the concluding chapter, the Republican party must shift to a consolidation mode, cutting the organizational waste and fat they often find in government, and making less do more for their nominees and state parties.

Democrats: Getting in the Game

Parties, like people, change their habits slowly. Democrats were reluctant to alter a formula that had been a winning combination for decades of New Deal dominance. The prevailing philosophy was, "Let a thousand flowers bloom"; candidates were encouraged to go their own way, to rely on organized labor and other interest groups allied with the Democrats, and to raise their own money, while the national party was kept subservient and weak. When the Democratic National Committee was heard from at all in the 1960s and 1970s, it was generally to attempt to regulate the state party selection of presidential convention delegates rather than to provide their party affiliates and candidates with assistance.

Like the effect a traumatic event on the personal level can have, the massive Democratic defeats suffered in 1980 forced a fundamental reevaluation of the party's structure and activities. Democrats, diverse and quarrelsome by nature, came to an unaccustomed consensus that the party must change to survive, that it must dampen internal ideological disputes, resist the temptation to meddle and regulate, and begin to revitalize its organization. Thus was born the commitment to technological and fundraising modernization, using the Republican party's accomplishments as a model, that drives the Democratic party today.

Comprehension of the task is but the first step to realization of the goal, so even after the better part of a decade, Democrats still trail their competitors by virtually every significant measure of party activity. Yet the financial figures of Table 3.1 can be read a different way. While the GOP has consistently maintained an enormous edge, the Democrats have considerably increased their total receipts. In 1976 the party received just $18.2 million, but by 1984 this total had increased to $98.5 million. (Like the GOP, Democrats recorded a decline in overall contributions in the 1986 off-year election cycle, when $61.8 million was raised.) In 1978 the Democratic party gave only $2.3 million to its candidates in direct contributions and coordinated expenditures; in 1984 and 1986, the gifts amounted to $11.6 million and $8.0 million, respectively. The Democrats lose the money competition with the Republicans by a country mile, but viewed in another context, the new Democratic party greatly outdistances the old. That is no small achievement.

The decision in 1981 to begin a direct mail program for the national party was a turning point. From a list of only 25,000 donors before the program began, the DNC's support base grew to 500,000 by 1987. Most of the early profits were wisely reinvested back into more direct mail to prospect for additional donors, insuring a bigger payoff later. Also in 1985 the party moved the program in-house, ending its contract with Craver, Mathews, Smith & Company, a major Democratic direct mail firm.[61] This shift saves the DNC about $300,000 annually, and builds the technology internally — where it can be transferred more easily to state party affiliates. Beyond direct mail, the Democrats have built strong relationships with labor and some trade PACs, which provide the national party committees with $5 million or more in an election cycle. (This amount is over and above the PAC donations given directly to individual candidates that the party helps stimulate for its nominees.) And the Democrats have tried to develop ties with more business leaders, particularly younger entrepreneurs with "new money." The Democratic Business Council, mainly composed of $10,000-level contributors, had 150 members by 1987.

The Democrats have imitated the Republicans not just in fundraising but also in the uses to which the money is put. In 1986 the party opened a $3 million media center financed with loans and a $550,000 grant from Pamela Harriman. Several dozen candidates took advantage of the center in the midterm congressional elections, producing television and radio spots at rates greatly reduced from those charged by independent political consultants. A communications media library has been established as a part of the center, containing video clips of statements by Republican officeholders — useful before and during campaign seasons for holding opposition candidates accountable for their public pronouncements. Even a few party institutional advertisements have been produced. As early as 1982, the Democrats had filmed a series of party spots keyed to the theme, "It Isn't Fair — It's Republican."[62] For the 1986 elections, radio ads and one television spot on the farm crisis were aired extensively in nine midwestern states. ("It wasn't just a farm, it was a family. Vote Democratic," intones the narrator as wind whistles through an abandoned barn and farmhouse with the phantom sounds of tractors and mealtime grace fading in and out.)

The DNC has also started to conduct some extensive survey research in an attempt to improve fundraising appeals as well as determine public opinion. In 1985 the DNC commissioned a $200,000 study consisting of forty-three "focus group" sessions (small discussion groups of nonrandomly selected voters) in six cities during which participants were interviewed. Complementing the focus groups was a randomly selected (and therefore representative) 5,500 person nationwide poll. Among other results, the research aided Democrats in targeting direct mail letters to an expanding middle-aged baby boom generation by emphasizing family economic concerns, such as housing costs and college tuition rates.

The Democratic party is attempting to do more for its candidates and their campaign staffs, too. In 1986 the Democrats selected two dozen of their potentially weakest incumbent House members and subjected them to what one party official described as "the political equivalent of a physical."[63] A thorough examination of their fundraising practices, congressional offices, and constituent services was conducted, and weaknesses were corrected well in advance of the election season. All of the supervised House members, including some who had been targeted for defeat by the Republicans, were reelected. In addition, the national party created the Democratic National Training Institute in 1985. With a $100,000 annual budget, the Institute coordinates so-called campaign schools for party workers from around the country. Finally, the Democrats have traditionally left much of the voter registration and contact effort to labor unions, black organizations, and privately financed nonprofit foundations.[64] But lately the party has been allocating some of its own money and attention to the task. In the 1986 midterm elections the DNC spent $160,000 for computerized voter identification and get-out-the-vote programs, mainly by means of small grants to thirty-one state parties.

The amounts of aid are, of course, minuscule compared to the Republican party's but the national Democrats' change of direction — from bureaucratic enforcers of party regulations to providers of vital services to candidates and state affiliates — is a profound one that will alter the course of its future. Under the leadership of DNC Chairman Paul Kirk, the shift to service orientation has been accompanied by a reduction in the power of the party's ideological interest groups and a strengthening of the role played by more centrist elected officials. The DNC withdrew official recognition from seven party caucuses claiming to represent blacks, women, Hispanics, gays, business, Asian-Americans, and liberals.[65] The party's midterm convention, a reform-spawned staple of the political calendar since 1974, was abolished, saving the party a substantial sum and avoiding the factional fractures often produced by this peculiar conclave.[66] Kirk also led the party to abandon its frenzy of reform in the presidential delegate selection process; for the first time in nearly two decades the Democrats are using basically the same set of nominating rules in successive presidential elections (1984 and 1988).[67] The one major rule change for 1988 reserves more unpledged seats at the national convention for elected party officials (members of Congress, governors, and the entire Democratic National Committee), increasing their stabilizing influence at the expense of ideologues. This shift in delegate allocation reverses the post-1968 direction of the Democratic party, and it will be discussed further in Chapter Six. Finally, Kirk made a major effort to keep his party's eye on the electoral ball — the recapture of the White House in 1988. Early in 1987 he enlisted the support of all the major Democratic presidential candidates for a "code of campaign conduct" that pledged them to give "early and unqualified support" to the eventual national ticket and forbade them from attacking the party and its constituency groups (as Gary Hart and Jesse Jackson had both done in 1984). At the same time, Kirk warned the party's constituencies against applying "narrow or single-issue litmus tests" to candidates and he warned state and local parties to refrain from conducting "straw poll" popularity contests since they require unnecessary expenditures of candidates' money and energy.

For all of these accomplishments, Kirk has not been able to make the Democratic party truly competitive in fundraising (and, consequently, in campaign service delivery). This condition is not always crippling electorally. The Democrats proved in 1982 and 1986 that money is not everything, winning major gains in congressional elections despite being substantially outspent in most key races. The Democrats make do in part because labor unions furnish Democrats with volunteer muscle unavailable to the GOP and because the Democratic label retains a significant edge in voter support in many parts of the country. Moreover, in any given election, there are only a few dozen districts and states with truly marginal, closely matched contests where money and services can make a difference to the outcome, permitting Democrats to conserve and target their limited resources in a manageable number of areas.[68] (If the Republican party succeeds in broadening the playing field by seriously contesting more districts, Democrats will be forced to spread their money thinly, but because most congressional districts are skewed to one party as a result of incumbency or redistricting, it is difficult for the GOP to accomplish this.) Earlier, Democrats and their labor PAC allies had been correctly accused of squandering too many precious dollars on safe incumbents, but in 1984 and 1986 the party and supportive PACs received generally high marks for intelligent resource allocation.[69]

Still, the relative lack of Democratic funds has unfortunate consequences for the party. Without a steady stream of polling data and tracking surveys, party and campaign officials are frequently forced to make crucial decisions blindly or to beg bits of information from independent pollsters. Candidate recruitment is also hurt, as Senator George Mitchell (D-Maine), chairman of the Democratic Senatorial Campaign Committee during the 1985 candidate recruitment season, explained: "There is no question there was a chilling effect because we weren't able to promise candidates we could give them the maximum."[70] Landslide defeats in the presidential elections of 1980 and 1984 obviously inhibited party fundraising, as did the Democrats' unwillingness to undertake party organizational renewal prior to 1980. The internal competition produced by the moderate-conservative Democratic Leadership Council (mentioned in Chapter Two) may also contribute to national party problems by showcasing party dissension and draining money that otherwise would be deposited in party coffers.[71] Greedy incumbents are yet another problem for the Democrats; in late 1986, at a time when most Democratic Senate challengers were being greatly outspent by Republican incumbents, Democratic senators who did not face re-election until 1988 or 1990 already had siphoned off $7.5 million from the pool of available campaign cash.[72] Nonetheless, real progress has been made, and the will to change is now a driving force in the Democratic party. Democrats are well positioned to move their party forward organizationally, especially when the leadership and fundraising opportunity afforded by control of the White House next presents itself. If a future Democratic president is as supportive of his party's development as Ronald Reagan and Gerald Ford have been of theirs, two-party technological parity will not seem quite so fanciful.[73]

The Transfused Revival of State Party Organizations

The transformation that has occurred in state party organizations is best illustrated by irony. The national parties were once creatures of the state affiliates and financed by them; today, the state parties are chartered chapters of Washington-based groups, and they owe much of their health and wealth to the national party committees. A relationship that V. O. Key once described as independent and confederative[74] has become integrated and centralized. Stimulated by new campaign finance laws that encourage collaborative efforts under national party direction, and in eleven states aided by public financing provisions that funnel money through the state parties (a subject discussed in Chapter Seven), most state parties are organizationally stronger now than at any time in their history. Much like the national parties, they have begun to offer a wide array of candidate services while recruiting candidates and providing direct financial assistance to nominees and some local parties.

The extent of state party revival is detailed in a study by James Gibson et al., and a recent survey of state parties by the Advisory Commission on Intergovernmental Relations.[75] Just two decades ago most state parties subsisted without paid staff or headquarters on paltry budgets of $50,000 or less. By the mid-1980s the average annual state party budget was $572,000,[76] and virtually all state parties had at least one full-time staffer, with 15 percent employing ten or more people. A large majority of both Democratic and Republican state parties now give campaign contributions to, and assist the fundraising of, state and congressional candidates as well.[77]

There is, of course, a significant variation in state party activity by region and by party. For example, Southern state parties have tended to be the least developed organizationally (historically a product of their relative lack of two-party competition), while the midwestern parties are especially likely to be well funded and programmatic.[78] Some individual states, for particularistic reasons, are exceptionally vibrant or comatose. Few if any Republican parties are as moribund as Massachusetts's; in the heavily Democratic Bay State, the GOP has actually resorted to placing newspaper and magazine advertisements to recruit state legislative candidates.[79] By contrast, Florida showcases one of the most impressive Republican superstructures in the country. Fed by in-migration from the Northeast and Cuban immigrants in Miami, the Florida GOP boasts an annual budget of $4.3 million and a high-tech headquarters crammed with up-to-date computer hardware, telephone banks, and printing facilities.[80] The Democrats feature a similarly wide variation from state to state.[81]

The most significant variance, though, is from party to party. As at virtually every level and category of campaign organization, Republican state parties have a major edge over their Democratic counterparts. Whereas three-quarters of the GOP state organizations provide polling and media consulting services to their nominees for state office, only about half of the Democratic parties do so.[82] Every single state Republican party sponsors campaign seminars to train legislative candidates and their staffs, but a quarter of the Democratic parties hold no such events.[83] The average Democratic organization recruits candidates for only one office (typically the state legislature) while the GOP usually searches out nominees for state legislature, United States Congress, and statewide constitutional offices.[84] And while 54 percent of the state Republican committees devote some portion of their budgets to assisting local party committees, 61 percent of the Democratic state organizations give not a single dollar to their local counterparts.[85]

The relative financial positions of the two national parties explain much (but not all)[86] of the gap, of course. Both parties have established what Leon Epstein calls a "grant-in-aid system," similar to the intergovernmental federal-to-state transfers of money and programs.[87] While the Democrats' approach has often been hierarchical and emphasized compliance with national party rules and delegate selection procedures, the Republicans have been more philosophically inclined and financially able to stress cooperative services. About three-quarters of all the state Republican parties receive money and fundraising assistance from the RNC, compared to the DNC's aid to under a fifth of state Democratic parties.[88] Nearly two-thirds of the GOP state parties receive polling, data processing, and candidate training services from Washington, while just a quarter of the Democratic state organizations derive similar benefits from their national party.[89] The GOP has also been successful in targeting support to its weakest state parties, particularly those in the South; 82 percent of the Southern Republican parties receives each major form of assistance provided by the RNC — the highest for any region.[90] In like fashion, the Republicans have selected 650 large "swing" counties across the country for special programs and substantial aid.[91] Inevitably, frictions arise when a national party invades the preserves of state and local leaders. This can be particularly true when the national party committee decides to endorse a certain candidate prior to nomination, as the RNC occasionally has done. A 1980 revolt by irate state and local party officials resulted in the adoption at the national party convention of a rule limiting RNC preprimary intervention to instances approved in advance by the state party chair and the elected national committee members from the state.[92] The rule does not apply to the party's congressional and Senate campaign committees, though, so frictions still arise from time to time.[93] These situations are rare, however. More typical is the collaborative arrangement between the RNC and the Wyoming party, which launched a joint telemarketing fundraising program in 1985 to help local party committees raise money in "phonathons."[94]

Major advances in the Democratic party's own "federalism" programs have been made in recent years, and the pace of progress has accelerated since Paul Kirk became DNC chairman in 1985. The national party manages the direct mail programs of many of the state parties (returning all of the net income to them), and substantial cash grants have been awarded to over two dozen state parties for compiling computerized lists of voters as well as targeted registration drives.[95] While the national party's help to the states remains modest in most categories, the Democrats have now nearly equaled the Republicans in the provision of organizational management aid and voter contact and registration programs.[96]

One of Chairman Kirk's primary goals has been to build up and strengthen ties with the state parties, and he established four regional desks at the DNC (East, Midwest, South, and West) to coordinate state-oriented programs and respond to the needs of state party leaders.[97] Former RNC chairman William Brock's 1978–1980 program for Republican state organizations served as Kirk's model.[98] Seeing a crippling lack of professionalism and continuity in most states, Brock recruited, trained, and paid the salaries of his own set of party executive directors in all fifty states. Kirk decided instead to create a nationally sponsored state field organization called the Democratic Party Election Force in sixteen target states during the 1986 midterm elections. In each selected state — usually the site of one or more key gubernatorial or Senate contests — the DNC paid for a full-time professional fundraiser plus one other party staff aide. In exchange for this $1.2 million allocation to state party operations, Kirk extracted some fascinating and unusual pledges from state chairpersons. First, they agreed to use the new staffers to help develop a comprehensive finance plan and organize a computerized voter file (for which additional money and consulting was granted by the DNC). Second, the chairs agreed to retain the services of these staffers (or similar individuals) at state party expense through the 1988 presidential election. (DNC funding extended only to October 1986.) Third, the state parties agreed to refrain from sponsorship or involvement in any presidential nomination "straw vote" — nonbinding preference polls of party activists that precede (sometimes by months or years) the actual nominating primaries or caucuses. Kirk correctly contended that these straw votes were little more than divisive and financially draining media sideshows that detracted from the goal of party building. Finally, and most usefully for a party often appearing fractured and fratricidal, Kirk obliged them:

> . . . to insist that Democratic candidates who benefit from this program do not run campaigns against, and instead, run with, the national Democratic Party. This means exerting all of the state party's influence and bringing all of the pressure it can to ensure that a positive, unified Democratic Party campaign develops. It also means that the state party and state committee shall disagree with and disavow

any remarks by a candidate or campaign that attack the national party.[99]

The remarkable aspect of this forced loyalty oath is that it was signed with almost no public controversy. As David Broder accurately observed, "Writing this requirement may be easier than enforcing it."[100] Its easy initial acceptance, however, suggests the recent homogenization and decline in ideological diversity within the Democratic party as well as the universal, urgent desire among state and national party leaders for competitive programmatic modernization. No longer just a jumble of ill-fitting parts, the emerging Democratic party may well find unity less elusive and technological near-parity with the Republicans not quite so far out of reach. In 1984 the Democrats collected centrally and disbursed to the state parties nearly the same amount of soft money, by some estimates, as the Republicans did,[101] and the DNC was similarly competitive in its 1986 investment in state legislative contests.[102]

For both parties, the revitalization of state organizations has major consequences — from the strengthening of party ties with voters and officeholders to the dramatic nationalization of a previously decentralized party system. These implications will be discussed more fully at the conclusion of this chapter, but the most significant meaning for America's victory-hungry major parties is simply an enhanced ability to win elections. The electoral relevance of muscled state parties is indisputable. In gubernatorial contests the organizationally stronger party tends to elect its candidates,[103] while in state legislative battles, even a little party help goes a long way.[104] These lessons have not been lost on political players over the years, and that is one major reason why many party-building measures are consensually supported by activists, candidates, and officeholders.

Where Party Works at the Local Level

When Americans think of local political parties, most quickly cite New York's Tammany Hall or Chicago's Daley Machine. But Tammany died before midcentury, and the Daley Machine has gradually faded since Mayor Richard J. Daley's passing in 1977, decimated by fratricide, by court rulings striking at the heart of the patronage system, and by opponents that one long-time machine alderman characterized as "intellectuals, troublemakers, and know-hows."

("When you give them a $10 bill, they can't even get a dog out of the dog pound for you!" he noted.)[105] That all local party organizations have gone the way of New York's and Chicago's is a commonly held belief, even among journalists and political observers.

Commonly held — and perhaps also mistaken. A recent study of the 7,300 county-level party organizations in the United States revealed that many local parties — Democratic as well as Republican — are surprisingly active, and have not really become less so over the past two decades.[106] While party organizational atrophy is unmistakable in many cities and counties and most county parties have no paid staff, central party headquarters, or even a telephone listing,[107] some local parties appear to have a life of their own, aided by substantial help from the state and (on the GOP side) national committees. These local organizations seem to endure and sometimes prosper despite party reversals at state or national levels.[108] In the most successful cases, that is due to one of two sources of strength: either a well-nourished grassroots organization fed by patronage or a technologically advanced party with a solid base of ideologically attuned contributors and supporters.

While in a decade's time there may well be more examples of the latter than the former, it is the big-city machine prototype that is still more common among vital local parties. One example is found in St. Clair County (East St. Louis), Illinois, where an electorally weighty Democratic organization holds sway. In a testament to old-time politics, the organization managed in 1986 to reelect Congressman Melvin Price, an 81 year old who had been ousted as chairman of the House Armed Services Committee in 1985 because of advanced age and debilitating frailty. Despite the efforts of an energetic, young, and attractive opponent, Price won a 52 percent to 39 percent victory by riding the back of the organization, which resented his opponent's attempt to secure office without having "paid his dues" to the machine.[109]

Another potent local organization, which many believe to have eclipsed Chicago's as the nation's most effective, is found in the Republican party of Nassau County, New York. No doubt Mayor Daley would have found much to like about this rigid and hierarchical machine that controls more than 20,000 jobs and features an elaborate superstructure of ward chairpersons, precinct committee members, and block captains who turn out the vote on election day.[110] Originally built on New York City's out-migration of blue-collar Irish and Italian ethnics who wanted to disassociate themselves from the city's liberal politics, the machine now takes great care to recruit young people, in part by distributing plum summer jobs, and many of these youths go on to base their whole careers on service to the party. In the best tradition of machine politics, aspiring officeholders are expected to work their way up the ladder slowly, toiling for years in the backrooms and the neighborhoods, delivering votes for the party candidates and dollars for the party war chest. Party chiefs encourage competition among committee members to see who can attract the most new registrants or sell the most tickets to a fundraiser. (About $2 million annually is raised in this single county for party activities.) The machine is not without its problems, of course. Corruption charges against some of its leaders have been proven, for instance, and its command of so many patronage positions is under attack. Yet electoral success keeps the organization humming, and it regularly wins a large majority of the area's county, state legislative, and congressional posts. The machine has even produced one of New York's United States senators, Alfonse D'Amato, first elected in 1980. D'Amato was a supervisor of Nassau's Hempstead township and a top leader of the party organization prior to his Senate bid. The conservative Republican learned constituency service politics well in the county machine, and he attended assiduously to the state's interests just as he had done for his township, earning a landslide reelection in 1986 that even included an endorsement from the liberal *New York Times*.

This description of the Nassau machine would once have seemed unremarkable or even tame, but with each passing year there appear to be fewer truly vibrant, grassroots, neighborhood-based parties. Indiana's local parties, especially on the Republican side, are often cited when the subject of strong organizations is raised. Yet there, too, parties have suffered recent body blows. Fundamentalist Christian congressional candidates embarrassed the local parties in two 1986 House primaries by defeating the party consensus choices by substantial margins.[111] (The GOP suffered for it in November; both nominees lost, including one from a reliably Republican district.) And the governor and state legislature, egged on by the news media and antipatronage public sentiment, voted to phase out the most unique and sustaining form of public financing in the nation.[112] In each Indiana county, the organization run by the governor's political party[113] had traditionally been allowed to retain a portion of the revenue from the state's motor vehicle licensing system. This delightful arrangement produced about $400,000 a year for the local parties.

Moreover, another $400,000 or so derived from the sale of personalized license plates was split between the two major parties. But no longer: as of 1987 the profits are going to the state.[114]

If Chicago, Nassau County, and Indiana represent the old-style party organization, then the Waxman-Berman machine in California may suggest the future directions of strong local parties.[115] Named after its founders, liberal Democratic Congressmen Henry A. Waxman and Howard L. Berman, this Los Angeles-based machine has built its success on direct mail and new campaign technologies rather than patronage and ward committee members. In many ways Waxman-Berman is the polar opposite of the Nassau County organization: informal, candidate (not party) centered, impersonal in the communication media it chooses, and a creation of California's basically antiparty environment. Also unlike their Nassau brethren, who virtually ignore national politics and concentrate on local offices, Waxman, Berman, and their allies care little about local politics; most of their energies are devoted to electing congressional candidates and influencing national and international policy. Yet a fundamental link between the two machines remains: they accumulate power by helping friends win elective and appointive office.

The Waxman-Berman machine (which prefers to call itself an "alliance") combines entertainment industry money and a firm liberal base in Los Angeles with the direct mail skills of Howard Berman's brother Michael (a well-known Democratic party consultant). Sophisticated fundraising and persuasive mail campaigns have enabled the machine principals to elect several dozen allies to congressional, state legislative, and major local posts. Moreover, the machine funnels money to a political action committee controlled mainly by Waxman. In the 1983–1984 election cycle Waxman gave about $140,000 from the PAC and his own campaign treasury to House and Senate candidates across the country.[116] Such gifts do not go unnoticed and unrewarded. After Waxman made similar contributions in 1979 to eight of his fellow members on the House Commerce Committee, he was able to win a key subcommittee chair over another, more senior member.[117]

If Waxman-Berman is the best example of the new technologically based party on the left, Senator Jesse Helms's (R-N.C.) Congressional Club may symbolize a similar development on the right.[118] Helms has built a formidable PAC, one of the nation's largest, on direct mail solicitation of right-wing Republican supporters. The Club has been a powerhouse in North Carolina politics, recruiting, training, and financing dozens of congressional and state legislative candidates. Though considered a divisive element by much of the state's GOP leadership and despite having suffered many setbacks over the years, the Club is still a force to be reckoned with in and out of North Carolina.

As I have already suggested, the newer technologically advanced model of strong local parties probably has more of a future than the older ethnically based or patronage-fed machine. Yet the latter should not be dismissed so easily, not only because it has proven hardier in some places than many expected but also because there is a great deal to be said for such personalized, neighborhood-oriented, "bottom-up" parties. The ideal self-sustaining and advancing party might well be a carefully crafted combination of modern technology and community service-centered organization. This is an idea to which I shall return in Chapter Six when I propose means to tie voters more closely to their parties.

Implications for Politics and Government

If this extended discussion of the strengthening of party organizations has proven anything, it is that the new technologies of politics, which have so often been used to weaken the parties by liberating individual candidates from party influence, are now being employed to build more vital political parties. No technology, after all, is inherently good or evil; the uses to which it is put determine its morality. Party advocates can only be delighted that these techniques are enabling parties to rebuild and fortify themselves at a time when either an antiparty mood prevails or people simply do not care very much about the parties' fate.

The consequences of reinvigorated party organization and financing are many. First of all, an obvious result is that parties are in a much better position to help their nominees win elections — a fact that does not escape the notice of candidates and officeholders. Already, it is apparent that elected officials are devoting more time and energy to party affairs in many states, as a recent survey of party chairpersons by the Advisory Commission on Intergovernmental Relations determined.[119] The ACIR also found that the more campaign assistance state parties provided to their candidates, the more likely it was that those candidates would take part in party activities.[120]

More importantly, the parties' new recruitment efforts, financial contributions, and provision of campaign services are bearing fruit in another way. The evolving ties between the parties and their elected decision makers may be helping to enact the party agenda and to increase cohesion among the party's officeholders. Gary Jacobson, among others, has suggested that the Republican party has been able to impose greater discipline on some policy matters through appropriate distribution of its campaign services.[121] For example, the large GOP Senate class of 1980, which owed its election in good measure to Ronald Reagan's presidential coattails and the lavish expenditures of the national party committees, showed unusual cohesion throughout the six-year term of its members. As a *National Journal* analysis of Senate voting records demonstrated, the members of the class of 1980 (with just a couple of exceptions) consistently voted with each other and with their party majority on almost all key domestic and foreign policy issues during their tenure.[122]

Interestingly, *both* congressional parties are displaying greater solidarity in the pattern of their floor votes in the 1980s compared to the 1950s, as Chapter Two noted. There are many reasons for this, of course, including the dwindling of the ranks of both Southern conservative Democrats and Northern liberal Republicans, which makes each party more ideologically and internally consistent. But the influence of party label seems to be an increasingly important aspect of the congressional voting calculus. The national parties' institutional advertising campaigns have made legislators accept basic party themes and realize that any single candidate's electoral fate is unavoidably bound up with that of his or her party. The parties have also created "chits" in exchange for their gifts of money and services that party leaders are able to "call in" on crucial matters. Thus, for perhaps the first time in decades, the parties have been able to counteract to some small degree the individualistic, atomizing forces that favor personalized, candidate-centered, interest group-responsive politics and legislative voting. There is even some evidence that the same phenomenon is occurring on the state level. Andrew Aoki and Mark Rom were able to conclude a study of Wisconsin party campaign contributions and the subsequent voting records compiled by state legislators by suggesting that "those candidates receiving more money may indeed be more likely to support the party in the following session than the candidates receiving less money."[123]

Nonetheless, there are considerable limitations on the influence American parties can exert on legislators under even the most favorable of conditions. Parties are certainly a more substantial source of cash and campaign technology than ever before, but they are not the only source by any means. While a legislator will not wish to offend any major benefactor, he or she will do so when necessary so long as other alternative support is available. Then, too, parties are hardly inclined at election time to discipline their incumbents — almost any incumbent, however uncooperative or obnoxious. Since the overriding objective is victory, the parties will normally choose the pragmatic course and aid any party candidate, rather than reward only some while punishing others and risking their defeat. After all, a candidate completely deprived of party assistance will be less pliable and even more hostile in the future. Still, it cannot be denied that the parties' influence has grown legislatively because of their enhanced electoral capabilities. This is potentially of great significance, even though in most votes, the effect may be minor. As Aoki and Rom conclude: "The changes are understandably small, but small changes can have big political effects, if they mean the difference between passing programs and indefinitely postponing them."[124]

There is another consequence of strengthened party organization that deserves mention. To this point, at least, party development has extended from the top down, from national to state party organizations. All politics may be local, but more and more, the key political decisions and allocations are being made nationally. Economies of scale and the new campaign finance rules have so far encouraged the centralization of electoral services and technology in the national party committees. While the national organizations were at one time financed by the state parties, the opposite pattern is closer to the truth today, and the national parties frequently also intervene to recruit state and local candidates.[125] This reversal of the flow of party power disturbs some federalists. As the Advisory Commission on Intergovernmental Relations expressed it:

> Throughout much of American history, the strongly decentralized structure of the political parties helped maintain a balance between national, state, and local authority . . . To the extent that the decentralized party system once contributed significantly to maintaining political balance in the federal system, that capacity has to some extent declined.[126]

Yet the health of federalism is also dependent on the vitality of the parties as a whole. The fact that the national party organizations have been revivified can only help the parties perform their linkage role in the federal configuration. If nothing else, the centralization of party resources permits the national parties to target weak state and local parties for special remedial help, freeing them from the demoralizing cycle of inbred defeat. By infusing money and services to anemic parties that otherwise might not have been competitive, vigorous two-party competition is spread in sometimes unlikely places. Surely, the federal division of power is fortified under such an arrangement. Beyond that, we must remember that the national parties are slowly but surely transferring the means and methods of the campaign technologies to the state and local parties themselves. Indisputably, centralization is probably a permanent feature of the new party system, but the dependency of state parties on their national counterparts will likely lessen somewhat as they develop quasi-independent capabilities. This process ought to be accelerated as much as possible, and the two concluding chapters will suggest some ways to build parties from the ground up, a goal that will serve the purposes of both parties and federalism. Then, too, the degree of centralization in party activity that has actually taken place can be exaggerated. The parties remain firmly rooted in the states both because the vast majority of party leaders and officeholders are elected and reside there and because the states, far more than the national government, regulate and control the parties.

Politically, there are other results of the parties' gain in campaign power, some of them almost universally recognized as beneficial. For instance, as the parties' clout rises, the influence of PACs and special interest groups is indirectly limited both in campaigns and in governing. The alternate source of financing provided by the parties is especially potent in checking PACs.[127] Furthermore, the expanding role of the parties as providers of campaign information to PACs and interest groups has gathered these organizations under the party umbrellas to a greater degree; many millions of dollars are contributed each year from PACs and interest groups to the party (not just candidate) coffers,[128] and many of the organizations, especially labor and education groups on the Democratic side and business and conservative religious interests on the Republican side, are participating in party activities more substantially.[129]

The mushrooming of party organizational strength has come at a crucial moment. All of the forces arrayed against the parties (discussed in Chapter One) have weakened them, and would have continued to do so except for the parties' self-initiated innovations. Now instead of continuing a slide into disfavor and oblivion, parties are battling those forces, using their expanded capacities to aid their candidates and to contact more voters — and thereby *perhaps* to develop stronger bonds with both groups. The parties may even have become, in the words of Cotter et al., "effective counter-dealigning agents" combating "the departisanization of the electorate" and "counteracting antiparty trends."[130] The effects these party efforts seem to be having on the voters, both in terms of their perceptions of the parties and in their choice of party, will be the subjects of examination in the next two chapters. The final two chapters will then focus on how the parties — on their own or with the help of government — can use their newly acquired skills, techniques, and organizational strength to broaden their reach and attraction still further, to translate money and technology into voter loyalty and devotion.

Notes

1. Personal interview with the author, July 24, 1979, New York City.
2. Many studies are cited later in this chapter that fully support this conclusion. See, for example, Paul Herrnson, "Do Parties Make a Difference? The Role of Party Organizations in Congressional Elections," *Journal of Politics* 48 (August 1986): 589–615.
3. See Michael Wolfe, "Personal Contact Campaigning in Presidential Elections," paper prepared for the annual meeting of the Midwest Political Science Association, Chicago, April 1979. Wolfe cites University of Michigan Survey Research Center data to show that only 12 percent of the public reported being contacted by party campaign workers in 1952, while by 1976 it was nearly 30 percent.
4. For more detailed treatment, see the author's *PAC POWER: Inside the World of Political Action Committees* (New York: W. W. Norton, 1984), 7–10. See also Joseph E. Cantor, *Campaign Financing in Federal Elections: A Guide to the Law and Its Operation* (Washington, D.C.: Library of Congress Congressional Research Service Report No. 86-143 GOV, August 8, 1986); Michael J. Malbin, ed., *Money and Politics in the United States: Financing Elections in the 1980s* (Washington, D.C.: American Enterprise Institute/Chatham House, 1984). The provisions of law discussed in the following paragraphs can be found in these key election statutes: Federal Election Campaign Act of 1971, Pub. L. No. 92-225, 86 Stat. 3 (1972); Revenue Act of 1971, Pub. L. No. 92-178, 85 Stat. 497, as amended, 87 Stat. 138 (1973); Federal Election Campaign Act Amendments of 1974, Pub. L. No. 93-443, 88 Stat. 1263; Federal Election Campaign Act Amendments of 1976, Pub. L.

No. 94-283, 90 Stat. 475; and Federal Election Campaign Act Amendments of 1979, Pub. L. No. 96-187, 93 Stat. 1339.

5. This assumes that the party committee or PAC is a multicandidate committee. See Sabato, *PAC POWER,* 7–8. If the committee or PAC has not qualified as a multicandidate committee, then a gift of only $1,000 maximum is permitted.
6. If there is a runoff election, another $15,000 from the three party committees combined can be added to the potential contribution total.
7. Under 2 U.S.C. 441a(d).
8. Based on 1974 dollars.
9. The original 1976 limit was $3.2 million; inflation and population growth account for the increase.
10. This limit applied only to House candidates in states with more than one House district; candidates in single-district states (such as South Dakota and Alaska) benefit from the higher Senate limits described in the following sentence.
11. In 1978 the Republican party established such "agency agreements" between a number of its state committees and the Republican National Senatorial Committee. The agreements were challenged by the Democrats, but the Supreme Court held in favor of the GOP in *Federal Election Commission v. Democratic Senatorial Campaign Committee,* 454 U.S. 27 (1981).
12. See Cynthia Cates Colella, "Parties, PACs, and Campaign Finance: An Intergovernmental Perspective," paper prepared for delivery at the annual meeting of the American Political Science Association, Washington, D.C., August 29–September 2, 1986, 7–8.
13. See Advisory Commission on Intergovernmental Relations, *The Transformation in American Politics* (Washington, D.C.: ACIR, August 1986), 121.
14. Sabato, *PAC POWER,* 7–8.
15. Ibid., 141–159.
16. See David E. Price, *Bringing Back the Parties* (Washington, D.C.: Congressional Quarterly Press, 1984), 242–245.
17. Granted, an independent is funded only *after* the general election *if* he or she has received at least 5 percent of the vote, and only in proportion to the vote actually received. Still, it can be argued that any provision at all is unnecessary and damaging to the two-party system. See Chapter Seven.
18. Price, *Bringing Back the Parties,* 244–245. For a comparison of media and organizational expenditures, see the author's *The Rise of Political Consultants: New Ways of Winning Elections* (New York: Basic Books, 1981), 197–205.
19. The Supreme Court in *Buckley v. Valeo* (96 S. Ct. 612, 1976 or 424 U.S. 1, 1976) ruled that limits on independent expenditures were an unconstitutional infringement of First Amendment rights.
20. ACIR, *The Transformation in American Politics,* 271–278.
21. Since the money is funneled to states, state law applies, and many states neither prohibit union or corporate treasury gifts nor require full

disclosure of campaign money given and received for these party activities.

22. Thomas B. Edsall, "'Soft Money' Will Finance Voter Signup," *Washington Post*, August 12, 1984, A4.
23. Ibid.; see also Peter Grier, "'Soft Money' and '84 Campaign Financing," *Christian Science Monitor*, June 19, 1984, 4. No exact accounting of soft money expenditure is possible since much of it is not disclosed at the federal or state levels.
24. See Institute of Politics, JFK School of Government, Harvard University, "An Analysis of the Impact of the Federal Election Campaign Act, 1972–78" (Cambridge, Mass.: JFK School of Government, May 1979), 1–3.
25. Services such as media production and polling are provided as in-kind contributions to candidates at drastically scaled down prices. Partially, this is a result of economies of scale. Also, Federal Election Commission rules permit such accounting practices, which have the practical effect of stretching the parties' campaign dollars and providing candidates with far greater support than the "party-to-candidate" dollar transfer may indicate. For example, a party may contribute a poll to a candidate, but depreciate its cost by 50 percent if it waits sixteen days after the poll's completion to deliver it to a candidate, and by a massive 95 percent if delivery is postponed more than sixty days after completion. (This is known as the *sixty-one day rule.*)
26. That is, the 15 to 17 percent estimate does not include the money PACs give to candidates at the urging of the parties. Both parties have active PAC solicitation programs to help their candidates secure PAC gifts. The Republican party committees are especially efficient at channeling friendly PAC funds to their contenders, and the GOP committees take little from PACs for their own organizational operation. In 1985–1986, for example, just 0.4 percent of the total funds raised by the Republican party committees came from PACs, whereas 9 percent of the Democratic committees' total was PAC-derived. Second, the 15 to 17 percent estimate also does not include the significant number of individual contributions that are collected by the GOP (in a process called bundling) and forwarded to specific candidates. The Republican party solicits these large and small denomination gifts on behalf of their most competitive or needy candidates, but even though the party channels the money and is the collecting agent, the donations are listed as individual contributions and are not reflected in the party fundraising total. No exact total is available, but the bundling operation almost certainly involves millions of dollars. For Senate candidates alone, the party estimated that $3 million was bundled in 1984 and $6 million in 1986. Obviously, if these gifts were counted toward the GOP totals, the proportion of congressional money supplied by the party would increase. The Democrats have no comparable program.
27. Leon D. Epstein, *Political Parties in the American Mold* (Madison: University of Wisconsin Press, 1986), 207.

28. Sabato, *The Rise of Political Consultants,* 295–296.
29. Ibid.
30. The GOP spending edge is actually even greater since the Republicans also have a large lead in bundled contributions, soft money donations, and cut-rate party services. See notes 21, 22, 25, 26 above. See also *National Journal* 18 (December 20, 1986): 3069.
31. Senator George J. Mitchell (D-Maine) as quoted in the *Washington Post,* February 9, 1986, A14.
32. Thomas B. Edsall, in the *Washington Post,* October 17, 1986, A1.
33. Dick Kirschten, "GOP Governors' Aide Offsets a Rough Year," *National Journal* 18 (January 10, 1987): 91.
34. See the *Washington Post,* October 13, 1985, A5, and November 2, 1986, A13. See also *National Journal* 17 (December 7, 1985): 2803.
35. For discussions and descriptions of the GOP's direct mail program, see Sabato, *The Rise of Political Consultants,* 290–300; *PAC Power,* 156–57; "Parties, PACs, and Independent Groups," in Thomas E. Mann and Norman J. Ornstein, eds., *The American Elections of 1982* (Washington, D.C.: American Enterprise Institute, 1983), 73–81; Xandra Kayden and Eddie Mahe, Jr., *The Party Goes On* (New York: Basic Books, 1986), 81; *Washington Post,* January 15, 1986, A15 and August 29, 1986, A1; and Maxwell Glen, "GOP Prospecting," *National Journal* 19 (January 31, 1987): 259–263.
36. See Sabato, *The Rise of Political Consultants,* 290–297; *PAC POWER,* 152–56; "Parties, PACs, and Independent Groups," 73–82.
37. See note 25 above. In 1986 the prices charged to Republican candidates for party polls ranged from under $100 to about $750, depending on certain factors, such as the number of candidates for whom the poll was taken and the amount of time lapsed between poll completion and delivery to the candidate(s).
38. See Sabato, "Parties, PACs, and Independent Groups," 76.
39. Ibid., 78–79.
40. Price, *Bringing Back the Parties,* 40.
41. Republican candidates clearly recognize that the party provides them with major assistance in issue development. See Herrnson, "Do Parties Make a Difference?" 598.
42. See *The New Republic* 191 (December 1, 1986): 22.
43. As quoted in a speech to the RNC by the Associated Press, January 24, 1987, and in the *Washington Post,* same date, A3.
44. The Republican senators most often cited as survivors thanks in part to financial and technological edges were Wisconsin's Robert Kasten and Pennsylvania's Arlen Specter.
45. Ronald Brownstein, "The Long Green Line," *National Journal* 18 (May 3, 1986): 1038–1042.
46. Thomas B. Edsall, "GOP Committees a Bonanza for Ex-Aides and Relatives," *Washington Post,* January 13, 1987, A1, A6.
47. Ibid., A6.
48. See the *Washington Post,* July 16, 1987, A1, A6.
49. See, for example, *Washington Post,* November 9, 1986, A1.

50. William McInturff, director of party development for the RNC, as quoted ibid.
51. It is possible, of course, that turnout would have been even lower and GOP incumbent senators would have lost by even more votes without the RNC's extensive 1986 voter contact program. But it strains credulity to believe that turnout could have been much lower than the nadir actually recorded; moreover, the program could hardly be called a success if winning means anything at all.
52. *Washington Post,* September 29, 1986, A1.
53. *Washington Post,* October 21, 1986, A11. The suit was settled out of court, with the GOP agreeing to halt the program in exchange for consent not to make public the embarrassing (for them) depositions filed in the case. See also ibid., July 24, 1987, A3.
54. *Washington Post,* October 31, 1986, A1.
55. Ibid.
56. See *Congressional Quarterly Weekly* 43 (October 13, 1985): 2050.
57. *Washington Post,* November 1, 1986, A10.
58. See, for example, Associated Press, "Democrats Tell Regan Negative Campaigning Would Harm Tax Bill," *Washington Post,* September 24, 1985, A3.
59. Jean Cobb and Lee Norrgard, "Sugar Daddy," *Common Cause* 12 (January/February 1986): 44–47; and *Washington Post,* August 29, 1986, A10.
60. *Washington Post,* January 13, 1987, A1, A6; and January 23, 1987, A16.
61. Dom Bonafede, "Kirk at the DNC's Helm," *National Journal* 18 (March 22, 1986): 703–707 at 707.
62. Sabato, "Parties, PACs, and Independent Groups," 84–86.
63. Martin D. Franks, executive director of the Democratic Congressional Campaign Committee, as quoted in the *Richmond Times-Dispatch,* October 21, 1986, A1.
64. See *National Journal* 18 (March 15, 1986): 636.
65. However, leaders of the black, women's, and Hispanic caucuses retained seats on the DNC's executive committee.
66. The Republican party has never had a midterm convention.
67. See *Congressional Quarterly Weekly* 44 (March 1, 1986): 509. See also James W. Ceaser, *Reforming the Reforms: A Critical Analysis of the Presidential Selection Process* (Cambridge, Mass.: Ballinger, 1982).
68. See Alan Ehrenhalt, "Campaign '86: Few Real House Contests," *Congressional Quarterly Weekly* 44 (January 25, 1986): 171.
69. Gary C. Jacobson, "Party Organization and Campaign Resources in 1982," *Political Science Quarterly* 101 (Winter 1985–1986): 603–625 at 618, 621. By 1986 Democratic party committees were devoting 68.3 percent of their direct contributions and coordinated expenditures to challengers and open-seat candidates for the House and Senate, and just 31.7 percent to incumbents. The GOP committees gave a larger proportion to their incumbents (44.4 percent), but even so Republican congressional challengers and open-seat candidates were much more

generously funded by the party committees in absolute dollars ($9.8 million) than their Democratic counterparts ($5.2 million).

70. As quoted in the *Washington Post,* October 27, 1986, A13.
71. The Democratic Leadership Council's annual operating budget is about $400,000.
72. See David S. Broder, "Democratic Money — But Not For the Party," the *Washington Post,* October 29, 1986, A19.
73. As noted in Chapter Two, party leaders report that both Ford and Reagan were unusually party-oriented, always willing to sign fundraising appeals and make appearances to benefit the GOP. Jimmy Carter, by contrast, kept the DNC weak and technologically primitive, preferring to centralize political activities in the White House.
74. V. O. Key, Jr., *Politics, Parties, and Pressure Groups* (New York: Thomas Y. Crowell, 1964), 334.
75. James L. Gibson, Cornelius P. Cotter, John F. Bibby, and Robert J. Huckshorn, "Assessing Party Organizational Strength," *American Journal of Political Science* 27 (May 1983): 193–222; and ACIR, *The Transformation in American Politics,* 112–116. See also David R. Mayhew, *Placing Parties in American Politics* (Princeton: Princeton University Press, 1986).
76. The median was a smaller but still sizeable $351,000. ACIR, *The Transformation in American Politics,* 112–116.
77. ACIR, ibid. Up to 95 percent of the GOP state parties give at least some financial aid, while up to 70 percent of the Democratic organizations do so. A slim majority of Republican state parties and about one-third of the Democratic parties seek to solicit and funnel PAC gifts to their candidates.
78. Ibid., 112; Price, *Bringing Back the Parties,* 35.
79. *Washington Post,* February 9, 1986, A14.
80. Paul Taylor, "GOP Offensives Produce Dramatic But Fragile Gains," *Washington Post,* May 20, 1986, A14.
81. ACIR, *The Transformation in American Politics,* 115.
82. Ibid.
83. Gibson et al., "Assessing Party Organizational Strength," 206.
84. ACIR, *The Transformation in American Politics,* 326.
85. Ruth S. Jones, "Financing State Elections," in Malbin (ed.), *Money and Politics in the United States,* 194.
86. Epstein, *Political Parties in the American Mold,* 223.
87. ACIR, *The Transformation in American Politics,* 120.
88. Ibid.
89. Ibid., 84–87.
90. Ibid.
91. Ibid.
92. This is Rule 26(f) of the party by-laws.
93. See Kayden and Mahe, *The Party Goes On,* 77–78.
94. See the RNC's *County Line* 5 (March 1986): 3.
95. See Dom Bonafede, "Kirk at the DNC's Helm," *National Journal* 18

(March 22, 1986): 705–707; and see also *National Journal* 18 (August 16, 1986): 2002.

96. ACIR, *The Transformation in American Politics,* 120.
97. Bonafede, "Kirk at the DNC's Helm," 705.
98. David S. Broder, "A Healthy Step," *Washington Post,* April 2, 1986, A23.
99. As quoted ibid.
100. Ibid.
101. See Ronald Brownstein and Maxwell Glen, "Money in the Shadows," *National Journal* 18 (March 8, 1986): 632–637.
102. See *Congressional Quarterly Weekly* 44 (November 15, 1986): 2893. The Democrats (through their "Project 500," a coalition of party, labor and liberal groups) and the Republicans (via the RNC's "1991 Plan," which refers to the year of the next legislative redistricting) each spent approximately $1 million in state legislative contests in 1986. Once again, though, the GOP retains an overall edge because of a well-funded political action committee called GOPAC — technically independent of the party but dedicated to precisely the same goals as the 1991 Plan. GOPAC raised over $2.6 million in the 1983–1984 election cycle alone.
103. See Cotter, Gibson, Bibby, Huckshorn, *Party Organizations in American Politics,* 104.
104. For a recent example in New Jersey, where Republicans turned a 43–37 Democratic edge in the lower house of the state legislature into a 50–30 Republican advantage in 1985, see Michael Barone, "GOP Benchmark," *Washington Post,* November 4, 1985, A15.
105. Alderman Vito Marzullo as quoted in the *Washington Post,* November 2, 1985, A3. Marzullo won 23 elections as a machine candidate and served for more than three decades on Chicago's city council before being forced to retire after unfavorable court-ordered redistricting in 1986. He spurned all offers of higher office over the years, explaining, "I just want to stay where I am . . . where I can help my friends and shaft my enemies."
106. Cotter, Gibson, Bibby, Huckshorn, *Party Organizations in American Politics,* 57. See also Epstein, *Political Parties in the American Mold,* 152.
107. Cotter, Gibson, Bibby, Huckshorn, 57.
108. See William Crotty, ed., *Political Parties in Local Areas* (Nashville: University of Tennessee Press, 1987); and Mayhew, *Placing Parties in American Politics.*
109. See *Congressional Quarterly Weekly* 44 (March 22, 1986): 660.
110. See Tom Watson, "All-Powerful Machine of Yore Endures in New York's Nassau," *Congressional Quarterly Weekly* 43 (August 17, 1985): 1623–1625.
111. See *Congressional Quarterly Weekly* 44 (April 26, 1986): 931–932, and (May 10, 1986): 1046.
112. *Washington Post,* September 23, 1985, A14. Also, it was an election issue in the 1984 gubernatorial race. While the Democratic candidate

who opposed the patronage system lost, he seemed to gain support based on the issue. The successfully reelected governor, Republican Robert Orr, received the electorate's message, and proposed abolition of the funding scheme in 1985.

113. The Republicans have been the major beneficiaries since they have controlled the Indiana governorship continuously since 1969.
114. Information supplied by Indiana Legislative Services. The bill that passed in 1986 was House Bill No. 1400 (IC 510-372).
115. See Rob Gurwitt, "Waxman, Berman and Allies Aim to Shape National Policy," *Congressional Quarterly Weekly* 43 (August 17, 1985): 1620–1623.
116. Ibid.
117. *Wall Street Journal,* November 10, 1983, 58; and *Congressional Quarterly Weekly* 41 (March 12, 1983): 505.
118. See Sabato, *PAC POWER.* See also Irwin B. Arieff, Nadine Cohodes, and Richard Whittle, "Senator Helms Builds a Machine of Interlinked Organizations to Shape Both Politics, Policy," *Congressional Quarterly Weekly* 40 (March 4, 1982): 479–505; and Paul Taylor, "Helms Modernizes GOP Political Machine for the Electronic Age," *Washington Post,* October 15, 1982, A2.
119. ACIR, *The Transformation in American Politics,* 116–118.
120. Ibid. This relationship was especially strong for Democratic candidates at all levels, but also was valid for the GOP in the case of congressional candidates.
121. Gary C. Jacobson, "Republican Advantage in Campaign Finance," in John Chubb and Paul Peterson, eds., *The New Direction in American Politics* (Washington, D.C.: The Brookings Institution, 1985), 169.
122. *National Journal* 18 (April 12, 1986): 866–868.
123. Andrew L. Aoki and Mark Rom, "Financing a Comeback: Campaign Finance Laws and Prospects for Political Party Resurgence," paper prepared for delivery at the annual meeting of the American Political Science Association, New Orleans, La., August 29–September 1, 1985, 14. In five of the six cases examined by the authors, the representatives who received the most money from the party during a campaign were more likely to support the party in the next legislative session than the group of representatives that received the least amount of money. However, the difference between the means of the two groups was never statistically significant.
124. Ibid., 17.
125. Kayden and Mahe, *The Party Goes On.*
126. ACIR, *The Transformation in American Politics,* 332, 360.
127. Sabato, *PAC POWER,* 141–159, 176–177.
128. Ibid.
129. ACIR, *The Transformation in American Politics,* 234.
130. Cotter, Gibson, Bibby, and Huckshorn, *Party Organizations in American Politics,* 989–991.

CHAPTER FOUR

• ☆ • ☆ •

The Parties and the People

A POLITICAL PARTY IS FAR MORE than its organizational shell, however dazzling the technologies at its command, and its reach extends well beyond the relative handful of men and women who comprise the party-in-government. In any democracy, where power is derived directly from the people, the party's real importance and strength must come from the citizenry it attempts to mobilize. The party-in-the-electorate — the mass of potential voters who identify with the Democratic or Republican labels — is the third and most significant element in the party triad, providing the foundation for the organizational and governmental parties. But in some crucial respects it is the most troubled of the three special components of the American political parties. In recent decades fewer citizens have been willing to pledge their fealty to the major parties, and many of those who have declared their loyalties have done so with less intensity. Also, as we shall see, voters of each partisan stripe are increasingly casting ballots for some candidates of the opposing party, and partisan identification is a less reliable indicator of likely voting choices today. The public's attitudes toward the parties is more critical or uncaring as well, and their image has deteriorated in some disturbing ways. The partisan affiliations, the voting practices, and the views about parties held by the American electorate will each be examined in turn in this chapter.

Trends in Party Identification

Most American voters *identify* with a party but do not *belong* to it. There is no universal enrolled party membership; no prescribed dues; no formal rules concerning an individual's activities; no enforceable obligations to the party assumed by the voter.[1] The party has no real control over or even an accurate accounting of its adherents, and the party's voters subscribe to few or none of the commonly accepted tenets of organizational membership, such as regular participation and some measure of responsibility for the group's welfare. Rather, party identification or affiliation is an informal and impressionistic exercise whereby a citizen acquires a party label and accepts its standard as a shorthand summary of his or her political views and preferences. Just because the acquisition is informal does not mean it is unimportant, however. As we discussed in Chapter One, the party label becomes a voter's central political reference symbol and perceptual screen, a prism or filter through which the world of politics and government flows and is interpreted. For many Americans, party identification is a significant aspect of self, the vital statistic of one's political personality and a way of defining and explaining oneself to others. The loyalty generated by the label can be as intense as any enjoyed by sports teams and alma maters; in a few areas of the country, "Democrat" and "Republican" are still fighting words.

On the whole, though, Americans regard their partisan affiliation with lesser degrees of enthusiasm, viewing it as a convenience rather than a necessity. The individual identifications are reinforced by the legal institutionalization of the major parties. Because of restrictive ballot laws, campaign finance rules, the powerful inertia of political tradition, and many other factors, voters for all practical purposes are limited to a choice between a Democrat and a Republican in virtually all elections — a situation that naturally encourages the pragmatic choosing up of sides. The party registration process that exists in many states, requiring a voter to state a party preference (or Independent status) when registering to vote and restricting participation in primaries to party registrants, also is an incentive for voters to affiliate.[2] Even the relentless drumbeat of public opinion surveys (to which this study, alas, has contributed) forces a choice of institutionalized party alternatives and may help to perpetuate the current alignment.

Whatever the societal and governmental forces undergirding party identification, the explanations of partisan loyalty at the individual's level are understandably more personal. Not surprisingly, parents are the single greatest influence in establishing a person's first party identification.[3] Politically active parents with the same party loyalty raise children who will be strong party identifiers, while parents without party affiliations or with mixed affiliations produce offspring more likely to be Independents.[4] Early socialization is hardly the last step in the acquisition and maintenance of a party identity; marriage and other facts of adult life can change one's loyalty.[5] So can charismatic political personalities, particularly at the national level (such as Franklin Roosevelt or, perhaps, Ronald Reagan), cataclysmic events (the Civil War and the Great Depression are the best examples), and maybe intense social issues (for instance, abortion). Interestingly, social class is not an especially strong indicator of likely partisan choice in the United States, at least by comparison to Western European democracies.[6] Not only are Americans less inclined than Europeans to perceive class distinctions — preferring instead to see themselves and most others as members of an exceedingly broad middle class — but other factors, including sectionalism and candidate-oriented politics, tend to blur class lines in voting.

Over the last two decades many political scientists as well as other observers, journalists, and party activists have become increasingly anxious about a perceived decline in partisan identification and loyalty. Many public opinion surveys have shown a significant growth in Independents at the expense of the two major parties. The Center for Political Studies/Survey Research Center (CPS/SRC) of the University of Michigan, for instance, has charted the rise of self-described Independents from a low of 19 percent in 1958 to a peak of 38 percent twenty years later.[7] Before the 1950s, while the evidence is more circumstantial because of the scarcity of reliable survey research data, there are indications that Independents were many fewer in number, and party loyalties considerably firmer.[8]

Yet as Table 4.1 suggests, the recent decline of party identification can be, and often has been, exaggerated. The most lasting impression left by the table's data is one of remarkable stability (at least in the aggregate). Over more than thirty years, during vast political, economic, and social upheavals that have changed the face of the nation, the Democratic party has nearly consistently drawn the support of a small majority (row A) and the Republican party has attracted a share of the electorate in the low-to-mid 30 percent range (row B). Granted, there have been peaks and valleys for both parties. The Johnson landslide of 1964 helped Democrats top the 60 percent mark, while the Reagan landslide of 1984 sent Democratic stock below the majority midpoint. The Goldwater debacle of 1964 and the Watergate disaster of 1974 left the Republicans with under a third of the populace; Reagan's reelection brought the GOP to the threshold of 40 percent. Some slight average erosion over time in Democratic party strength is certainly apparent, as is a small Republican gain during the Reagan era. Yet these sorts of gradations are more akin to rolling foothills than towering mountain ranges, or (to mix metaphors) gentle merry-go-rounds than turbulent roller coasters. The steady-state nature of modern partisanship goes beyond the fortunes of each party. Since we are concerned here with partisan loyalty as a whole, Row D — which adds Democratic and Republican strength together — is even more reassuring. Support for the two parties in modern times has never dipped below 83 percent of the American electorate (recorded during the disillusionment spawned by Watergate in 1974), and can usually be found in the mid-to-upper 80 percent range. A small gradual downward drift from the 1952 and 1964 zeniths of 92 percent is obvious, but recent party gains have restored the partisanship proportion to near its thirty-year average of 87 percent. (See also Figure 4.1.)

Critics will properly point out that I have relied upon the strictest definition of "Independent" in the foregoing analysis. When pollsters ask for party identification information, they generally proceed in two stages. First they inquire whether a respondent considers himself or herself a Democrat, Republican, or Independent. Then the party identifiers are asked to categorize themselves as a "strong" or "not very strong" supporter, while the Independents are pushed to reveal their leanings with a question such as, "Well, which party do you normally support in elections — the Democrats or the Republicans?" It may be true that some Independent respondents are thereby prodded to pick a party under the pressure of the interview situation, regardless of their true feelings. But research clearly demonstrates that Independent "leaners" in fact vote very much like real partisans, in some elections more so than the "not very strong" party identifiers.[9] There is reason to count the Independent leaners

TABLE 4.1 Party Identification, 1952–1986[a]

PARTISAN CATEGORY	PERCENT, BY YEAR																	
	1952	1954	1956	1958	1960	1962	1964	1966	1968	1970	1972	1974	1976	1978	1980	1982	1984	1986
A. Democrat	57	57	50	56	51	53	61	55	55	54	52	52	52	49	51	55	48	50
B. Republican	35	33	37	33	37	34	31	32	34	32	34	31	33	31	33	32	39	36
C. Independent[b]	6	7	9	7	10	8	8	12	11	13	13	15	15	14	13	11	11	12
D. Partisan total (D&R)[c]	92	90	87	89	88	87	92	87	89	86	86	83	85	84	84	87	87	86
E. Strong Democrats	22	22	21	27	20	23	27	18	20	20	15	18	15	15	17	20	17	18
F. Strong Republicans	14	14	14	17	14	16	14	15	15	15	13	14	14	13	14	14	15	10
G. All Independents (including leaners)[d]	23	22	23	19	23	21	23	27	29	30	35	37	37	38	34	30	34	33

H. Partisan total minus Independent leaners[e]	75	75	73	77	75	74	77	71	70	68	64	61	63	60	63	68	64	65

SOURCE: Center for Political Studies/Survey Research Center of the University of Michigan, made available through the Inter-University Consortium for Political and Social Research. Also, Leon D. Epstein, *Political Parties in the American Mold* (Madison: University of Wisconsin Press, 1986), Table 8.1, 257.

[a]Partisan totals do not add to 100% since "apolitical" and "other" responses were deleted. Sample size from poll to poll varied, from a low of 1,130 to a high of 2,850.

[b]Pure Independents only. Independent "leaners" have been added to Democratic and Republican totals.

[c]That is, total percentages for Democrats and Republicans listed immediately above have been added together in this row.

[d]That is, Independent Democrats + Independent Republicans + Pure Independents.

[e]That is, partisan total as listed above minus Independent Democrats and Independent Republicans.

FIGURE 4.1 Trends in Party Identification, 1952–1986

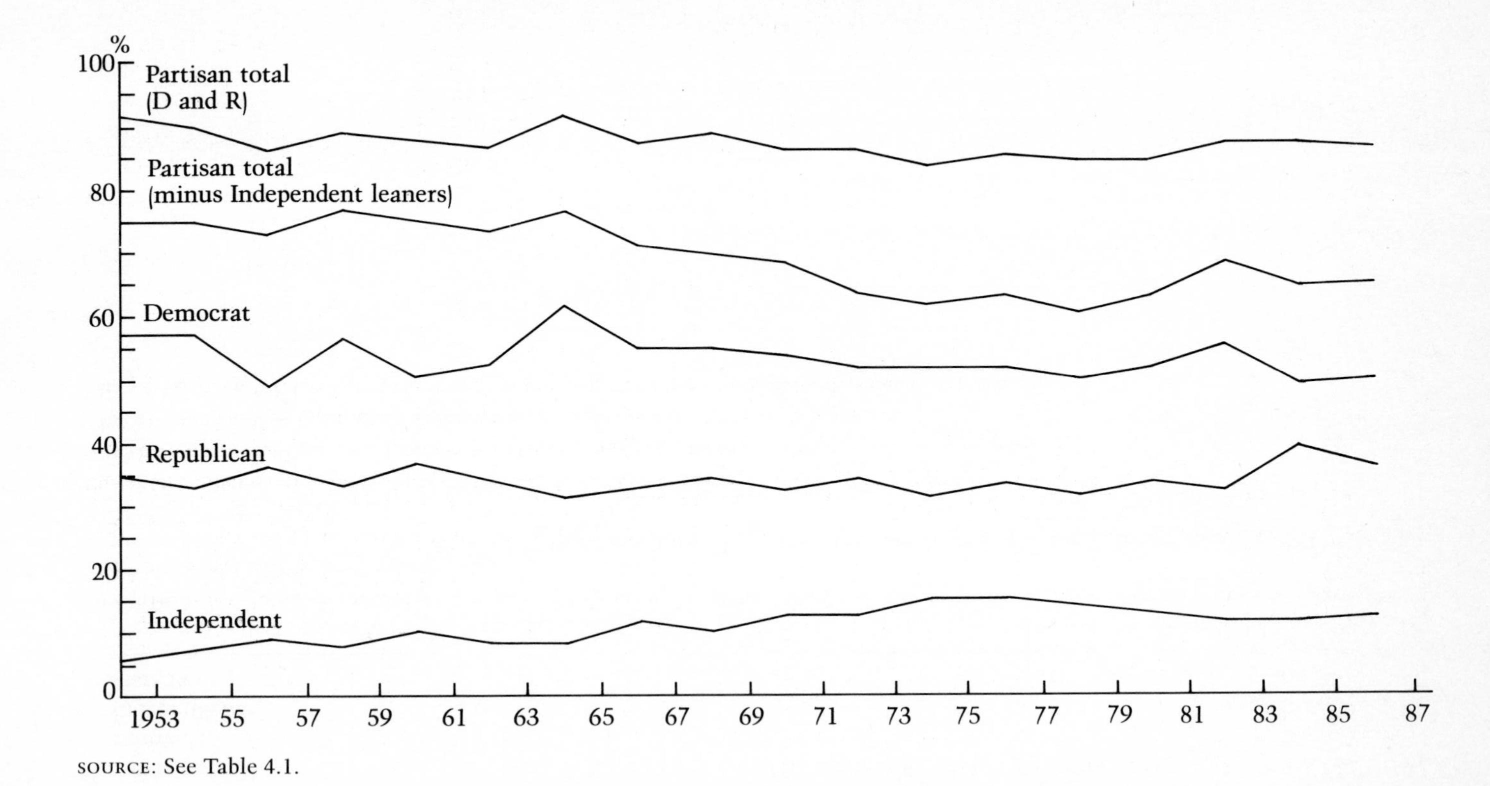

SOURCE: See Table 4.1.

as closet partisans, though voting behavior is *not* the equivalent of real partisan identification. If it were, we would not bother to ask poll respondents about their party affiliations, quizzing them only about how they normally vote.

In fact, the reluctance of "leaners" to admit their real party identities in itself is worrisome because it reveals a sea change in attitudes about political parties and their proper role in our society. Being a socially acceptable, integrated, and contributing member of one's community once almost demanded partisan affiliation; it was a badge of good citizenship, motherhood, and apple pie, signifying that one was a patriot. Today the labels are shunned as an offense to a thinking person's individualism, and a vast majority of Americans insist they vote for "the man, not the party." These antiparty attitudes will be examined in more detail shortly, but the reasons for their prevalence are not hard to find. The growth of an issue-oriented politics that cuts across party lines for those voters who feel intensely about certain policy matters is partly to blame.[10] So too is the emphasis on personality politics by the mass media (especially television) and political consultants.[11] Others cite the broad-based higher educational levels achieved in recent decades, which supposedly enables voters to gain enough information to judge candidates on issues and character apart from party labels,[12] though this suggestion has been seriously disputed by additional research.[13] Underlying all of these causes, though, is a far more disturbing and corrosive long-term phenomenon: the perceived loss of party credibility and the decline of the party's tangible connections to the lives of everyday citizens. This development — and possible mechanisms to reverse it — will be the focus of the concluding chapters, but for now it is enough to note that while total real partisanship has not declined significantly since 1952 (as discussed earlier), voter-admitted partisanship has dropped considerably. Referring again to Table 4.1 (row H), about three-quarters or more of the electorate volunteered a party choice without prodding from 1952 to 1964, but since 1970 an average of under two-thirds has been willing to do so. Self-professed Independents (including leaners)[14] have increased from around a fifth of the electorate in the 1950s to a third or more in the 1970s and 1980s (row G), although during the latter decade there has been a welcome if minor recession from the peak 37–38 percent Independency reached from 1974 to 1978. Also cause for concern is the marginal decline in strong Democrats (row E) and strong Republicans (row F). The failure of the GOP to make any substantial gain in strong Republicans despite the favorable electoral trends of the 1980s is particularly noticeable, as is the sharp 1986 drop in strong Republicans to the lowest level in at least three and a half decades (just 10 percent). Strong partisans are a party's backbone, the source of its volunteer force, candidates, and dependable voters. Even slight shrinkage in these ranks can be troublesome. Finally, when we consider only *pure* Independents — the voter category least friendly to political parties — considerable growth is apparent (row C). Despite a tiny partisan advance in the last few years, the proportion of pure Independents has doubled since 1952.

The Subgroup Continuum of Party Loyalty

The national summary data on party identification are deceptive and simplistic, as all averages can be. There are enormous variations in the patterns of party loyalty from one region or demographic group to another, as Table 4.2 demonstrates:

□ While all other geographic regions are relatively closely contested between the parties, the South still exhibits the Democratic party affinity cultivated in the last century and stoked in the fires of the Civil War. In all regions, party strengths vary by locality, with central cities almost everywhere being heavily Democratic, the swelling suburbs serving as the main source of GOP partisans, and the small towns and rural areas split evenly between the two major parties.

□ Women and men differ sharply in their partisan choice, a phenomenon called the *gender gap,* which has yawned at least since 1980. The sixteen-point gap in our poll finds women favoring the Democratic party by 10 percent and men giving the GOP a 6 percent edge. Besides women's rights issues, female concerns for peace and social compassion may be providing much of the gap's foundation. For instance, women are much less likely than men to favor American military aid to the contra rebels fighting the procommunist Sandinista government of Nicaragua,[15] and they are less inclined to support cuts in government funding of social welfare programs.[16] The gender gap persists at about the same magnitude for all ages,[17] but the divide is much greater for whites

TABLE 4.2 Party Identification in the Electorate, by Selected Subgroups[a]

	SELECTED SUBGROUP	DEMOCRATIC	REPUBLICAN	INDEPENDENT[b]	OVERALL DEMOCRATIC ADVANTAGE
	National sample	*45%*	*40%*	*13%*	+ *5%*
Geography	Northeast	40	44	13	− 4
	Midwest	39	44	16	− 5
	South	53	35	11	+18
	West	42	42	14	0
Demography	City dweller	53	31	16	+22
	Suburban	35	50	16	−15
	Small town	44	44	12	0
	Rural	46	44	10	+ 2
Sex	Men	39	45	16	− 6
	Women	50	40	11	+10
Race	Black	86	4	10	+82
	White	41	46	14	− 5
	Hispanic[c]	69	14	16	+55
Age	18–34	42	46	12	− 4
	35–49	47	38	15	+ 9
	50+	46	40	14	+ 6
Occupation	Executive/professional	32	54	12	−22
	Other white collar	34	51	13	−17

(continued)

TABLE 4.2 *(continued)*

	SELECTED SUBGROUP	DEMOCRATIC	REPUBLICAN	INDEPENDENT[b]	OVERALL DEMOCRATIC ADVANTAGE
Occupation (continued)	Blue collar	48	35	15	+13
	Unemployed	55	33	13	+22
	Retired	41	47	11	− 6
	Student	36	58	6	−22
	Homemaker	49	44	7	+ 5
Labor union	Union members	56	22	19	+34
Income (annual family)	Under $12,000	62	25	11	+37
	$12,000–$23,999	47	37	13	+10
	$24,000–$34,999	44	39	14	+ 5
	$35,000–$41,999	43	40	14	+ 3
	$42,000+	37	48	15	−11
Education	Less than high school	59	23	14	+36
	High school graduate	48	38	11	+10
	Some college[d]	41	43	12	− 2
	College graduate[d]	39	47	13	− 8
	Graduate school[d]	41	44	15	− 3
Religion	Protestant	41	46	13	− 5
	Catholic	49	39	12	+10
	Jewish	52	28	20	+24
	Born-again[e]	38	49	13	−11

Marital status	Married	42	43	15	− 1
	Never married	45	46	9	− 1
	Widowed	49	40	11	+ 9
	Divorced/separated	55	33	12	+22
Ideology	Very liberal	76	14	10	+62
	Somewhat liberal	63	27	9	+36
	Middle-of-the-road	47	34	19	+13
	Somewhat conservative	29	58	12	−29
	Very conservative	31	59	10	−28
Voter registration[f]	Registered to vote	45	40	13	+ 5
	Unregistered to vote	39	43	15	− 4

SOURCE: Poll 1 (see Appendix).

[a]The question wording was as follows: "Generally speaking, do you consider yourself a Democrat, Republican, or an Independent? (*IF INDEPENDENT*) Well, which party do you normally support in elections — the Democrats or the Republicans? (*IF DEMOCRAT/REPUBLICAN*) Would you say you are a strong (Democrat/Republican) or not a very strong (Democrat/Republican)?" "Don't know," "refuse to answer," and "other party" responses are not listed in table; therefore, row percentages do not total to 100%.

[b]Pure Independents only. Party leaners (those pushed to identify their partisan leanings after first categorizing themselves as "Independent") are included in Democrat and Republican totals.

[c]The Hispanic population is a subset of whites. About 4 percent of the white respondents classified themselves as being of Hispanic, Mexican, or Central/South American heritage. This is not enough of a subsample to produce precise, reliable findings but at least the general direction of Hispanic party leanings is clear.

[d]"Some college" includes two-year, technical, and community college graduates; "College graduate" includes *only* graduates of four-year institutions; "Some graduate school" includes all graduate professional degrees as well as nondegree graduate training.

[e]A separate question was asked only of those who gave "Protestant" as their religious preference: "Do you consider yourself a born-again Christian resulting from a personal experience with Jesus Christ?"

[f]Self-reported unregistered N = 330.

than blacks, due to the unique Democratic solidarity of blacks described below.

- Blacks are the most dramatically different population subgroup in party terms. The 82 percent advantage they offer the Democrats dwarfs the edge given to either party by any other segment of the electorate, and their proportion of strong Democrats (39 percent) is three times that of whites. There are actually more black Independents (10 percent) than black Republicans (4 percent).[18] Blacks account almost entirely for the lead in party affiliation that Democrats enjoy over Republicans, since the GOP has been able to attract a narrow plurality of whites (46 percent to 41 percent for the Democrats) to its standard. Perhaps as a reflection of the massive party chasm separating blacks and whites, the two races differ greatly on many policy issues, with blacks overwhelmingly on the liberal side and whites closer to the conservative pole. An exception, incidentally, is abortion, where religious beliefs may lead blacks to the more conservative stance.[19] The much smaller population group of Hispanics[20] supplements blacks as a Democratic stalwart; by 69 percent to 14 percent, Hispanics prefer the Democratic label, and 27 percent of the Hispanics classify themselves as strong Democrats.
- Young people are trending more Republican. While polls in 1972 indicated that the 18–24 age group, and particularly students, were the only cohort to support Democratic presidential nominee George McGovern,[21] by 1986 the 18–34 age group was the only one with a Republican party identification edge. Age managed to override the gender gap in one sense: among whites, young women 18–34 joined young men in favoring Republicanism (though women did so by a 7 percent margin and men by a 22 percent margin).[22] Much of that margin was derived from strong student affiliation with the Republicans; by a 22 percent margin, the GOP was the party of choice for students. The most Democratic age group, by contrast, was the 35–49 year olds, whose political views were shaped in part by the era of civil rights, Vietnam, and Watergate.
- Some traditional strengths and weaknesses persist for each party by occupation, income, and education. The GOP remains predominant among executives, professionals, and white-collar workers, while the Democrats lead substantially among blue-collar workers and the unemployed. Labor union members are also Democratic by 2½ to 1, as one would expect, though the

GOP's share of 22 percent suggests the labor membership, unlike labor PACs,[23] is not monolithic. The more conservative retired population leans Republican, though not by a great measure, owing perhaps to Democratic skill in exploiting the Social Security issue. Homemakers, less liberal than working women, are nonetheless Democratic by about 5 percentage points — half the pro-Democratic margin of women as a whole. Occupation, income, and education are closely related, of course, so many of the same partisan patterns can be detected in all three classifications. Democratic support drops steadily as one climbs the income scale; from a massive 37 percent lead among those whose families make under $12,000 a year, Democrats gradually move to an 11 percent deficit among those whose families earn more than $42,000 annually. Similarly, as years of education increase, identification with the Republican party climbs — until graduate school, when the Democrats rally a bit and only narrowly trail GOP partisans.

□ The party preferences by religion are also traditional, but with modern twists. Protestants, especially Methodists, Presbyterians, and Episcopalians, favor the Republicans by a few percent, while Catholics and, even more so, Jews are predominantly Democratic in affiliation. Less polarization is apparent all around, though.[24] Democrats have made inroads among many Protestant denominations over the last three decades, and Republicans can now claim more than a quarter of the Jewish population and nearly 40 percent of the Catholics. The "born-again" Christians, who have received so much attention in recent years, are somewhat less Republican than commonly believed. The GOP has just an 11 percent edge among them, primarily because so many blacks classify themselves as born-agains.[25] These fundamentalists' attitudes on politics are often quite similar to those not of their religious stripe, yet their sometimes apocalyptic and pessimistic outlook is readily apparent. As a group they are somewhat more likely to believe that "things have gotten pretty seriously off on the wrong track" in America, and they stand in stark contrast to the rest of the country in their views on tradition and change. When asked, "Do you feel that America needs more conservative, traditional values of earlier days or do we need to adapt our thinking to the modern changes that are occurring?" born-agains chose traditional values by a margin of 52 percent to 35 percent, while the rest of the population preferred adaptation to change by a larger 55 percent to 30 percent majority.[26]

- Even marital status reveals something about partisan affiliation. Those who are married, a traditionally more conservative group, and those who have never married, a segment weighted toward the premarriage young who are currently Republican-leaning, are closely divided in party loyalty. But the widowed are Democratic in nature, probably because there are far more widows than widowers, and the gender gap is once again expressing itself. The divorced and the separated, who may well be experiencing economic hardship and appear to be more liberal than the married population, are a substantially Democratic group.
- Ideologically, there are few surprises. Lending credence to the belief that both parties are now relatively distinct philosophically, liberals are overwhelmingly Democratic and conservatives are staunchly Republican. One source of the overall Democratic edge in the general electorate is apparent from the ideological breakdowns. Democrats control the center, or at least are able to attract far more moderates to their banner than the GOP can. Moreover, the Democratic defection rate among the party's natural philosophical constituency is much lower than the Republicans'. Democrats lose just one-seventh of the "very liberal" population to the GOP, but thanks mainly to continued Democratic strength in the South, the Republican party is deserted by nearly one-third of the "very conservative" voters.
- Finally, contrary to popular political mythology, the unregistered population is not necessarily more Democratic than the registered electorate. Since young people are very mobile and have not become fully integrated into their communities, they have the lowest rate of voter registration. In our survey fully a third of the 18–34 year olds admitted to being unregistered, compared to 17 percent of those aged 35–49 and just 11 percent of those over 50 years of age.[27] Thus, the Republican proclivities of the 18–34 age group help to produce a slight lead for the GOP among those presently ineligible to vote.

These subgroup partisan loyalties yield a kind of continuum of party identification in the American electorate, as Figure 4.2 depicts. Even a quick glance at the figure confirms some of the assertions made earlier. First, the Republicans have nothing remotely comparable to the truly remarkable position of blacks in the Democratic constellation. Second, Democrats maintain their edge partly by drawing disproportionately from the GOP's base; the whole con-

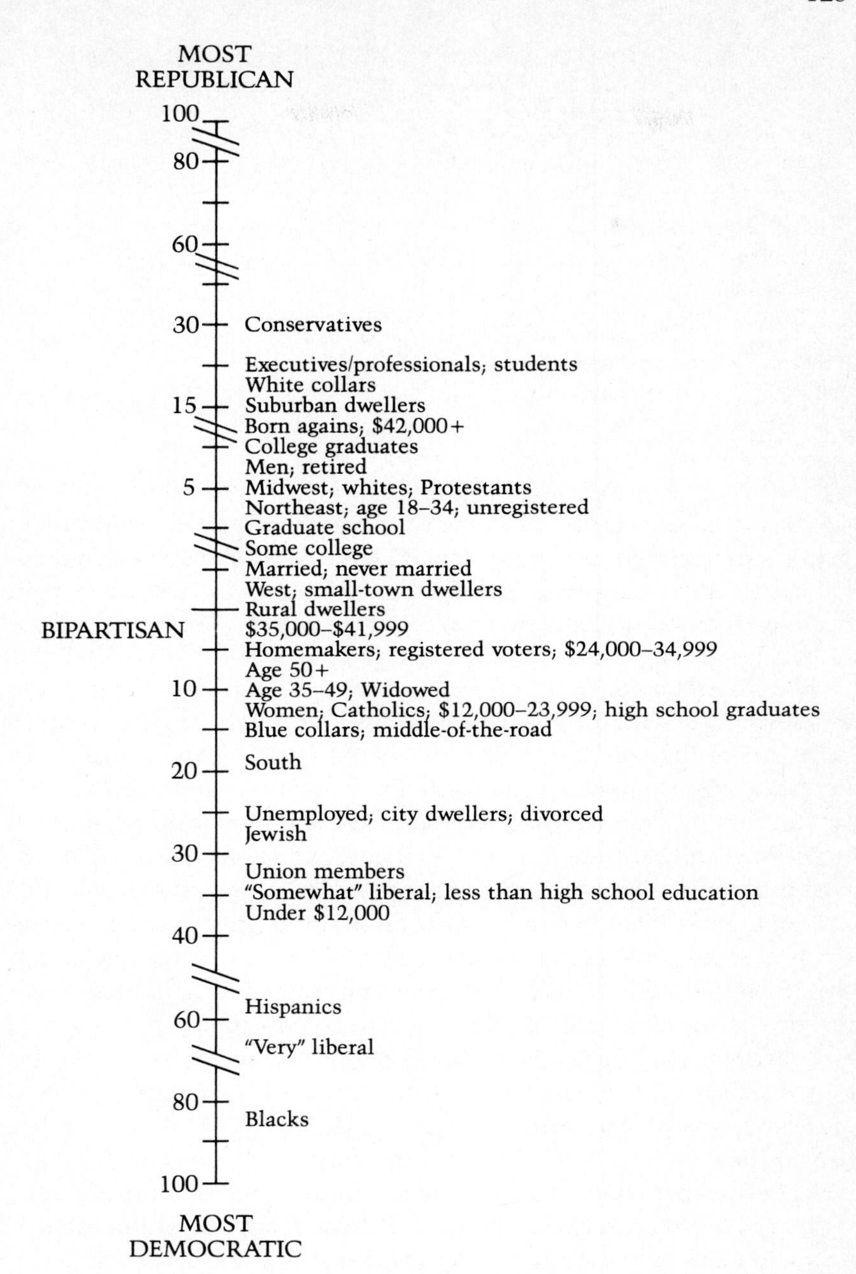

FIGURE 4.2 The Continuum of Subgroup Party Identification[a]

[a]See Table 4.2 and its footnotes.
Break in graphic's numerical scale.

TABLE 4.3 Changes in Party Identification, June–November 1986 (in Percentages)[a]

	STRONG DEMOCRAT	NOT STRONG DEMOCRAT	INDEPENDENT DEMOCRAT
June 1986[b]	16	17	12
November 1986[c]	20	17	8
Gain (or loss)	+ 4	0	(−4)

[a]See Table 4.2 and its footnotes. Totals do not add to 100% because "other party" and "don't know" responses are not included.

[b]Poll 1 (N = 1400). See Appendix.

[c]Poll 3 (N = 1399). See Appendix.

tinuum seems to be shifted in the Democratic direction rather than being symmetrical. And third, while Democratic subgroup margins have shrunk considerably from Franklin Roosevelt's heyday, the outline of the New Deal coalition is still apparent. (This is a subject to which we will return in the next chapter.)

The subgroup continuum of Figure 4.2 is certainly not immutable. Real events and personalities can affect dramatically individual segments of the population. For instance, a Republican presidential nominee who is Hispanic and Catholic might very well move these two normally Democratic groups into the GOP column by potentially large pluralities. But by and large, when the political drift pushes the electorate toward one or the other party, a marginal shift of just a few percent occurs in most or all of the subgroupings; save in special circumstances or during a full-scale party realignment, they tend to slide back and forth along the scale in roughly the same formation, flowing with the tidal currents of politics.

Perhaps as expected, many of the subgroups clustered toward the most partisan ends of the continuum have the greatest proportions of strong party identifiers, especially on the Democratic side. While the national average for strong Democrats was 16 percent, blacks, Hispanics, those whose families make under $12,000 annually or who have less than a high school education, Jews, and union members all had concentrations of strong Democrats of between 27 and 41 percent of their totals.[28] In both parties, born-again and older voters rather than younger ones tended to exhibit firmer partisan identification. The composition of each party was strikingly similar in another way: strong identifiers comprised nearly 40 percent of the

PURE INDEPENDENT	INDEPENDENT REPUBLICAN	NOT STRONG REPUBLICAN	STRONG REPUBLICAN
13	12	13	15
17	9	12	15
+ 4	(−3)	(−1)	0

total, not very strong partisans supplied about 35 percent of the party base, and the remaining quarter was made up of Independent leaners.

The pure Independents do not appear in the party subgroup continuum, of course, but like the parties, they are differentiated. As Table 4.2 indicates, men, urbanites, and middle-of-the-roaders, among others, are slightly more likely to be pure Independents than women, rural dwellers, and those closer to the ideological poles. More importantly, there are what we might call ignorant Independents and erudite Independents.[29] The former group are uninvolved, uninterested, and unaware politically, the apolitical "dregs" of the American electorate.[30] But the pure Independents also include an erudite corps who are better educated, higher on the socioeconomic scale, and generally informed about government and politics. They participate and vote in elections at rates not unlike weak partisans, and they ticket-split with abandon, primarily on the basis of candidate personality, image, and issue stands.

These erudite Independents add to the volatility of elections, but by no means are they the only factor involved. As we will discuss in the next chapter, some Americans change parties outright. More frequently, though, voters shift in the strength of their identifications within their chosen party. During the presidential election year of 1980, for example, a study by Richard Brody and Lawrence Rothenberg found that 31 percent of the electorate became more committed or less committed to their parties at least once, floating among the strong, not very strong, and Independent-leaning partisan affiliations.[31] The short-term forces of the 1986 midterm congressional elections also resulted in marginal changes in partisan categories. (See Table 4.3.) From June to November strong Democrats and pure Independents each gained 4 percent of the total while Democratic Independent leaners as well as Republican "not strong" and

TABLE 4.4 Party Identification in Selected States[a]

	NATIONAL	FLORIDA	KANSAS	LOUISIANA	OHIO
Democratic (%)	45	48	37	62	45
Republican (%)	40	37	49	24	40
Independent (%)[b]	13	11	13	12	13
Strong Democrats	16	22	12	30	19
Strong Republicans	15	13	17	10	14

[a]The party identification question wording in each poll reported in this table is identical to the one noted in Table 4.2. All polls were random-sample telephone surveys taken by William R. Hamilton and Staff in the spring or summer of 1986, as detailed below. For each state two or four separate surveys were averaged to produce the results listed here:

Poll	*N*	*Date*
National	1400	June 1986
Florida	601	April 1986
	703	August 1986
Kansas	508	May 1986
	601	August 1986
Louisiana	601	April 1986
	600	July 1986
	801	July 1986
	500	September 1986
Ohio	599	June 1986
	603	September 1986

[b]Pure Independents only. Party leaners are added into Democratic and Republican totals.

Independent leaners together lost 4 percent. This aggregate trend in the Democratic direction is slight, and within the sampling error, but it undoubtedly masks greater movement between the gradations of party loyalty, similar to that of the Brody/Rothenberg findings. Most of the time, people seem to move in half-steps, from "not strong" Democrat to strong Democrat, for instance, rather than all the way across the party spectrum. This was probably the pattern in 1986, with the party continuum sliding just a few degrees in the Democratic direction.

As I noted earlier, these national averages hide the richer and far more complex changes occurring simultaneously in individuals, population subgroups, and particular states. The diversity in the fifty states is not as dramatic as in subgroups and individuals, of course, but it is substantial. Table 4.4 presents the results of ten surveys taken in four states during 1986. Compared to the national partisan breakdown, there is wide variation. Florida still retains a somewhat Democratic cast, despite the tremendous industrialization and influx of migrants that have transformed it from a sleepy Southern backwater into a megastate. By contrast, Kansas is much more Republican than the country as a whole, the only state listed where strong Republicans outnumber strong Democrats. Louisiana is at the opposite party pole, more in the Old South mold. Democratic identifiers dominate the GOP band by 2½ to 1 among all voters and 3 to 1 among strong party identifiers. Finally, two-party competitive Ohio comes closest to the national model, matching the country's partisan composition nearly precisely.

Not incidentally, a state party identification can operate somewhat independently of a voter's national party affiliation; that is, some voters appear to identify with one party at the state and/or local level, and the other party at the national level.[32] This bifurcated, federalist pattern of party affiliation has perhaps been most common in the South, where the liberal national Democratic party has often seemed out of step with the traditional conservatism that has characterized many state Democratic parties.

The Decline of Partisan Voting and the Rise of Ticket-Splitting

Party identification is only one measure of party loyalty, of course. Just as important is the willingness of voters to support their party's nominees at election time. For those who hope for party-voter solidarity, there is little reason to be encouraged by modern electoral trends. Citizens have been increasingly deserting their party affiliates in the polling booths, and the practice of ticket-splitting — voting simultaneously for candidates of both parties — has soared dramatically. It is abundantly clear that while some recent deterioration in partisan identification has occurred, the decay is minor compared to the decline of party-line (also called straight-ticket) voting.

The evidence of this development abounds. Republican presidential landslides in 1956, 1972, 1980, and 1984 were accompanied by the election of substantial Democratic majorities in the House of Representatives. Divided government, with the presidency held by one party and one or both houses of Congress by the other party, has never been as frequent in American history — nor as troubling, since split control makes any sort of party-responsible government much

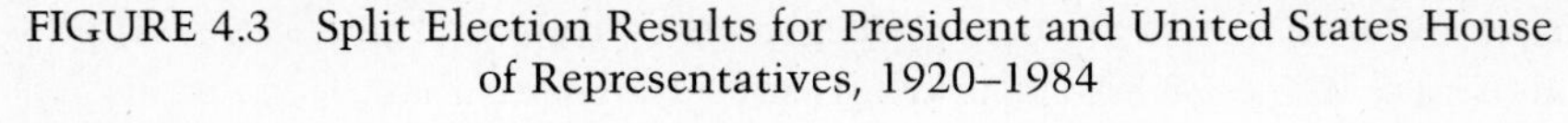

FIGURE 4.3 Split Election Results for President and United States House of Representatives, 1920–1984

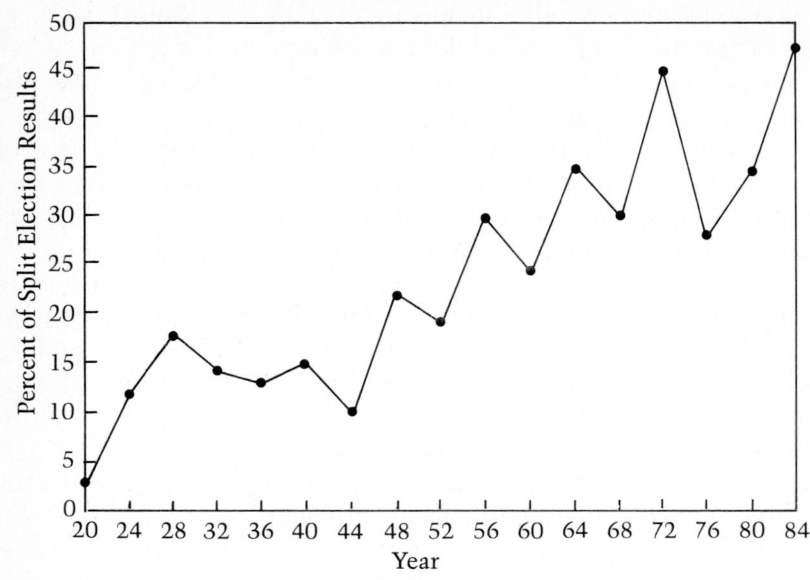

SOURCES: Advisory Commission on Intergovernmental Relations, *The Transformation of American Politics* (Washington, D.C.: ACIR, 1986), 56; Richard Boyd, "Electoral Trends in Postwar Politics," in *Choosing the President,* James Barber, ed. (Englewood Cliffs, N.J.: Prentice-Hall, 1974), 185; and Norman Ornstein et al., *Vital Statistics on Congress, 1982* (Washington, D.C.: American Enterprise Institute, 1982), 53.

more difficult to achieve. From 1920 to 1944 fewer than 15 percent of the congressional districts voted for presidential and House candidates of different parties, but from 1960 to 1984, no less than a quarter of the districts cast split tickets in any presidential year, and in 1984 nearly half the districts did so. (See Figure 4.3.) Similarly, at the statewide level, only 17 percent of the states electing governors in presidential years between 1880 and 1956 elected state and national executives from different parties. Yet from 1960 to 1984 fully 40 percent of states holding simultaneous presidential-gubernatorial elections recorded split results.[33]

These aggregate numbers actually understate the degree of ticket-splitting by individual voters. The Gallup poll has regularly asked its respondents, "For the various political offices, did you vote for all the candidates of one party, that is, a straight ticket, or did you vote for the candidates of different parties?" Since 1968 the proportion of voters reporting the casting of a straight ticket in presidential years has consistently been just 37 percent to 43 percent of the total.[34] Other polls and researchers have found reduced straight-ticket balloting and significant ticket-splitting at all levels of elections, especially since 1952.[35] In my own surveys for this study, respondents reported widespread ticket-splitting in the 1986 midterm election. For example, 65 percent said they voted for both parties' candidates in state and local contests on a poll taken only days after the election (when the public's memory was presumably fresh and self-reporting error would be reduced).[36] Even when only the set of purely local posts (such as state legislator, county officials, and constitutional officers) is considered — positions which are low in visibility and where voters might tend to rely more heavily on their party identification as a voting cue — fully 46 percent reported having split their tickets.[37]

Not surprisingly, the intensity of party affiliation is a major determinant of a voter's propensity to ticket-split. Strong party identifiers are the most likely to cast a straight-party ticket; pure Independents are the least likely. Somewhat greater proportions of ticket-splitters are found among high-income and better-educated citizens, but there is little difference in the distribution by sex or age. As expected, blacks exhibit the highest straight-party rate of any population subgroup; about three-quarters of all black voters stay in the Democratic party column from the top to the bottom of the ballot.

Just as the drop in partisan identification levels can be exaggerated, so too can the rise of ticket-splitting. In elections for the House of Representatives the proportion of voters casting ballots for their party's candidate has never fallen below 69 percent since 1956, and in recent years about three-quarters of all House voters have remained loyal to their party's House nominee.[38] Moreover, among those party identifiers who have strayed to the other party's standard-bearers, many have defected in only one or a few contests on a crowded ballot in any given year. Still, even a resolute optimist would need to strain to see the electorate's cup as half-full for the parties in the area of voting behavior today.

There are a number of explanations for the modern rise of ticket-splitting, many of them similar to the perceived causes of the dip in party identification levels. The growth of issue-oriented politics, the mushrooming of single-interest groups, the greater emphasis on candidate-centered personality politics, and broader-based education are all often cited. So too is the marked gain in the value of incumbency. Thanks in part to the enormous fattening of congressional constituency services, incumbent United States representatives and senators have been able to attract a steadily increasing share of the other party's identifiers.[39] Once again, though, the most powerful and telling explanation for yet another antiparty phenomenon may well be this: the parties simply do not matter a great deal anymore to many voters,[40] and they seem to have little relevance to the lives and daily needs of most Americans. The disconnection between the party and its voter may be more fundamental and pervasive than any of the other factors mentioned above, but at least it is a situation the parties can do something about, as we will argue anew in Chapter Six.

Partisan Images and Popular Attitudes

In a country where politics is generally unappreciated and is viewed suspiciously as a source of duplicity, intrigue, and corruption, it should come as no surprise that Americans have skeptical if ambivalent opinions about partisan activity. On one hand, people recognize the civic virtue inherent in party work; on the other, they lack confidence in the parties, fail to appreciate their political centrality in our system, and resist ceding their individual political prerogatives to them. The political parties have experienced a measurable decline in their perceived legitimacy in the last quarter-century.[41] There has been a steady drop, for instance, in the proportion of people who believe that "political parties help to make the government pay attention to what the people think"; 41 percent thought parties helped "a good deal" in 1964 but only 18 percent did so by 1980.[42] Political scientists differ about whether the public is more negative and openly hostile toward the parties or merely more indifferent and neutral about them,[43] but whichever description may be more accurate, it is indisputable that the political parties are not as highly respected and regarded as they once were.

Certainly the results of my surveys offer little cheer to those concerned about the parties. As Table 4.5 shows, public attitudes on partisan subjects suggest that while opinion is mixed and support for the parties has not collapsed by any means, there is no ringing endorsement for the parties. Americans say they vote for "the person, not the party" by as close to a unanimous margin as public opinion usually gets. Whether phrased in an antiparty fashion (state-

TABLE 4.5 Citizen Attitudes about the Political Parties (in Percentages)[a]

STATEMENT[b]	AGREE	DISAGREE
A. I always vote for the person who I think is best, regardless of what party they belong to.	92	8
B. I always support the candidates of just one party.	14	85
C. People who call themselves Independent are really indecisive and are unwilling to commit themselves.	34	63
D. If I don't know anything else about a candidate for public office, the political party a candidate belongs to tells me a lot how to vote.	47	51
E. It would be good if a new political party would form that would better represent the views of people like me.	35	61
F. The two political parties we have now in America are enough; we don't need any new ones.	63	34
G. Political parties don't really make any difference anymore.	37	61

SOURCES: Polls 1, 2, 3 (see Appendix).

[a]Percentages do not add to 100 since "don't know" responses are not included.

[b]Statements A, B, E, F from Poll 1; statements C, D from Poll 2; statement G from Poll 3. (See Appendix.) Statements were scattered throughout the polls and were not asked in the order appearing in this table.

ment A) or a proparty way (statement B), Americans are quick to assert their independence from party labels. These sentiments are expressed even by most of those who voted a straight ticket in 1986 or admitted a strong party identification. And though most citizens have at least a weak partisan affiliation, by a nearly 2-to-1 margin Americans are unwilling to criticize Independents for being "indecisive" and "unwilling to commit themselves" (statement C). Naturally enough, 84 percent of the Independents disagree, but so do 55 percent of the Democrats and 51 percent of the Republicans. Furthermore, those who strongly dispute this characterization of Independents comprise a healthy 57 percent of the "disagree" total.

Other findings were slightly more encouraging. A near-majority (47 percent) in one poll acknowledged that "the political party a candidate belongs to tells me a lot how to vote" if other information was lacking (statement D), and there was reasonably strong opposition to the creation of third parties: 63 percent agreed "the two political parties we have now . . . are enough" while only 35 percent believed "it would be good if a new political party would form that would better represent the views of people like me" (statements E and F). Finally, a 61 percent majority disagreed — including 38 percent who strongly disagreed — that "political parties don't really make any difference anymore." Still, the fact that 37 percent could assent to such an extreme comment about the parties is unsettling. Nearly as many respondents (32 percent) answered no when asked, "Do you think it matters which political party controls the U.S. Senate or not?"[44] Their evaluation is preposterous to even a casual observer of Congress and legislative-executive relations, yet a third of the American public apparently believes party control of the Senate is immaterial.

At the same time the electorate as a whole does not seem to be hostile toward the parties. The institutions themselves are judged highly. (See Table 4.6.) Not only do both parties achieve favorability ratings in the mid-60s percentile, but their "very favorable" scores exceed that of Congress and most well-known public figures, and their "very unfavorable" totals are quite small. Naturally, each party is rated most highly by its own primary constituency groups, but even population segments who vote heavily for one party are inclined to give a somewhat favorable evaluation to the other party. So, for instance, 44 percent of blacks and 41 percent of all Democrats rate the GOP favorably, and 52 percent of the professionals and 37 percent of the Republicans rate the Democrats favorably. Part of this may simply be the American propensity to award high ratings on these sorts of scales and to refrain from harsh judgments in such matters,[45] but regardless, the absence of generalized hostility toward the parties is clear and welcome.

Respondents to one of our surveys were also asked open-ended questions about the two major parties. (See Tables 4.7 and 4.8.) Slightly under 40 percent offered a positive comment about one or both parties, while about a third of the sample gave a negative characterization of one or both parties. The mixture of old and new stereotypes is instructive. The Democrats are still viewed as the champions of the "little guy," concerned about the poor and disadvantaged, yet they are seen as big spenders, high taxers, and proponents of wasteful "big government" giveaway programs. The chaos of an out-of-power party that depends so heavily on interest group aggregation has crept into the party's image as well, with 10 percent

TABLE 4.6 Party vs. Personality Favorability Ratings

QUESTION:[a] "Now I'd like to ask you your impressions of some people and institutions in public life. As I read each one, just tell me whether you have a very favorable opinion of that person, a somewhat favorable opinion, a somewhat unfavorable opinion, or a very unfavorable opinion. If you don't recognize them, just say so. Here's the first one . . ."

NAME/INSTITUTION	VERY FAVORABLE	SOMEWHAT FAVORABLE	A LITTLE OF BOTH (VOLUNTEERED)	SOMEWHAT UNFAVORABLE	VERY UNFAVORABLE	RECOGNIZE NAME, BUT CAN'T RATE	DON'T RECOGNIZE
Mario Cuomo	14	23	1	10	4	9	38
George Bush	17	48	2	18	10	3	2
Pat Robertson	6	16	1	9	10	8	50
Jim Wright	3	15	1	4	2	8	67
Ronald Reagan	41	31	2	12	13	—	1
Walter Mondale	12	38	3	26	18	3	1
Jesse Jackson	11	34	2	26	21	4	2
Jack Kemp	7	22	1	10	4	13	43
Gary Hart	15	47	2	15	6	8	7
Lee Iacocca	33	34	2	9	7	7	8
The Republican party	20	47	3	19	9	—	2
U.S. Congress	13	56	4	19	5	3	—
The Democratic party	16	48	3	23	7	—	3

SOURCE: Poll 1 (see Appendix).

[a]Actually, two separate questions were asked, the first one for public figures and the second one for institutions. The order of the names and institutions was rotated by the interviewers. The survey was taken in June 1986, before the effects of the Iran-contra scandal had diminished the popularity of Ronald Reagan and George Bush, and before Gary Hart was forced to drop out of the 1988 presidential contest because of alleged womanizing.

TABLE 4.7 Citizens' Descriptions of the Parties

QUESTIONS:[a] "What word or phrase do you think best describes the Republican party? What else?" and "What word or phrase do you think best describes the Democratic party? What else?"

	DESCRIPTION CATEGORY	% OF N (= 1400) DEMOCRATIC PARTY	REPUBLICAN PARTY
Positive comments	General positive[b]	11	15
	Performance	4	12
	Philosophy	8	7
	Responsiveness	16	3
	Help the poor	2	0
	Business-oriented	0	1
	Specific social and moral issues	1	1
	Economic policies	0	3
	National defense	0	1
	Honesty	1	1
	Independent	0	1
	Well-organized	0	1
	Other specifics	1	1
Total comments		37	39
Negative comments	General negative[b]	6	7
	Performance	6	1
	Philosophy	8	7
	Unresponsiveness	2	5
	For the rich	0	13
	Specific social and moral issues	2	0
	Economic policies	3	0
	National defense	1	1
	Disorganized	10	0
	Dishonest	0	1
	For big government	1	0
	Too political	3	0
	Other specifics	1	1
Total comments		35	29

SOURCE: Poll 1 (see Appendix).

[a]Multiple responses for these open-ended questions were encouraged. Neutral comments were also recorded but disallowed in the tabulations presented in this table. (About 9 percent of the comments about the Democratic party and 13 percent of the remarks about the GOP were essentially neutral in content.)

[b]Responses too general to be categorized under any specific grouping.

TABLE 4.8 Sample Comments of Citizens' Party Descriptions[a]

POSITIVE COMMENTS	
DEMOCRATIC PARTY	REPUBLICAN PARTY
"Looking out for the small guy." "More idealistic and more concerned for the disadvantaged." "Fair and responsive to all the people." "They consider the average American." "Camelot."	"Hardworking, patriotic, and conservative." "They're doing a good job and turning things around." "They promote individual enterprise and are against government giveaway programs." "Breath of spring; they brought back good living without spending money indiscriminately." "Pragmatic, like business."
NEGATIVE COMMENTS	
DEMOCRATIC PARTY	REPUBLICAN PARTY
"Disorganized, incompetent political hacks." "Well meaning but wasteful." "Too socialistic — they foster government spending, welfare, and the laziest." "Unrealistic pollyannas — too inclined to think government can solve everything." "Confused — it's tried to embrace so many different elements."	"A bunch of old conservative males." "Ultraconservative and war-minded." "I'm not a rich person and that's who they're for." "Selfish, always looking out for those who already have it made." "They always look backwards and think things were just fine in the past."

[a]See notes for Table 4.7. The comments in this table are generally representative of the recorded responses, though on the whole the selected remarks are more thoughtful and well articulated than the average.

citing "disorganization" as the word best describing the Democratic party. The Republicans, on the other hand, retain "for the rich" and "backward-looking" as their shibboleths, but at least until the Iran-contra scandal, they had made significant progress based on the perceived performance and success of the Reagan administration. "They're turning things around" was the most common positive remark about the GOP. These evaluations are always in flux, of course, depending on current events and the cycle of power. This survey was taken five and a half years into a Republican presidency, which James L. Sundquist described as a point when voters "are beginning to rediscover what it is they do not like about Republicans [while] they have not yet forgotten what it is they disliked about the Democrats."[46]

Party Personalities and the Voters[47]

A party's image is also shaped to a great degree by the men and women who seek or secure its presidential and vice-presidential nominations, or become prominent in the national spotlight in other ways. Which candidates — from the past and present — do voters most identify with each political party? During one of the polls conducted for this study, respondents were asked, "Which person — either from the past or present — do you associate most with each party?" (Multiple choices were permitted.) The results are presented in Table 4.9.

For the Democrats, John F. Kennedy is still the brightest star in the firmament, with 46 percent of the total population and 55 percent of the Democrats naming him. JFK was the special pick of those aged 35–49, but he was also the first choice of those too young to remember his presidency. The dominance of the Kennedy name is even more impressive when the 4 percent who mentioned Senator Edward Kennedy and the 3 percent who named the late Senator Robert Kennedy are added to JFK's total. Franklin Roosevelt is a distant second at 20 percent. Northeasterners and those over 50 years old were somewhat more likely to remember FDR, while blacks were especially unlikely to do so. Interestingly, Republicans picked FDR more frequently than Democrats. The most recent Democratic president, Jimmy Carter, is a poor third (13 percent), though he does somewhat better in his native South and among 18-to-34 year olds. The GOP-leaning members of this latter group frequently cited Carter as the reason for their Republican identification, so his remembrance by the young is a mixed blessing for Democrats. Harry Truman is a surprisingly strong fourth (10 percent), perhaps the residue of the "Truman revival" that took place in the 1970s. The Democratic party's recent landslide losers barely register on the public screen. Walter Mondale was mentioned by only 6 percent, and not a single respondent recalled George McGovern. A few notables managed a 1 to 3 percent showing: former President Lyndon Johnson

(3 percent), former Vice-President Hubert Humphrey (2 percent), New York Governor Mario Cuomo (2 percent), former House Speaker Tip O'Neill (2 percent), former United States Senator Gary Hart (1 percent), and 1984 vice-presidential nominee Geraldine Ferraro (1 percent). Presidential candidate Jesse Jackson was not named by any whites and only 3 percent of blacks.

For the Republicans, a very different image emerges. As might be expected, Ronald Reagan dominates the field, though not to the extent one might have thought. A solid majority (54 percent) chose Reagan, with white men, Democrats, and 18-to-34 year olds especially likely to do so. (While 72 percent of white 18-to-34 year olds named Reagan, just 43 percent of the over-50 whites did.) Richard Nixon placed second, at 21 percent, and he was disproportionately recalled by Democrats. Each party's identifiers seem to have remembered best the other party's most objectionable figures or biggest losers; thus, more Democrats than Republicans named Nixon, Barry Goldwater, and Herbert Hoover, while more Republicans recalled Mondale and Tip O'Neill. (The reverse of this "devil theory" is also true: each party's identifiers were more likely than their adversaries to name their party's past heroes. Thus, Democrats cited JFK in larger numbers than Republicans, while GOP voters pointed to Abraham Lincoln and Dwight Eisenhower more frequently than did Democrats.) Overall, Eisenhower is the third most frequently recalled Republican, at 18 percent. Whites over 50 named him most often; blacks and young people least often. Finally, the GOP's image is neither a Ford nor a Lincoln. Abraham Lincoln at 6 percent outdoes former President Gerald Ford (4 percent), Vice-President George Bush (3 percent), and a host of one-percenters (former Senator Barry Goldwater, Senator Robert Dole, former President Theodore Roosevelt, Senator Jesse Helms, and former Senator Howard Baker).

Public Evaluations of the Parties on the Issues

Despite the emphasis on personality politics in our society, issues still matter a great deal, and a voter bases his or her overall evaluation of the parties on the substantive positions they take as well as on the individuals they nominate for office. As suggested in Chapter One, many citizens have come to believe that the two major parties

TABLE 4.9 Party Personalities and the Voters

QUESTION: "Which person — either from the past or present — do you associate most with [each] party? Who else?"

DEMOCRATIC PARTY FIGURES	TOTAL	BY PARTY: DEM.	IND.	REP.
John Kennedy	46%	55%	43%	39%
Franklin Roosevelt	20	17	20	24
Jimmy Carter	13	14	13	12
Harry Truman	10	13	9	8
Walter Mondale	6	3	7	7
Edward Kennedy	4	5	2	5
Lyndon Johnson	3	3	3	4
Robert Kennedy	3	4	3	2
Hubert Humphrey	2	2	3	1
Mario Cuomo	2	3	1	1
Tip O'Neill	2	1	1	5
Gary Hart	1	1	1	—
Geraldine Ferraro	1	1	1	—
Others	9	13	6	7

REPUBLICAN PARTY FIGURES	TOTAL	BY PARTY: DEM.	IND.	REP.
Ronald Reagan	54%	57%	53%	54%
Richard Nixon	21	25	19	20
Dwight Eisenhower	18	14	19	21
Abraham Lincoln	6	3	8	7
Gerald Ford	4	4	2	4
George Bush	3	3	2	2
Herbert Hoover	2	3	2	1
Howard Baker	1	1	2	1
Robert Dole	1	1	1	—
Barry Goldwater	1	3	1	1
Jesse Helms	1	1	—	1
Theodore Roosevelt	1	1	1	4
Others	8	6	9	7

SOURCE: Poll 1 (see Appendix).

NOTE: Multiple choices were permitted, so totals add to more than 100 percent.

BY RACE:		BY AGE (WHITES ONLY):			BY AREA:			
WHITE	BLACK	18–34	35–49	50 & UP	NORTH-EAST	MID-WEST	SOUTH	WEST
45%	50%	40%	56%	44%	45%	49%	44%	48%
21	8	9	13	38	27	16	18	23
13	13	23	11	6	11	10	16	12
11	3	—	8	23	12	10	9	11
6	5	8	7	2	3	10	5	3
4	3	3	9	3	6	3	4	5
3	3	2	5	3	4	3	2	5
3	3	4	5	1	2	4	3	3
2	3	2	5	1	1	2	4	—
2	—	3	1	2	5	2	—	—
2	—	4	1	2	3	—	3	—
1	—	2	1	—	—	2	—	3
1	—	1	1	—	2	1	—	—
9	16	11	7	7	7	9	10	10

BY RACE:		BY AGE (WHITES ONLY):			BY AREA:			
WHITE	BLACK	18–34	35–49	50 & UP	NORTH-EAST	MID-WEST	SOUTH	WEST
57%	26%	72%	61%	43%	51%	55%	54%	56%
21	29	18	25	21	25	21	19	23
19	11	2	20	30	26	12	20	12
6	8	2	7	7	9	4	6	5
4	—	5	3	3	3	5	3	2
3	5	2	3	3	4	1	4	2
3	—	1	2	4	1	3	1	5
1	3	1	2	1	1	—	3	—
1	—	—	—	2	—	1	—	3
2	—	1	1	3	2	1	1	3
—	5	1	—	—	—	—	1	2
2	—	1	2	2	2	1	1	3
9	—	12	6	8	6	8	5	15

SOURCE: Poll 1 (see Appendix).

NOTE: Multiple choices were permitted, so totals add to more than 100 percent.

are relatively indistinguishable. A solid majority (54 percent) asserts that there is "*only some* difference . . . between the candidates and policies of the Republican party and the candidates and policies of the Democratic party." ("A lot" of difference is seen by 35 percent, but "none at all" by 7 percent.)[48] Fortunately, though, many of those who find only some party differences also realize that those disagreements are significant. The proportion of the electorate saying that there are "important differences" between the parties has steadily risen from 46 percent in 1972 to 62 percent by 1984.[49] Because of this and other trends,[50] political scientists Stephen Craig and Michael Martinez have concluded that there is "increasing party differentiation in the American electorate."[51]

This differentiation can certainly be seen in Table 4.10, which lists the public's views on which party would do a better job on a host of issues. The contrast in party scores from item to item comprises a fascinating commentary on modern American politics. Democrats are stronger as preservationists of the governmental, programmatic status quo (such as Social Security), protectors of the threatened or weak (the poor, the disadvantaged, the elderly, the unemployed, farmers, the middle class), and as defenders of the environment and opponents of the nuclear arms race. The Republicans' image is quite different. They are seen as prodefense, tough on drugs, and advocating the traditional American values of family, hard work, and patriotism. More importantly, the GOP under Ronald Reagan has claimed a significant advantage on such key economic issues as controlling inflation and keeping the lid on government spending. The Republicans also secure a slight edge on the crucial question of having "the foresight to deal with America's future in the next twenty to thirty years." On this issue and almost all the others, between a fifth and a third of the respondents rated the parties' abilities to do the job "about the same"; in every case fewer than 15 percent believed that neither party was up to the job — a welcome absence of cynicism.

Public opinion on the parties' issue performance is subject to rather rapid change, of course, depending on the circumstances of current politics. The data presented in Table 4.10 were derived from a poll taken in the immediate aftermath of the Democratic resurgence that occurred in the 1986 midterm election. In the short period from June to November of 1986[52] the Democrats gained an additional 13 percent advantage on "reducing unemployment" after they highlighted local and regional joblessness around the country

TABLE 4.10 Public Views of the Parties on Specific Issues (in Percentages)[a]

QUESTION: "Now, I'd like to ask you about some specific issue areas and for each, I'd like you to tell me which political party you think would do a better job — the Democratic party, the Republican party, both about the same, or neither?"

ISSUE AREA	DEMOCRATIC	REPUBLICAN	BOTH	NEITHER	NET DEMOCRATIC ADVANTAGE
Helping the poor and disadvantaged people	58	11	22	7	+47
Helping farmers in the U.S.	50	13	22	9	+37
Protecting Social Security	43	13	30	1	+30
Protecting the middle class	43	18	25	10	+25
Putting a limit on the nuclear arms race	42	18	24	9	+24
Reducing unemployment	39	23	26	8	+16
Protecting our citizens from toxic waste storage and transport accidents	30	14	36	12	+16
Effectively running your state government	35	28	26	5	+ 7
Best able to handle the U.S. trade problems	21	23	34	11	(− 2)
Holding taxes in line so they are fair	28	31	22	12	(− 3)
Having the foresight to deal with America's future in the next 20–30 years	21	26	33	11	(− 5)
Preserving traditional American values like family, hard work, and patriotism	23	30	34	8	(− 7)
Dealing with the drug problem in the U.S.	13	24	42	14	(−11)
Keeping government spending at a reasonable level	22	37	22	14	(−15)
Controlling inflation	21	41	21	12	(−20)
Keeping U.S. national defense as strong as we need	15	50	25	4	(−35)

SOURCE: Poll 3 (see Appendix). Poll was taken in November 1986.

[a]Rows do not total 100 percent since "don't know" responses are not listed. Items were rotated by interviewers and the four response alternatives were repeated after every fourth item.

during the campaign. Similarly, by stressing the United States' international trade imbalance, Democrats picked up 11 percent in the "best able to handle the trade problem" category. Also, perhaps because attractive young Democratic candidates were showcased in many states, the Republican lead in "foresight to deal with the future" was shaved from 12 percent to 5 percent.

The partisan pattern over a lengthier period of time is instructive as well. Figure 4.4 plots the public's evaluation of the parties on six issues from 1981 to 1986. As the furor over alleged GOP attempts to cut Social Security gradually died down, the Republican deficit on the subject dropped nearly 20 percent in five years. In the glow of Reagan's economic successes, the Democrats lost their traditional edge on the unemployment issue in 1984, but regained it during the 1986 election. With enormous federal deficits mounting during the Reagan administration, not even the GOP's age-old identification with governmental frugality could stop a 23 percent Republican deterioration on that issue. Two other policy areas remained relatively stable throughout the period. Democrats kept a substantial margin on "limiting nuclear arms," while Republicans were consistently viewed as the party better able to support a strong national defense.

This chapter has identified some disturbing developments in the relationship between the American people and their political parties. Ticket-splitting has become rampant and there has been a near doubling of the proportion of pure Independents in the electorate over the last several decades. Moreover, a slight reduction in the group of *strong* partisans has been observed. Most worrisome and revealing of all is the reluctance of a growing number of partisans (the so-called Independent leaners) to readily acknowledge their party affiliations. The swelling ranks of leaners may *act* like partisans in their voting habits, but they do not necessarily *think* like partisans in their conception of the political world and their place in it.

Why have more citizens moved from categories of weak or strong partisan affiliations into the classification of Independent leaner? Partly, it is because the parties have been weakened generally by the forces described throughout this study, from the rise of primaries to the fall of patronage. Then, too, parties and partisanship are simply out of fashion, unchic in an era when individualism is celebrated. The television news media, in particular, have encouraged the de-

FIGURE 4.4 Public Evaluations of Party Performance on Specific Issues, 1981–1986[a]

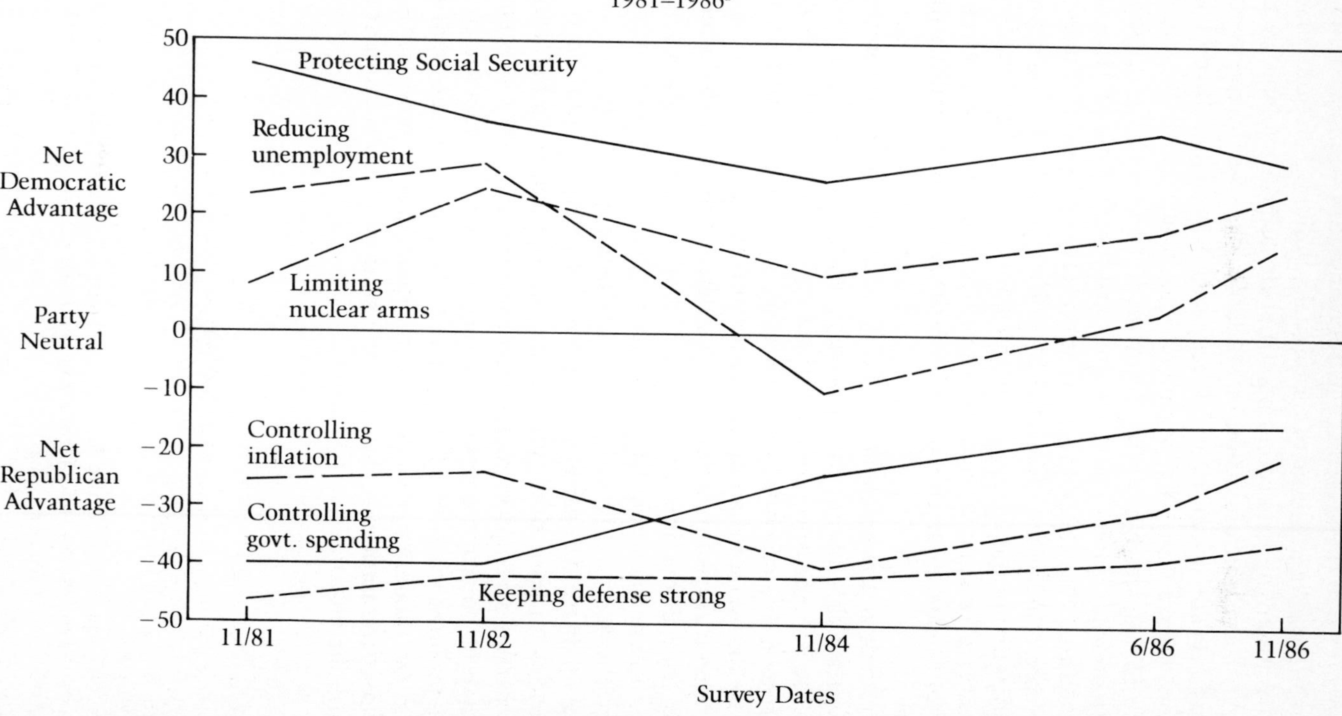

[a]Question wording is noted in Table 4.10. All surveys were random-sample telephone polls taken by William R. Hamilton and Staff. Sample sizes were as follows: Nov. 1981 (N = 1261), Nov. 1982 (N = 1401), Nov. 1984 (N = 1351), June 1986 (N = 1400), Nov. 1986 (N = 1399).

partisanization of the electorate by focusing almost all attention on the personalities and issues of individual candidates and officeholders rather than the partisan superstructure of politics, and by persisting in the communication of outdated, negative stereotypes of the party role and operations. Yet the prevailing media line probably could not have sold well if people had not been inclined to believe it in the first place. While the survey results presented in this chapter indicate that voters generally are not hostile to the parties, and in broad terms they judge the institutions favorably, neither does the public care much about the parties' welfare or see the importance and centrality of parties in American political life. The steady deterioration in the perceived legitimacy of the political parties recorded in the last quarter-century underlines the modern difficulties they face.

Nonetheless, the prospects for party renewal in the electorate are brighter than this dismal portrait might suggest. The absence of outright hostility and the presence of generalized favorability toward the parties offer some hope; after all, apathy and neutrality are much easier to counteract than open enmity and antagonism. The underlying partisanship of many supposed Independents, the slight recent reversal in the decline of partisan identification, and the voter's sharper differentiation of the parties also give cause for optimism.[53] Finally, the reasonably large cadre of strong party loyalists, who number in the millions, as well as the increasingly vital party organizations on both sides, provide a firm foundation to build upon as the parties attempt to regenerate and intensify voter allegiance. What can be constructed on this base, and how, is proposed in the two concluding chapters. First, however, we turn to the final element in the modern party calculus: the condition of two-party competition at the national level, and the state of party alignment and realignment.

Notes

1. See E. E. Schattschneider, *Party Government* (New York: Rinehart, 1942), 55–56.
2. See Steven E. Finkel and Howard A. Scarrow, "Party Identification and Party Enrollment: The Difference and the Consequence," *Journal of Politics* 47 (May 1985): 620–642.

3. Angus Campbell et al., *The American Voter* (New York: John Wiley and Sons, 1964), 86–96.
4. Paul A. Beck and M. Kent Jennings, "Parents as 'Middlepersons' in Political Socialization," *Journal of Politics* 37 (1975): 83–107.
5. Morris P. Fiorina, *Retrospective Voting in American National Elections* (New Haven: Yale University Press, 1981), 102.
6. See, for example, Angus Campbell and Henry Valen, "Party Identification in Norway and the United States," *Public Opinion Quarterly* 25 (1961): 514–515. More precisely, I refer here to socioeconomic status (SES), one's place in the pecking order of society.
7. Data are contained in Table 4.1, discussed in the text that follows.
8. Leon D. Epstein, *Political Parties in the American Mold* (Madison: University of Wisconsin Press, 1986), 253–255. If nothing else, the much greater degree of straight-ticket voting earlier in the century would strongly suggest this.
9. See Bruce E. Keith, David B. Magleby, Candice J. Nelson, Elizabeth Orr, Mark C. Westlye, and Raymond E. Wolfinger, "Further Evidence on the Partisan Affinities of Independent 'Leaners,'" paper presented at the 1983 meeting of the American Political Science Association, Chicago, Ill., September 1–4, 1983.
10. Norman H. Nie, Sidney Verba, and John R. Petrocik, *The Changing American Voter* (Cambridge, Mass.: Harvard University Press, 1979), 374–375.
11. Larry Sabato, *The Rise of Political Consultants: New Ways of Winning Elections* (New York: Basic Books, 1981), 284–290.
12. Everett Carll Ladd, Jr. and Seymour Martin Lipset, *Academics, Politics, and the 1972 Election* (Washington, D.C.: American Enterprise Institute, 1973), 46.
13. Martin Wattenberg, *The Decline of American Political Parties, 1952–1980* (Cambridge: Harvard University Press, 1984), 114–117.
14. This is usually the way the public pollsters (Gallup, Harris, et al.) report Independent affiliation. See *Public Opinion* 9 (January/February 1987): 35.
15. In Poll 1 (see Appendix) we asked respondents whether certain issue positions would make them more or less likely to support a congressional candidate. Men favored a candidate who wanted to give military aid to the contra forces by 47 percent to 45 percent (with 8 percent undecided), while women were opposed to such a candidate 56 percent to 34 percent (with 10 percent undecided).
16. Ibid. Men were more likely to vote for a candidate who favored "reducing the budget deficit by making major cuts in *all* government programs including defense and social programs" by 59 percent to 36 percent (with 6 percent undecided), but women opposed such a candidate by 51 percent to 41 percent (with 9 percent undecided).
17. While the gender gap is about the same for all age groups, the partisan loyalties of the age groups differ considerably, with those below the age of 35 favoring the GOP and those 35 and over preferring the Democratic

party, as Table 4.2 and the following breakdown for whites shows:

	18–34	*35–49*	*50+*
White men	−22 (R)	−7 (R)	−5 (R)
White women	− 7 (R)	+7 (D)	+8 (D)
Gender gap	15%	14%	13%

SOURCE: Poll 3 (see Appendix).

18. See also John E. Stanga and James F. Sheffield, "Black and White Attitudes Toward the Parties: The Myth of Zero Partisanship," paper prepared for the annual meeting of the American Political Science Association, Washington, D.C., August 27–31, 1986.
19. Blacks are less likely to vote for a congressional candidate who takes a prochoice position on abortion by a margin of 49 percent to 43 percent (with 8 percent undecided), while whites favor such a candidate by 54 percent to 36 percent (with 9 percent undecided). See note 15 above for details of poll and question wording.
20. Hispanics comprised about 4 percent of Poll 1's sample, compared to about 10 percent for blacks.
21. Even the 18–24 year olds were very closely split between McGovern and Nixon in most polls, but McGovern ran more than a dozen percentage points better among the very young than among the electorate as a whole.
22. See note 17 above.
23. Labor PACs consistently give 95 percent or more of their contributions to Democratic candidates each federal election cycle.
24. The presidential election of 1960 may be an extreme case, but John Kennedy's massive support among Catholics and Nixon's less substantial but still impressive backing by Protestants demonstrates the polarization that religion could once produce. See Philip E. Converse, "Religion and Politics: The 1960 Election," in Angus Campbell et al., *Elections and the Political Order* (New York: John Wiley, 1966), 96–124.
25. Women and younger people are also disproportionately self-classified as born-again Christians.
26. Poll 1 (see Appendix). Ten percent of both groups volunteered a response of "both," and 3 percent of the born-agains and 5 percent of the nonfundamentalists were undecided.
27. Ibid. The real rates of nonregistration are undoubtedly higher because of many respondents' natural reluctance to admit their lack of good citizenship. Still, one would expect the ratio of real nonregistration from age group to age group to be somewhat similar to the poll's findings.
28. The exact percentages were: blacks (39), Hispanics (27), under $12,000 income (38), less than a high school education (37), Jews (41), and union members (30).
29. See Walter Dean Burnham, *Critical Elections and The Mainsprings of American Politics* (New York: W. W. Norton, 1970), 126–129; Nie, Verba, Petrocik, *The Changing American Voter;* and Wattenberg, *The*

Decline of American Political Parties. See also V. O. Key (with the assistance of Milton C. Cummings), *The Responsible Electorate* (Cambridge, Mass.: Harvard University Press, 1966); and Keith et al., "Further Evidence on the Partisan Affinities of Independent 'Leaners.' "

30. Key, *The Responsible Electorate.*
31. Richard A. Brody and Lawrence S. Rothenberg, "Dynamics of Partisanship During the 1980 Election," paper prepared for the 1983 annual meeting of the American Political Science Association, Chicago, August 28–September 1, 5.
32. See Michael Maggiotto, "Party Identification in the Federal System," paper prepared for delivery at the annual meeting of the American Political Science Association, Washington, D.C., August 27–31, 1986.
33. Larry Sabato, *Goodbye to Good-Time Charlie: The American Governorship Transformed* (Washington, D.C.: Congressional Quarterly Press, 1983), 139, Table 4–12. Data has been modified to reflect 1984 election results.
34. Cited in Everett Carll Ladd, Jr., "On Mandates, Realignments, and the 1984 Presidential Election," *Political Science Quarterly* 100 (Spring 1985): 23.
35. See, for example, Wattenberg, *The Decline of American Political Parties,* 20.
36. Poll 2 (see Appendix).
37. Poll 3 (ibid.) About 79 percent of the sample reported voting in local contests. The percentages cited in the text are proportions of this 79 percent subsample.
38. See ACIR, *The Transformation in American Politics,* 55, Table 3–4.
39. Thomas E. Mann and Raymond E. Wolfinger, "Candidates and Parties in Congressional Elections," *American Political Science Review* 74 (September 1980): 617–632; Albert D. Cover, "One Good Term Deserves Another: The Advantage of Incumbency in Congressional Elections," *American Journal of Political Science* 21 (August 1977): 535; and Gary C. Jacobson, *The Politics of Congressional Elections* (Boston: Little, Brown & Co., 1983), 86.
40. Wattenberg, *The Decline of American Political Parties,* 25–27.
41. See Jack Dennis, "Trends in Support for the American Party System," *British Journal of Political Science* 5 (April 1975): 187–230; and Dennis, "Changing Public Support for the American Party System," in William J. Crotty, ed., *Paths to Political Reform* (Lexington, Mass.: D. C. Heath, 1980), 40–44.
42. To the question, "How much do you feel that political parties help to make the government pay attention to what the people think? A good deal, some, or not much," here is the pattern of responses from 1964 to 1980:

	1964	*1968*	*1970*	*1972*	*1974*	*1976*	*1978*	*1980*
A good deal	40.7%	36.7%	32.8%	26.0%	21.8%	17.2%	20.9%	17.9%
Some	9.4	40.5	42.9	51.9	54.6	52.5	52.7	51.1
Not much	2.8	16.4	19.2	18.2	19.1	25.9	21.7	28.1
Don't know	7.1	6.4	5.1	3.9	4.5	4.4	4.8	2.9

SOURCE: As reported in Stephen Earl Bennett, "Changes in the Public's Perceptions of Governmental Responsiveness, 1964–1980," paper prepared for delivery at the annual meeting of the Midwest Political Science Association, Milwaukee, Wisconsin, 1982, 32.

43. See Wattenberg, *The Decline of American Political Parties;* Stephen Craig, "The Decline of Partisanship in the United States: A Reexamination of the Neutrality Hypothesis," *Political Behavior* 7: 1 (1985): 57–58; Martin Wattenberg, "Do Voters Really Care About Political Parties Anymore? A Response to Craig," a paper delivered at the annual meeting of the American Political Science Association, Washington, D.C., August 27–31, 1986; and John Stanga, Patrick Kenney, and James Sheffield, "The Myth of Zero Partisanship: Attitudes Toward American Political Parties, 1964–1984," a paper delivered at the annual meeting of the American Political Science Association, Washington, D.C., August 27–31, 1986.
44. Poll 1 (see Appendix); 61 percent said yes, and 7 percent had no opinion.
45. Pollsters report that favorability scales such as the one in Table 4.6 almost always produce inflated ratings in an electoral sense; that is, many people supportive of one candidate will still award a high favorability rating to his opponent.
46. James L. Sundquist, "Has America Lost Its Social Conscience?" paper delivered at the Florence Heller Graduate School for Advanced Studies in Social Welfare, November 21, 1985, 25.
47. A version of this section was published in *The Polling Report* 2 (October 20, 1986): 1–3.
48. Poll 1 (see Appendix). Just 4 percent answered "don't know." Independents and women were least likely to see "a lot" of difference between the parties, while strong party identifiers, men, and executives/professionals were most likely to see a considerable difference.
49. Stephen Craig and Michael Martinez, "Not a Dime's Worth of Difference: Perceived Choice and Partisanship in the U.S., 1964–1984," paper delivered at the annual meeting of the American Political Science Association, Washington, D.C., August 27–31, 1986, 5.
50. These other trends included the greater identification of voters with one or the other party as being better able to handle important national problems and the placing of the parties further apart on the liberal-conservative continuum.
51. Craig and Martinez, "Not a Dime's Worth of Difference," 7.
52. Polls 1 and 3 (see Appendix).
53. See also Stanga, Kenney, and Sheffield, "The Myth of Zero Partisanship: Attitudes Toward American Political Parties, 1964–1984"; and Craig and Martinez, "Not a Dime's Worth of Difference."

CHAPTER FIVE

• ☆ • ☆ •

Realignment: Reality or Reverie?

NO SUBJECT FASCINATES POLITICAL OBSERVERS quite as much as major party realignment. Have individual voters and groups changed partisan loyalties in sharp and durable ways? Have these shifts been sufficient to make the GOP the dominant party? Have Democrats relinquished the majority status they secured at the onset of the New Deal in the 1930s? Of course, Republican analysts have been busily attempting to convince the political world of the reality of major realignment ever since Ronald Reagan's decisive presidential victory in 1980, just as another contingent had tried to do following Richard Nixon's successes in 1968 and 1972. As evidence, the GOP boosters point to increased levels of Republican identification, especially by the young, and a string of presidential victories that supposedly imply a Republican "lock" on an Electoral College majority. Democrats have been equally preoccupied with insisting that the Republican claims are nothing more than wishful thinking and reverie. Resurrecting a popular 1984 campaign slogan, Democrats ask, "Where's the beef?" noting their overwhelming edge in local offices, continuous firm control of the House of Representatives, and recapture of the Senate in 1986.

Clearly, major changes in the American electorate have been occurring, but these changes may or may not constitute a major, critical realignment of party balance. This chapter explores the possibilities of realignment from both parties' perspectives, and examines the relevance of existing realignment tendencies to the current state of political parties in the United States.

Realignment and Contemporary Political Conditions

Major realignments — circumstances when relatively swift and permanent alterations in existing partisan alignments occur — are rare events in American political life, with the last confirmed realignment happening in the 1928–1936 period.[1] A major realignment is precipitated by one or more *critical elections,* which may polarize voters around new issues and personalities in reaction to crucial political, economic, or social developments. Three tumultuous eras in American history produced major party realignments. First, during the period leading up to the Civil War, the Whig party gradually dissolved, and the Republican party developed and won the presidency. Second, the radicalization of the Democratic party in the 1890s enabled the Republicans to greatly strengthen their majority status and make lasting gains in voter attachments. Third, the Great Depression of the 1930s propelled the Democrats to power, causing large numbers of voters to repudiate the GOP and embrace the Democratic party. In each of these cases, fundamental and enduring alterations in the party equation resulted.

The process of major realignment occurring during Franklin D. Roosevelt's presidency has served as a hopeful model for Reagan Republicans. Beginning the electoral phase of realignment in 1932, the electorate decisively rejected the party previously in power. This dramatic vote of "no confidence" was followed by substantial changes in policy by the new president, who demonstrated in fact or at least in appearance that his policies were effective. The people responded to his success, accepted his vision of society, and ratified their choice of the new president's party in subsequent presidential and congressional elections. Simultaneously, the former majority party reluctantly but inevitably adjusted to its new minority role. So strong was the new partisan attachment for most voters that even when short-term issues and personalities that favored the minority party dislodged the majority party from power, the basic distribution of party loyalties did not shift significantly. Thus in 1952, 1956, 1968, and 1972 Republicans could win the presidency but the

New Deal Democratic majority coalition could survive. These four examples of alignment-*deviating* elections can be contrasted to the alignment-*maintaining* elections of 1940, 1944, 1948, 1960, 1964, and 1976, when the New Deal coalition prevailed in the presidential contests — but in all ten cases, regardless of the party identity of the presidential winner, the underlying distribution of party affiliation was essentially the same.

Until recent times, at least, major realignments had been spaced about thirty-six years apart in the American experience. With the aid of catalytic circumstances, realignments are accomplished in two primary ways.[2] Some voters are simply converted from one party to the other by the issues and candidates of the time. New voters may also be mobilized into action: immigrants, young voters, and previous nonvoters may become motivated and then absorbed into a new governing coalition. However vibrant and potent they may be at first, party coalitions age, tensions increase, and grievances accumulate. The original *raison d'être* of the majority fades, new generations do not remember the traumatic events that originally brought about the realignment and they lack the stalwart party identifications of their ancestors. New issues arise, producing conflicts that can only be contained by a breakup of old alignments and a reshuffling of individual and group party loyalties. Viewed in historical perspective, party realignment has been a mechanism that ensures stability through the management of unavoidable change.

By no means is a critical realigning era the only occasion when changes in partisan affiliation are accommodated. In truth, every election produces realignment to some degree, since some individuals are undoubtedly pushed to change parties by events and by their reactions to the candidates. Recent research suggests that partisanship is far more responsive to current issues and personalities than had been believed earlier, and that major realignments are just extreme cases of the kind of changes in party loyalty registered every year.[3] While the term *realignment* is usually applied only if momentous events produce enduring and substantial alterations in the party coalitions, political scientists have long recognized that a more gradual rearrangement of party coalitions could occur.[4] Called *secular realignment,* this piecemeal process depends not on convulsive shocks to the political system but on slow, almost subterranean demographic shifts — the shrinking of one party's base of support and the enlargement of the other's, for example, or simple generational replacement. A recently minted version of this theory, termed *rolling realignment,*[5] postulates that in an era of weaker party attachments, a dramatic full-scale realignment may not be possible. Still, a critical mass of voters may be attracted to one party's banner in waves or streams, extending over many years, if that party's leadership and performance are consistently exemplary. This theory has been advanced most avidly by Republican strategists who, of course, have hoped for such an occurrence during the Reagan presidency. And some contend that the decline of party affiliation has in essence left the electorate *dealigned* and incapable of being realigned as long as party ties remain tenuous for so many. Voters shift with greater ease between the parties during dealignment, but little permanence or intensity exists in identifications made and held so lightly. The obsolescence of realignment theory may be indicated by the calendar if nothing else; if major realignments occur roughly every thirty-six years, we are long overdue.[6]

As the trends toward ticket-splitting, partisan independency, voter volatility, and delay of voting decisions until nearer election day (discussed in previous chapters) have suggested, there is little question that we have been moving through an unstable and somewhat "dealigned" period. The foremost political question today is whether dealignment will continue (and in what form) or whether a major realignment is in the offing. Each previous dealignment has been a precursor of realignment,[7] but there is no immutable law that requires realignment to succeed dealignment, especially under modern conditions. It may be that the outlines of the Democratic New Deal coalition will continue to be seen and to prevail in American politics, or that the system may be so dealigned that only short-term and transitory majority coalitions are possible. The other alternative is one more to the liking of Republican activists: a full-scale or rolling realignment of the electorate building on the electoral successes of the Reagan years and producing a stable GOP majority. The realignment hopes and fears of each party will be examined in turn.

The Reagan Revolution and the Republican Renaissance

Undeniably there has been a general loosening of partisan ties by the voters, and in at least one important way the development has worked to the benefit of the Republican party: far more Democrats have become "less committed" to their party over the last five years.

FIGURE 5.1 Five-Year Change in Commitment to Party

QUESTION:[a] "Would you say you are more committed or less committed to your political party today than you were five years ago?"

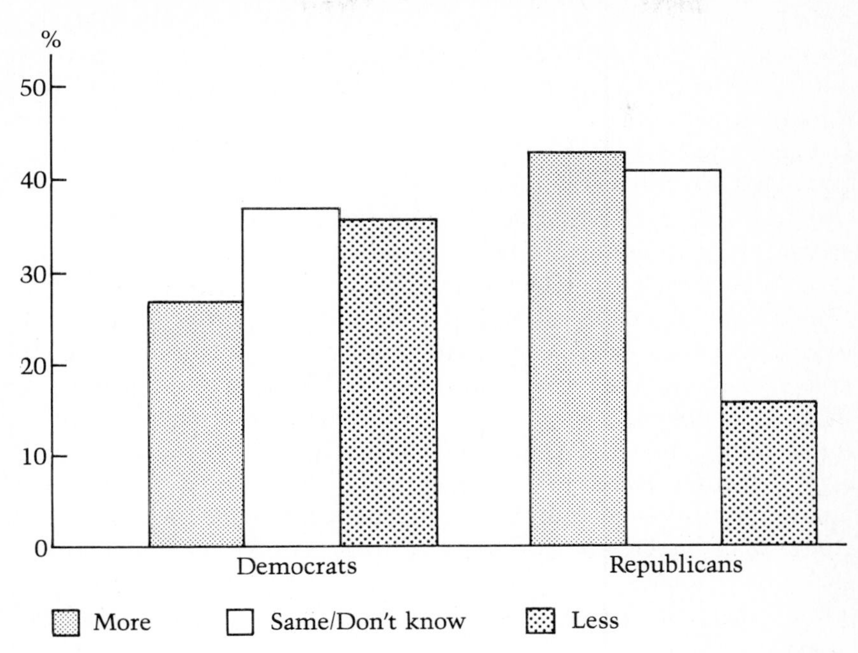

SOURCE: Poll 1 (see Appendix).

[a]Question was not put to pure Independents but to party "leaners."

(See Figure 5.1.) More than a third (36 percent) of current Democratic identifiers report that they have become somewhat estranged from their party, compared to just 16 percent of the Republicans. Furthermore, 43 percent of the GOP adherents say they are "more committed" today than five years ago, while only 27 percent of the Democrats can make the same claim. Put another way, seven out of every ten Americans who are less committed to their party today are Democrats, while six of ten who are more committed are Republicans. Whites and blue-collar workers are particularly likely to have loosened their Democratic ties recently; young voters, executives/professionals, and whites have been the most inclined to move closer to the Republican standard.

Among those who have actually broken ranks with their party, the Republicans have also been the major beneficiaries. A surprisingly high 42 percent of all Americans say that they have changed their minds at some point about which political party they "felt closest to."[8] (See Table 5.1.) (This is well above the 24 percent rate reported by the Center for Political Studies of the University of Michigan in 1976.)[9] By a decisive margin of three to one those who had "become closer" to another party had moved in the Republican direction. As Table 5.1 shows, exactly half of the changers became closer to the GOP, over a quarter edged toward Independent status, and just a sixth had gravitated to the Democrats.

These shifts are remarkably undifferentiated among population groups, with some notable exceptions. (See Table 5.2.) Far more current Republicans than Democrats have switched allegiances, of course, since the GOP has gained most of the defectors.[10] Half of all pure Independents originally were partisans or have been attracted at some time to one party or the other, and by a five-to-one margin Independents have been more inclined to have an alliance with the Republicans than the Democrats. (This result is a double-edged sword, though, because it suggests the GOP has failed to solidify a bond with the larger number of Independents who have found it rather than the Democratic party alluring.) A massive racial difference is also visible, with just 21 percent of blacks but 44 percent of whites reporting a change in party allegiance. Most of the white party shift was to the Republicans, as expected, while the lesser movement among blacks was bipartisan. Substantial Republican advances among the born-agains and executives/professionals are again apparent, as is more modest GOP improvement among men and Southerners. The increased modern ideological polarization of the two parties is seen once more in the disproportionate tendency of liberal switchers to adopt the Democratic party label while conservative changers have found a home in the GOP. Not incidentally it is the "very" liberals and the "very" conservatives who say that they are more committed to their current parties in higher proportions than all other ideological groupings.[11]

About half of the shifts in party allegiance have taken place just since 1980, emphasizing the importance of the Reagan election and presidency to recent partisan movement. The year 1980 itself was clearly a watershed in shaping attitudes for many voters in both parties. For example, current Republicans who date their conversion to the GOP at 1980 are much more likely to "strongly approve" of Ronald Reagan's performance as president than Republicans

TABLE 5.1 Changes in Party Preference, in Percentages

QUESTION: "Have you ever changed your mind about which political party you felt closest to?"		
Yes	42	
No	57	
Don't know	1	
↓		
IF YES, QUESTION: "Which of the following best describes how you changed?"		
Became closer to Democrats	7	
Became closer to Republicans	21	
Became closer to Independents	12	
Don't know	2	
(No response)	(58)	
↓		
QUESTION: "And about how many years ago did this change occur?"		
Since 1984	4	20
Between 1980 and 1984	16	
Between 1974 and 1979	11	19
Between 1961 and 1973	6	
Before 1960	2	
Don't know	3	
(No response)	(58)	
↓		
QUESTION: "What was the main thing that made you change? What else?"[a]		
General disenchantment	10	
Candidates	14	
Reagan — 3%		
Carter — 2		
Others — 1		
General statements — 9		
Policies/issues/platforms	17	
Economy — 3%		
Defense — 1		
Spending — 1		
Social issues — 1		
Other issues/general statements — 11		
Other reasons	3	
(No response)	(58)	

SOURCE: Poll 1 (see Appendix).

[a]Multiple responses were accepted.

TABLE 5.2 Changes in Party Preference, by Selected Subgroups,[a] in Percentages

QUESTION: (1) "Have you ever changed your mind about which political party you felt closest to?"[b]

QUESTION: (2) "Which of the following best describes how you changed?"[c]

		QUESTION 1	QUESTION 2. BECAME CLOSER TO		
	SELECTED SUBGROUP	YES	DEMOCRATS	REPUBLICANS	INDEPENDENTS
	National sample	*42*	*7*	*21*	*12*
Party[d]	Democrats	36	12	13	9
	Republicans	48	4	31	11
	Independents	50	4	19	23
Geography	Northeast	40	7	20	12
	Midwest	46	9	21	14
	South	42	7	23	10
	West	38	6	18	12
Sex	Men	43	6	23	12
	Women	42	8	20	12
Race	Black	21	6	8	7
	White	44	7	22	13
Age	18–34	41	6	21	13
	35–49	46	8	23	14
	50+	42	8	21	10
Occupation	Executive/professional	47	6	26	11
	Other white-collar	42	5	22	12
	Blue-collar	45	8	22	13
	Unemployed	29	4	13	11
	Retired	39	7	21	9
	Student	32	11	8	14
	Homemaker	42	10	20	9

Demography	City dweller	44	7	23	11
	Suburban	47	6	24	15
	Small town	36	7	18	10
	Rural	45	8	21	13
Mobility	Born in current state	40	7	21	12
	Moved there	46	8	23	12
Religion[e]	Protestant	42	8	21	12
	Catholic	41	6	21	13
	Born-again	38	3	24	10
Marital status	Married	44	8	21	13
	Never married	40	9	15	13
	Widowed	41	11	12	16
	Divorced	45	6	25	13
Ideology	Very liberal	42	15	10	15
	Somewhat liberal	40	11	15	13
	Middle-of-the-road	44	8	18	14
	Somewhat conservative	44	4	29	11
	Very conservative	42	4	29	6
Voter registration	Registered to vote	43	7	21	12
	Not registered to vote	43	7	22	13

SOURCE: Poll 1 (see Appendix).

[a]See also Table 5.1.

[b]Nationally, 57 percent answered "no" and 1 percent said "don't know." No subgroup had a "don't know" percentage higher than 3, so the approximate proportion of "no" responses can be easily deduced from the data in the table.

[c]Only those respondents who answered "yes" to the first question were asked this follow-up query. Percentage figures shown are of total sample. "Don't know" responses are again omitted.

[d]Party totals include Independent "leaners." Independent total includes only pure Independents.

[e]The subsample of Jewish voters (N = 25) is too small to give statistically reliable results.

who converted before or after 1980, or indeed those who have been lifelong members of the GOP. Similarly, new Democrats from 1980 were the most likely of any group of Democrats to express strong disapproval of Reagan. Not only do the 1980 converts have the most polarized view of Ronald Reagan, they tend to be more strongly partisan and somewhat more likely to have contributed time and money to their newfound parties.

What made the switchers change their minds about their partisan affiliations? As Table 5.1 summarizes, most people cited policies, issues, or platforms in generalized terms to justify their move, with the economy being the most frequently mentioned example. Nearly as many people cited party candidates, especially Reagan and Carter. Vague and unspecified disenchantment accounted for most of the rest of the defections.

This movement toward the Republicans has not been restricted to polling measures of party affinity; it has been reflected in voting patterns from the courthouse to the White House. Republicans have captured nearly 80 percent of the two-party Electoral College votes cast since 1968,[12] and have won four of the last five presidential contests, three of them by landslides (1972, 1980, and 1984). The GOP's one loss (in 1976) was by a narrow margin even though the party was severely hobbled by the Watergate scandals and a serious split in party ranks. The Senate fell to the Republicans for the first time in more than a quarter-century in 1980, and GOP control was maintained for six uninterrupted years. Even in the House of Representatives, consistently a bastion of Democratic strength in modern times, Republican candidates received 48 percent of the total votes cast for House seats in 1980, and fully half the votes in 1984.[13] (Artful redistricting favoring the Democrats and the pattern of voting[14] kept the actual Republican House contingent smaller in both years than the proportion of votes cast for their nominees.[15]) At the state level, Republicans have rebuilt their statehouse corps from a post-Watergate low of 12 governors in 1976 to almost half of the total (24) in 1986. During the same decade the GOP boosted its share of state legislators from 31 percent to 40 percent.[16]

As noted in earlier chapters, the Republican party has strengthened its ability to elect more of its nominees by improving its organizational, financial, and electoral base. For the first time in modern history, voter identification with the GOP has been nearly on a par with Democratic affiliation during some of the Reagan years, and the public's image of the Republicans has been polished considerably. The GOP has achieved favorability ratings equal to or exceeding the opposition, and the electorate views the GOP as better able to tackle many vital issues than the Democrats. Important population groups, such as fundamentalist Christians, have moved decisively in a Republican direction,[17] while many other blocs that remain mainly outside the GOP orbit, including blue-collar workers and Roman Catholics, are much less monolithically Democratic than they once were.[18] The tendency of the youngest voters to identify predominantly as Republicans may offer the greatest hope of eventual dominance to the GOP — realignment through generational replacement.[19] Even blacks in the 18-to-29 age group are slightly more Republican and much less likely to be "strong Democrats" than their elders.[20] Finally, Republicans can rightly point to the South, where a realignment of some magnitude has unmistakably taken place since the 1960s.[21] While Democrats retain the partisan advantage in the South, their edge is greatly reduced from the days when the only contest worth participating in was the Democratic party's primary. Victory there was considered tantamount to election since the November general election with the Republicans was a foregone conclusion. Now the GOP has elected at least one governor or United States senator in every Southern state, and Republican presidential candidates have swept or nearly swept the South in each election since 1968, with the exception of Southern native Jimmy Carter's maiden White House run in 1976. A combination of demographic factors have produced the South's new two-partyism, including (in order of their occurrence) the black exodus to the North (depriving Democrats of nearly guaranteed votes), an influx of Yankee Republicans seeking jobs and retirement comfort, the younger generation of white southerners (which has been measured at up to 70 percent Republican[22]), and the conversion of older, conservative, formerly Democratic natives.[23]

The combination of Ronald Reagan and issues that pre-dated Reagan but often flowered during his tenure explain much of the GOP's recent advances in party identification, in youth support, and in the South. While Richard Nixon's goal was to construct a personal presidential majority and Gerald Ford preferred to concentrate on the traditional Republican base, Ronald Reagan's vision has been a new GOP majority coalition that combines working-class elements of his New Deal past with newly active fundamentalists, the idealistic and impressionable young, and the age-old Main Street/Wall Street backbone of the Republican party. His partial success, which may yet prove enduring despite the Iran-contra scandal, has been in transcending the natural barriers that divide these groups by inspirationally appealing to their hopes and shrewdly invoking their fears. The Democratic chairman of Maine, Anthony Buxton, illustrated the power of Reagan's rhetoric and performance with a revealing story:[24]

> In 1984 I was in Portland, Maine to register voters. A very poor woman came up to me. She wasn't clean. She carried a dirty child. I asked for identification and she showed me her welfare card, her social security card, and her Medicare i.d. I said, "Would you like to register to vote?" She said "yes." I asked if she'd like to join a political party. She said, "Well, I think I'd like to be a Republican — I've always liked Ronald Reagan." I said to myself "Holy shit, it's *all over* if *this* lady, who is thoroughly existing on the programs Reagan would like to eliminate, wants to be a Republican." I asked her why and she said, "He gives me hope." John Kennedy made millions of people Democrats. Ronald Reagan is making millions of people Republicans.

Commentators have frequently focused on Reagan's lack of success in transferring his popularity to other GOP candidates. In 1986, for example, most of the Republican senatorial nominees for whom Reagan campaigned extensively were defeated for election or reelection. While Reagan undeniably was unable to reverse the Democratic Senate tide in the midterm elections, his visits alone would sometimes shift the partisan balance several percent in the Republican direction. For example, the president's barnstorming in Florida in late October 1986 reduced Democratic party affiliation by 4 percent and boosted GOP and Independent totals by 2 percent each, as measured by two unusually extensive large-sample surveys taken right before and right after Reagan's appearance.[25]

Beyond Reagan, stands on specific policy issues and divergent party images have also helped to produce a pro-Republican change in the electorate. The Democratic party of Franklin Roosevelt, Harry Truman, and John Kennedy had the appearance of firmness and toughness, not just compassion and fairness, particularly in foreign affairs. Their party was in the mainstream on important social and moral issues, and it always seemed to be the guarantor of economic prosperity for the "little guy" — not like the Republican party of the Wall Street barons and the Main Street well-to-do. The Democratic party's carefully nurtured image has eroded if not crumbled since the mid-1960s. First, the issue of race sent white southerners to the GOP in droves, then the war in Vietnam bitterly split the party into "hawks" and "doves." With the eventual triumph of the dovish forces within the Democratic party from 1969 to 1973, white southerners, northern ethnics, and foreign policy conservatives generally became alienated, or in the case of southerners, further estranged. The Democratic party, primarily because of the growing prominence of its liberal wing, became identified in some quarters with other unpopular positions: a kind of "blame America first" internationalism, softness on crime, social permissiveness, militant feminism, homosexual rights, and opposition to school prayer. In stark contrast to its New Deal salad days as the party of broad vision and the national interest, the modern Democratic party often gave the impression of being less than the sum of its parts, an organization increasingly driven by the special interests who made numerous nonnegotiable demands as the price of their participation and votes. As former Iowa Democratic chairman David Nagle once characterized his party:

> This is the most Balkanized political organization in America, barring none. We've allowed ourselves to be caught and trapped into talking about the more controversial issues as opposed to the ones that are consensus-attracting. And part of the way we've done that is that any group which walked into our party and agreed to support our party if we supported their special issue, we've immediately embraced.[26]

The crowning indignity for the Democrats may have been the severe economic dislocations that occurred during the Carter administration. Skyrocketing inflation and interest rates as well as high unemployment in 1979 and 1980 effectively destroyed, at least for the short term, the Democrats' single most valuable asset: the voters' belief that it was the party of prosperity. The Reagan presidency complemented and encouraged these Democratic economic woes by eventually presiding (after a deep recession in 1982) over relative boom times coupled with very low inflation. Reagan's rhetoric also highlighted many popular aspects of the Republican party's conservative philosophy in vivid contrast to the less appealing planks of the Democratic platform: patriotism and nationalism, low taxes and reduced government spending, opposition to many forms of affirmative action and all racial quotas, support of the school prayer movement, a "law and order" stance, a pro-defense posture, and so on. These positions were attractive to precisely the groups most alienated by the Democrats. Furthermore, by the late 1970s the Republicans managed to convey a coherent, consistent, unified message by purging their liberal wing so extensively that only a rump of the once powerful liberal GOP faction still exists. This tiny contingent is considered so politically leprous that the only 1988 Republican presidential candidate who would even agree to address the premier liberal GOP forum, the Ripon Society, did so in order to denounce their views.[27]

The Democrats' Realignment Rejoinder

By now the reader may be convinced that not only has a major realignment transpired but that the Democratic party's electoral position is resting somewhere between hopeless and terminal. Nothing could be further from the truth, as a glance at congressional election results during the Reagan era would suggest. Even though historically, realignment usually has been accompanied by large House gains for the ascendant party, the Republicans control only eighteen more House seats in the twilight of Reagan's presidential tenure than they did before his initial election. And despite a sustained effort the GOP has not succeeded in building a broad grassroots party at the local level in many areas, and this has enabled the Democrats to maintain control of a large majority of state legislatures and local offices.[28] The ongoing revitalization of Democratic fundraising and organizational capacity will probably help to reduce somewhat the GOP's technological advantage and aid Democrats in holding their own in congressional, state, and local contests in the post-Reagan era.

The electoral auguries for that era are not as forbidding for the Democrats as many analysts have claimed. First of all, in an age of loosened party ties and candidate-centered campaigns, much depends on the identities of the presidential nominees in 1988 and beyond. Not only does a president have the opportunity to reshape his or her party's image but victory alone frequently boosts the public's evaluation of and identification with the presidential party.[29] Obviously Democrats will have to win the presidency to reap these rewards, but their chances of doing that are not at all bad. Even before the Iran-contra scandal, only 30 percent of the electorate agreed with the statement, "Given President Reagan's success in governing the country, we should stick with a Republican as our next president."[30] After the scandal broke Democrats quickly gained a substantial advantage as the party people preferred to win the White

House in 1988,[31] and other important perceptions were also reversed. In September 1986, for example, the GOP was chosen as the party better equipped to cope with the main problems facing the country by a 47 percent to 36 percent margin, but by January the Democrats held the advantage by a nearly identical plurality of 46 percent to 38 percent.[32] Whether the Democrats prevail in 1988 or not, these figures suggest how rapidly political events can reverse field. They also cast doubt on the belief that any lasting realignment has taken place, since one would expect deeply held partisan loyalties to weather storms of the Iran-contra variety better than early indications suggest they have. Absent a major realignment and given the natural cycle of American politics, it is almost inevitable that the Democrats will capture the presidency again in the next several elections, and with a new leader will come a fresh start and partial absolution for the party's past sins (in anticipation, perhaps, of new transgressions).

Moreover, as Table 5.3 shows, there has been no massive shift in party identification during Reagan's presidency. Until the Iran-contra scandal Republicans had gained marginally and Democrats had drifted downward slightly, but the overall Democratic advantage, while reduced, was never really eliminated. And as the previous chapter reviewed, few radical alterations have occurred in the coalition of population groups that comprise each party's base.[33] The New Deal coalition has eroded but is still clearly visible, and while it may well be fading, it has staged one of the longest goodbyes in American history.[34] Obviously, the arrival of a new electoral majority does not require the complete destruction of its predecessor,[35] and the ascending coalition may be simply a relatively minor rearrangement of the old one. Still, one is struck by the enduring quality and stability of the political alliance that continues to fuel most Democratic victories in subpresidential contests.

The Democratic party's coalition has proven lasting partially because of the popular staying power of many of the party's issues and ideas.[36] Public support for trimming government expenditure does not imply backing for a dismantling of the welfare state. On the contrary, Democratic innovations such as Social Security, Medicare, and even basic support programs for the poor are considered politically sacrosanct — untouchable by the Republicans when they hold office. Protection of the environment, equal rights for women and minorities, opposition to policies unfairly benefiting big business

TABLE 5.3 Party Identification During the Reagan Presidency[a]

PARTISAN AFFILIATION	DATE OF SURVEY					
	NOV. 1981	NOV. 1982	NOV. 1984	JUNE 1986	NOV. 1986	JULY 1987
Democrat	51%	46%	46%	45%	45%	47%
Republican	35	34	41	40	36	38
Independent[b]	13	16	11	13	17	14
Net Democratic advantage	+16	+12	+ 5	+ 5	+ 9	+ 9

[a]Question wording in all surveys was the same as that listed in footnote a of Table 4.2. Column percentages do not add up to 100% because "don't know," "refuse to answer," and "other party" answers are not included. All surveys were random-sample telephone polls taken by William R. Hamilton and Staff. Sample sizes were as follows: Nov. 1981 (N = 1261), Nov. 1982 (N = 1401), Nov. 1984 (N = 1351), June 1986 (N = 1400), Nov. 1986 (N = 1399), July 1987 (N = 1200).

[b]Pure Independents only. Party leaners are included in Democrat and Republican totals.

and the wealthy — all positions clearly associated in the public mind with the Democrats — are also as popular or more popular today than in the pre-Reagan period. So long as issues and principles this fundamental to American politics are strongly identified with the Democratic party, it is difficult to believe the party would be forced into a permanently secondary electoral role. Reagan's broad personal appeal often has obscured the fact that a large proportion of his supporters are not in sympathy with many of his policies. Fully 41 percent of those who gave Reagan a favorable personal popularity rating in one of our polls admitted that they like only "about half" to "almost none" of the Reagan administration's policies.[37] Clearly, many of these individuals may prove susceptible to the charms of a *likeable* Democratic candidate with whom they *do* agree.

The Democratic party has not been condemned to the past, then, because voters consider many of its main concerns to be central to contemporary life. As Table 5.4 shows, voters during the Reagan presidency have consistently disagreed, usually by 2 to 1, with the statement, "The Democratic party is the party of the past — holding

TABLE 5.4 Party Perceptions in the Reagan Years, in Percentages

	DATE OF SURVEY[a]				
	NOV. 1981	NOV. 1982	NOV. 1984	NOV. 1986	JULY 1987
STATEMENT: "The Democratic party is the party of the past — holding onto tired, outdated ideas that no longer work."					
Agree	30	33	46	30	34
Disagree	60	60	49	68	62
Don't know	10	7	5	4	4
STATEMENT: "The Republican party is the party of the future — it has the fresh ideas to deal with America's problems."					
Agree	39	46	48	44	40
Disagree	49	46	47	50	56
Don't know	12	8	5	6	4

[a]All surveys were random-sample telephone polls taken by William R. Hamilton and Staff. Sample sizes were as follows: Nov. 1981 (N = 1261), Nov. 1982 (N = 1401), Nov. 1984 (N = 1351), Nov. 1986 (N = 1399), July 1987 (N = 1200).

onto tired, outdated ideals that no longer work." Furthermore, by 1986, 34 percent strongly disagreed with that proposition and only 9 percent strongly agreed. And while Americans in the heyday of Reagan's Republican renaissance were closely divided about whether or not "the Republican party is the party of the future [with] the fresh ideas to deal with America's problems," support for that belief has dropped to near the pre-1982 level. Once again, by 1986, those who strongly disagreed outnumbered those who strongly agree (by 21 percent to 12 percent). Incidentally, Reagan's own successes may be at least as responsible as his most prominent failure (the Iran-contra fiasco) for the resurgence in Democratic fortunes. By his second term, the most antigovernment president since Calvin Coolidge had restored the public's faith in the federal government by reducing some of its perceived excesses; he had bolstered support for domestic spending programs by allegedly cutting the waste out of them; and he had built up the nation's defenses so fully that backing for further defense spending had plummeted.[38] In dissipating anger directed at Washington and scaling back government about as far as most people wanted to go, Reagan also calmed the passions of those who blamed the Democratic party for the problems, and indirectly and unintentionally prepared the way for the Democrats' eventual comeback.

It is also inevitable that the Democrats will sooner or later draw considerable strength from the inherent tensions and contradictions in the current GOP coalition. The flammable mix of the predominantly blue-collar, socially traditionalist fundamentalist Christians, the libertarian young (especially affluent yuppies), and the Main Street business establishment cannot forever coexist without political combustion. Recent economic and foreign policy issues as well as Reagan's personal appeal have united these disparate groups. But as cultural issues (lifestyle choice, creationism, etc.) become more prominent and as the fundamentalists become more insistent that "their issues" be moved to the top of the agenda, the GOP could easily be torn by dissension and deserted by a significant share of its base.[39] A possible harbinger of elections future is apparent in a survey conducted for this study. Voters under the age of 35 believed that "we need to adapt our thinking to the modern changes that are occurring" rather than "America needs more conservative, traditional values of earlier days" by the decisive margin of 52 percent to 34 percent. The "born-again" population was the mirror image, choosing tradition over change by 52 percent to 35 percent. (Other predominantly Republican groups were closely split on the question.[40]) It is certainly true that for many decades the Democrats held together groups at least as diverse as the modern GOP's, but conditions were quite different. Broad-based education, instant mass communications, the growth of issue-oriented politics, and the weakening of party identification all make it much more difficult to submerge disputes and paper over disagreements. Put another way, the costs today of changing parties and the stimulus necessary to do so probably both are reduced compared to the New Deal's period of dominance. This may be especially true for the volatile young, whose partisan identities are not firmly set and who can sometimes swing dramatically in their voting choices from election to election.[41]

Finally, the Democrats themselves deserve some credit for staving off what might have turned into a realignment of sorts had they proved oblivious to their own faults and to the lessons of recent party defeats. In essence, the Democrats changed organizationally and adapted philosophically to survive. They are rapidly and with a measure of success becoming technologically and financially modernized, enabling them to compete on more equal terms. Additionally, the Democrats undeniably have moderated in tone and substance. As mentioned in Chapter Three, the "special-interest" caucuses (representing various minority groups) no longer have official recognition in party councils. And just as major parties incorporate the popular planks of third party platforms, so too does each major party absorb most of the ideas made broadly acceptable by the other major party. The Republicans might never have won the presidency again if they had not made their peace (however uneasy) with the New Deal, and pledged preservation of the major social welfare gains achieved in that era. Similarly, the Democrats have come to understand that the presidency may continue to elude their grasp without the party's acquiescence to the public's desire for lower taxes and less government "giveaway" waste. After the Democrats recaptured the Senate in 1986, the proposals made by new committee chairs were remarkably cautious and frugal compared to those of their previous tenure.[42] Instead of comprehensive national health insurance, a system of private insurance with fairly minimal governmental requirements was suggested. Instead of a flood of new educational aid, a mere trickle to targeted needy districts was slated for action. Instead of massive government "make-work" jobs programs, states might be rewarded with some additional federal aid for getting citizens off the welfare rolls and into productive employment. The crown prince of American liberalism, Senator Edward Kennedy (D-Massachusetts), gave the party's shift to the right an unmistakable imprimatur when he declared, "America does not have to spend more to do more."[43] The Democrats' programmatic sights have been lowered, but their party's chances for victory have been raised as a consequence.

Realignment's Relevance in an Antiparty Age

Every presidential election offers a new test of realignment theories, and whichever party wins in 1988, pundits will be proclaiming the start of an era of dynamically altered political realities. The truth is, sadly, that the party label of 1988's victor will probably not herald any new era at all. If the Democrats win, one doubts that it will happen because of any potentially enduring issues or coalitional rearrangements; the Iran-contra scandal, an appealing nominee, and the natural cycle of change after eight years of Republican rule will more likely be the root causes. If the Republicans win, it is hard to imagine the GOP nominee carrying in a Republican House and Senate, too — and such a straight-ticket coattail result is one essential ingredient of any actual party realignment as opposed to a candidate's mere personal triumph. In some respects, voters may be ready for realignment: the intensity of partisan loyalty has dropped, there is a relatively large number of unaffiliated voters, most citizens have no memory of the cleavage that took place in the 1930s, and so on. The problem with this scenario is that for real realignment to occur, for a large percentage of the population to change parties, people must believe that political parties really matter and that partisan affiliation is a vital element of their lives. In fact, *there is little proof that most of the electorate cares about parties and there is considerable evidence to the contrary,* as I have discussed in previous chapters. The painful reality is obvious: most citizens do not understand or appreciate the role that political parties play in running government, organizing elections, or stabilizing society. Moreover, they do not see much if any party connection to their everyday lives. As long as the parties remain irrelevant to the public's view of the political world, ticket-splitting will flourish, volatility in the electorate will be the norm, and shifts between party identification and Independency or "leaning" status will be casual in response to the current fads in issues and personalities. Further, the concept of realignment itself will not be germane, both because voters will not take parties seriously enough to adopt a new label with any permanency and because realignments under these conditions can be nothing more than lightly held, easily changeable, seesaw associations — transient adjustments to the candidates and circumstances of the moment.

The realignment debate is a pleasant enough way to pass the political time of day, but it is not pertinent to the central question at hand: how to strengthen the tie between the voter and the party. Only when partisan loyalty at the individual level is firmed or regenerated will realignment be possible and the full benefits of a vibrant party system (as described in Chapter One) be realized. It is to that critical task that we now turn in the concluding chapters.

Notes

1. On the subject of realignment, see V. O. Key, Jr., "A Theory of Critical Elections," *Journal of Politics* 17 (February 1955):3–18; Walter Dean Burnham, *Critical Elections and the Mainsprings of American Politics* (New York: W.W. Norton, 1970); Kristi Andersen, *The Creation of a Democratic Majority* (Chicago: University of Chicago Press, 1979); Robert S. Erikson and Kent L. Tedin, "The 1928–1936 Partisan Realignment: The Case for the Conversion Hypothesis," *American Political Science Review* 75 (1981): 951–962; Jerome M. Clubb, William H. Flanigan, and Nancy H. Zingale, *Partisan Realignment* (Beverly Hills: Sage, 1980); James L. Sundquist, *Dynamics of the Party System: Alignment and Realignment of Political Parties in the United States* (Revised ed.) (Washington, D.C.: The Brookings Institution, 1983); Stanley Kelley, Jr., "Democracy and the New Deal Party System," Project on the Federal Social Role, Working Paper No. 10, Democratic Values (Washington, D.C.: National Conference on Social Welfare, 1986); and John R. Petrocik, "Realignment: New Party Coalitions and the Nationalization of the South," *Journal of Politics* 49 (May 1987): 347–375.
2. See especially Andersen, *The Creation of a Democratic Majority* and Clubb et al., *Partisan Realignment.* See also Barbara Farah and Helmut Norpoth, "Trends in Partisan Realignment, 1976–1986: A Decade of Waiting," paper prepared for delivery at the annual meeting of the American Political Science Association, Washington, D.C., August 27–31, 1986.
3. See Charles H. Franklin, "Party Identification and Party Realignment," paper prepared for delivery at the annual meeting of the American Political Science Association, Washington, D.C., August 27–31, 1986; Morris Fiorina, *Retrospective Voting in American National Elections* (New Haven: Yale University Press, 1981); and Charles H. Franklin and

John E. Jackson, "The Dynamics of Party Identification," *American Political Science Review* 77 (1983): 957–973.

4. See, for example, Key, "A Theory of Critical Elections."
5. The less dynamic term *creeping realignment* is also sometimes used.
6. Since the last major realignment took place between 1928 and 1936, the next one might have been expected in the late 1960s and early 1970s.
7. See Paul Allen Beck, "The Dealignment Era in America," in Russell J. Dalton et al., *Electoral Change in Advanced Industrial Democracies: Realignment or Dealignment?* (Princeton: Princeton University Press, 1984), 264. See also Philip M. Williams, "Party Realignment in the United States and Britain," *British Journal of Political Science* 15 (January 1985): 97–115.
8. One would presume that at least a few respondents have changed their party affiliations more than once. The interviewers did not specifically probe for this, though, and no respondent volunteered such information. Our guess is that the last such change would be best remembered and reported.
9. The wordings of our poll question and the CPS survey's question were different, however, and that may account for some of the disparity. CPS asked, "Aside from times when you may have voted for a candidate of another party, was there ever a time when you thought of yourself as a [other two labels]?" Still, one strongly suspects that the Reagan years have increased the proportion of party-switchers, perhaps significantly.
10. Note also that the 13 percent of Democrats who reported moving closer to the GOP nonetheless identified themselves earlier in the survey as Democrats (though many had become Independent "leaners.") Just a tiny percentage of the Republicans (4) had moved closer to the Democrats yet still retained the GOP identification.
11. The distribution from poll 1 (see Appendix) is as follows:

QUESTION:"Would you say that you are more committed or less committed to your political party today than you were five years ago?"

	Very liberal	*Somewhat liberal*	*Moderate*
More	38%	35%	33%
Less	20	30	31
Same	10	11	16
Don't know/not asked*	33	24	21

	Somewhat conservative	*Very conservative*	*Don't know*
More	37%	50%	23%
Less	23	18	27
Same	17	12	14
Don't know/not asked*	23	20	36

*Pure Independents were not asked this question, but Independent "leaners" were.

12. Of the 2,689 Electoral College votes cast from 1968 to 1984, the GOP has won 2,075 (77 percent), the Democrats 567 votes (21 percent), and others 47 votes (2 percent). When the "other" total is not considered, the Republicans have secured about 79 percent of the total.
13. See *Congressional Quarterly Weekly* 44 (November 15, 1986): 2896.
14. For example, Republican votes were often cast heavily in districts where GOP control was assured; any vote beyond the minimum majority needed to win a seat is wasted, in the sense that a vote for the party could be better used in other districts where the Republican candidate needed more votes to win.
15. The Republicans won just 44 percent of the House seats in 1980 and 42 percent in 1984.
16. The upward trend is clear, though the vagaries of each election year's politics have made the progression inconsistent, as the following figures indicate. The proportion of Republican state legislators, in percentages, from 1976 to 1986 has been:

1976	*1978*	*1980*	*1982*	*1984*	*1986*
31	36	39	37	41	40

17. See, for example, the survey results reported in the *Washington Post*, December 22, 1985, B1; May 22, 1986, A9; and January 11, 1987, C2.
18. See *Public Opinion* 7 (October/November 1985): 29; and *Washington Post*, January 25, 1986, A4.
19. See Everett Carll Ladd, Jr., "On Mandates, Realignments, and the 1984 Presidential Election," *Political Science Quarterly* 100 (Spring 1985): 18; and Farah and Norpoth, "Trends in Partisan Realignment," 14–18.
20. See *The Polling Report* 2 (November 10, 1986): 2–3.
21. See Ray Wolfinger and Michael G. Hagen, "Republican Prospects: Southern Comfort," *Public Opinion* 7 (October/November 1985): 8–13, 24; David S. Broder, "GOP Gaining Strength in Political Cauldron," *Washington Post*, May 18, 1986, A1, A12; and Petrocik, "Realignment."
22. See surveys cited in Bill Peterson, "To Southern White Youth, Ronald Reagan Heads the Class," *Washington Post*, May 23, 1986, A1.
23. Wolfinger and Hagen, "Republican Prospects," 9.
24. In the course of research for this study, twelve Republican and ten Democratic state chairpersons were interviewed about the condition of their political parties at the national and state levels. Buxton was interviewed by telephone in March 1986.
25. The telephone surveys of about 3,500 respondents each were taken before and after Reagan's Florida visit on October 25, 1986 by William R. Hamilton and Staff. The survey results before Reagan's trip showed 51 percent Democrats, 39 percent Republicans, 10 percent Independents; afterwards there were 47 percent Democrats, 41 percent Republicans, and 12 percent Independents. (Independent "leaners" are included in the party totals.) Interestingly, Reagan's stumping for GOP United States Senator Paula Hawkins, opposed by well-known and liked Democratic Governor Robert Graham, had no perceptible effect on the Senate race, despite the party identification shift. But in the gubernatorial

election, where both candidates were relatively little known, Reagan seemed to provide the Republican nominee (Tampa Mayor Robert Martinez) with a lift almost comparable to the party affiliation change. Martinez won and Hawkins lost a week later. This example appears consonant with the studies cited earlier in this chapter that conclude that party identification is more responsive to short-term political events and personalities than is often believed. See note 3 above.

26. As quoted in Rob Gurwitt, "Democrats' Links with Gays Come under Fire," *Congressional Quarterly Weekly* 43 (September 14, 1985): 1826.
27. The Candidate was former Delaware Governor Pete DuPont. See the *Washington Post,* April 27, 1986, A18.
28. Between 1978 and 1986, for instance, the Democrats controlled between 63 and 71 of the 99 legislative chambers (counting each House and Senate separately). Republicans were in charge of only 26 to 35 chambers. (In each year a few chambers were tied or — for Nebraska's unicameral legislature alone — nonpartisan.)
29. The same phenomenon is often observed on the state level. For instance, after Virginia's Democrats swept all statewide posts in November 1985, Democratic party identification increased by six percentage points, and GOP identification fell by five compared to the preelection period. The surveys were taken by Mason-Dixon Opinion Research and reported in Kent Jenkins, "Poll shows shift to Democratic Party in Virginia," *Virginian-Pilot,* December 6, 1985, A1, A3.
30. Fifty-two percent disagreed, and 18 percent said "not sure," in a Yankelovich Clancy Shulman random-sample telephone survey for *Time* magazine, September 8–10, 1986. N = 1,014 adults.
31. In a random-sample telephone survey of 781 registered voters conducted December 7–8, 1986 by the *New York Times* and CBS News, 39 percent said they "will probably vote" for the Democratic presidential candidate in 1988, 27 percent for the Republican, and 34 percent were unsure. In October 1986 the parties had been essentially tied on this question, with 32 percent preferring the Democrat and 33 percent the Republican.
32. Both random-sample telephone polls were conducted by the *Washington Post* and ABC News. See the *Washington Post,* January 27, 1987, A4.
33. See Figure 4.2 in Chapter Four.
34. See Harold Stanley, William Bianco, and Richard Niemi, "Partisanship and Group Support Over Time: A Multivariate Analysis," *American Political Science Review* 80 (September 1986): 970–976; and Seymour Martin Lipset, "Beyond 1984: The Anomalies of American Politics," *PS* 19 (Spring 1986): 222–236.
35. See James L. Sundquist, "Whither the American Party System? — Revisited," *Political Science Quarterly* 99 (Winter 1983–1984): 573–593.
36. See Lipset, "Beyond 1984"; Thomas Ferguson and Joel Rogers, *Right Turn: The Decline of the Democrats and the Future of American Politics* (New York: Hill and Wang, 1986); and William Schneider, "Win Now, Pay Later," *The New Republic* 192 (August 21, 1986): 19–20.

37. Poll 1 (see Appendix). Of the 72 percent who said they had a "very favorable" or "somewhat favorable" opinion of Reagan, 7 percent liked "all the policies of his administration," 51 percent supported "most" of them, 36 percent liked "about half," and 5 percent supported "almost none" (1 percent said "not sure").
38. Note the surveys cited in *National Journal* 18 (August 2, 1986): 1891.
39. This clash has already occurred in some state, local, and congressional contests. See, for example, *Congressional Quarterly Weekly* 44 (April 12, 1986): 802–803.
40. Poll 1 (see Appendix).
41. See the surveys cited in the *Washington Post*, September 14, 1986, D1, and November 5, 1986, A36.
42. See Helen DeWar, "Reagan's Themes, Deficits Alter Course of Democratic Mainstream," *Washington Post*, March 9, 1987, A3.
43. As quoted ibid.

CHAPTER SIX

• ☆ • ☆ •

Toward Party Renewal, American Style Part I

. . . the parties are alive, if not well in America . . . What seems likely . . . is a politics of greater fluidity and instability . . . The new challenge for the parties in this fragmented politics is to fight, for the first time, for a place and a role in American politics — to cope with the fact that they do not have a guaranteed future. — *Frank Sorauf*[1]

. . . it is possible that new loyalties to the old labels will be built in response to new issues and new leaders associated with the Republican or Democratic labels. What is frayed may be mended or restored. — *Leon Epstein*[2]

. . . the door remains open for party renewal. — *Martin Wattenberg*[3]

POLITICAL SCIENTISTS HAVE BEEN at once pessimistic and hopeful about the future of the political parties. The reality is that Americans evidence increasingly little fealty to their party identifications, while the personalities of individual candidates continue to be at the center of the nation's electoral show. The deeply rooted bias of individualistic Americans against parties often combines with the vested (if shortsighted) interest of candidates and officeholders who treasure their independence from party leaders and thus prefer that parties remain in a weakened state. The result is that even special interest groups are often held in higher regard than the parties; a

1983 Gallup poll taken for the Advisory Commission on Intergovernmental Relations found that nearly half the population (45 percent) saw interest groups as best representing the respondent's political needs compared to only about a third (34 percent) who believed that either of the parties did so.[4] Because of disturbing statistics like these, a recent random-sample survey of political scientists revealed that of all major American institutions the parties were rated least effective and successful.[5]

Yet room for some optimism remains. There seems to be a growing appreciation of the role parties can play — an appreciation that can be fostered by the parties themselves in ways that will be described below. Many influential journalists have joined political scientists in lavishing attention and often praise on the work of the parties. Candidates and officeholders have witnessed and benefited from the revolution in party-sponsored services and campaign technologies. The voters, too — as survey data presented later in this chapter and the next one will suggest — appear more receptive to a strengthened role for parties in at least some ways.

Part of the change in attitude can be attributed to fear of the consequences of continued party decline. Political fragmentation, multiparty elections without majority winners, additional emphasis on candidates' personalities to the exclusion of broader issue themes, a still greater empowerment of the news media — all could become reality if current trends persist. Whereas a half-century ago the energies of reformers were devoted to dismantling and restricting the parties, today many concerned citizens and political elites are determined to strengthen them. The value of such a sea change among influential reformist elements should not be underestimated.

To capitalize on these conditions, though, the parties will have to take the initiative themselves. Not only are remedies requiring governmental action usually slow in coming, but they inevitably will be compromised by partisan politics, the ambitions of elected officials, and lingering public mistrust of centralized parties. Luckily, both national parties have demonstrated the resolve and the institutional capacity necessary to enact at least some of the internal reforms proposed in this chapter. And a few of the government-sponsored changes to be discussed in Chapter Seven are more than pipe dreams as well.

Governing my choice of proposals were ten attributes that I believe strong parties ought to display in the American context:[6]

1. *Equity and Legitimacy:* The appearance and the reality of equity and legitimacy in the eyes of the electorate, which are absolutely essential to the public acceptance of the parties' role in democracy.
2. *Electoral Appeal:* A broad-based electoral appeal that enables a party to mobilize support, aggregate power, unify disparate groups and interests, and provide stability to representative democracy;
3. *Participation and Education:* Internal mechanisms that encourage participation by voters in the party and educate voters about the party's candidates and ideas.
4. *Accountability:* Internal mechanisms that help to hold party leaders and officeholders accountable to the party and its supporters for their actions.
5. *Conflict Control:* Sufficient power to control, contain, or successfully arbitrate dissension, conflict, and fragmentation in the party ranks.
6. *Resources:* Sufficient resources (money, people, technology, etc.) to accomplish important party goals and perform party functions well.
7. *Autonomy:* The autonomy and power to make fundamental decisions and choices about party structure, organization, method of nomination, and so forth.
8. *Policy Capacity:* The capacity to formulate, refine, and promote its philosophy, policies, ideas, and issues.
9. *Incentives:* The possession of enough rewards, incentives, and penalties to enable the party to induce cooperation from its officeholders and partisan activists — cooperation not only with the party but with each other in government so as to project a coherent image and to produce solid accomplishments.
10. *Candidate Assistance:* The ability to assist its candidates to win elections in substantial, sophisticated, and effective ways.

I would argue that each of the proposals contained in this chapter and in Chapter Seven shores up or fulfills one or more of these crucial "strong-party attributes." (Those attributes reinforced by each proposal will be designated following every reform subtitle.)

In selecting and promoting ideas for party renewal, I was also guided and motivated by a fundamental belief in the case for parties that was made in the opening chapter. *So crucial is their role that the two major parties deserve what we might term "most favored nation" status in our laws and political practices.* Since the two-party system manifestly assists in preserving the stability of our nation's democracy, we have every right — indeed, the obligation, since it is in our vital interests — to assist them by enabling the parties to perform their functions better.

An Agenda for Party Renewal: Party-Initiated Actions

OMBUDSMAN/MOBILE OFFICE PROVISION

Build modern grassroots parties on an old-style model by designating party "ombudsmen" in key constituencies and establishing mobile party offices. Strong-party attributes:

EQUITY AND LEGITIMACY
PARTICIPATION AND EDUCATION
RESOURCES

Compared to European parties or even American parties of a century ago, United States political parties today maintain remarkably little personal contact with average voters. Fully 77 percent of the electorate report that they have never "been helped with a problem by a member of a political party."[7] A party representative would also be among the last individuals a voter in need of assistance would call: when asked, "if you had a problem or concern with the government, whom would you most likely contact for help — an elected official, or an official of your political party, or someone else?" only 14 percent of the respondents named the party.[8]

There can be no surprise here. Party officials and scholars alike have long noted the atrophy of many local party organizations. Even when the local party committee rosters are at full strength, relatively few of the individual committee members tend to be active or particularly well known in the precinct they are charged with organizing. The rewards (social and political) for energetic service are often too small or nonexistent to encourage any other kind of behavior; committee posts are unpaid and there are generally no sanctions (save expulsion) to be levied for indolence. The result, of course, is that the party becomes invisible in the community, and people fail to see a useful connection between their party and their lives. Precisely this disjunction is cited by some scholars to explain the growing estrangement between voter and party.[9]

Both parties, in different ways, have recognized the problem in the last few years and made some minor effort to remedy it. The Republicans established the Working Partners program in 1982, which puts local GOP leaders to work on well-publicized community projects.[10] In several hundred successful outings, party activists have cleaned up litter in the Grand Canyon; refurbished a facility for autistic adults in Santa Rosa, California; held job fairs (with the NAACP) in Tulsa, Baltimore, and St. Paul; organized food banks for the needy in a half dozen cities and towns, and sponsored safety fingerprinting of children in San Diego and La Mesa, California. The national Democratic party has no organizational counterpart, but individual local committees, often spurred by Democratic candidates and officeholders, have orchestrated similar events in scattered locales around the country.

The question might reasonably be asked: do people really want the parties to strike out in the direction of community involvement, and would it make much difference to voters' partisan loyalties even if the parties did adopt an activist posture? An historical answer is certainly provided by the big-city machines of old; their devotion to their constituents' daily needs made them a dominant element of urban life and was richly rewarded at election time with votes from grateful beneficiaries.[11] But there is also evidence to support party activism from modern public opinion. In one survey taken for this study,[12] respondents were asked this question:

> It has been suggested that there be a basic change in the role played by political parties in America. Some people want political parties to be more active as social and civic organizations to help people deal with government and better their communities. Do you believe that such a change should happen, or should political parties stay the way they are now?

As Table 6.1 indicates, a substantial majority (58 percent) favored a shift in party activity. The proposal was popular among all major segments of the population, and it was viewed especially favorably by groups that have sometimes been excluded from the party mainstream (women, blacks, and young people). Interestingly, Americans

TABLE 6.1 Basic Change in Party Role

	CHANGE IN PARTY ROLE[a]	
SELECTED SUBGROUP	% FAVOR	% OPPOSE
National sample	*58*	*36*
Northeast	64	31
Midwest	52	39
South	59	37
West	62	33
Democrats	60	34
Republicans	55	40
Independents	60	34
Men	53	42
Women	63	30
Black	67	31
White	59	35
18–34	58	37
35–49	64	31
50 +	52	41
Executive/professional	58	37
Other white collar	58	35
Blue collar	58	38
City dweller	62	32
Suburban	63	30
Small town	55	38
Rural	58	38
More committed to party[b]	57	38
Less committed to party[b]	67	28
Registered to vote[c]	58	36
Unregistered to vote[c]	65	28

SOURCE: Poll 1 (see Appendix).

[a]See text for exact question wording. Totals do not add to 100 percent since "don't know" responses are not listed in table.

[b]Respondents with any party identification or leaning were asked: "Would you say you are more committed or less committed to your political party today than you were five years ago?"

[c]Self-reported unregistered N = 330.

who live in the sprawling suburbs — the *least* organizable demographic unit, where parties are currently *least* in evidence[13] — are *most* supportive of change, signaling both their desire for visible party assistance and an opening for the parties to appeal to them. Perhaps most importantly, the idea of a party role change appeals particularly to segments of the electorate who are more alienated from the parties and the political system: the unregistered and those who admit becoming "less committed" to their political party over the last five years. This finding suggests at least the possibility that the least involved, most party-neutral citizens might establish or strengthen their partisan loyalties if a party tangibly contributed to their lives.

The abstract concept of greater civic involvement by the parties is certainly attractive to many, then, but how could the idea be practically applied? One appealing way would be the designation of certain party precinct or ward committeepersons as "community ombudsmen." As a designated "red tape cutter," the ombudsman's job would be akin to the ward heeler of old: to keep in touch with his or her neighbors, to be alert to their needs, and to act as their advocate when problems arise. From getting potholes filled to organizing "crime watch" neighborhood security programs, ombudsmen could perform valuable services for voters who surely would be grateful and perhaps more receptive to their benefactor's party as well. As offensive as it may be to political purists and ideologues, there is nothing inherently wrong with the time-honored, pragmatic American tradition of "votes given for favors done"; it is, in fact, the operating premise of the constituency service operations so carefully nurtured by incumbent members of Congress. Undoubtedly, volunteer spirit and party fealty alone will not be enough to spur the designated ombudsmen to energetic action. They should receive a stipend commensurate with such part-time work, perhaps several thousand dollars a year. Both parties are now in a financial position to do this in at least some states and localities, though obviously the Republicans currently have a vastly greater opportunity to set up an ombudsman scheme. (My proposal on tax refund "add-ons" for the parties, however, which follows in Chapter Seven, would help to make the Democrats competitive.) Even the GOP could not afford to include every precinct or ward, of course, so the program would inevitably be targeted (at least at first) to marginal, closely contested areas where the political payoff would be greatest.

A less expensive alternative to the ombudsman program — or,

more grandiosely, a supplement to it — would be the establishment of party "mobile units" that would travel from precinct to precinct and locality to locality on a regular schedule. Staffed by both volunteers and paid workers, these mobile units could raise the party's profile in nonelection seasons, assist residents with governmental problems, and serve as a field base for party operations such as canvassing. If these units sound suspiciously like the mobile offices many members of Congress send throughout their districts, they are intended to be. In fact, one of the purposes of these units should be to provide service competition to incumbent members of Congress, and the party's mobile offices should be used heavily in marginal districts controlled congressionally by the opposition party. (The mobile units will probably of necessity be restricted to these kinds of districts, given limited resources and the objections that would be raised by same-party incumbents who would see the party units as unwarranted intrusion and unwanted competition.) At present, incumbent legislators are essentially "unopposed" in their delivery of assistance to voters, using several hundred thousand dollars of taxpayer funds each year to do it — a fact that accounts in part for a House incumbent reelection rate that regularly exceeds 90 percent and reached a post–World War II peak of 98 percent in 1986.[14] Such massive reelection rates are delightful for officeholders, but of questionable value to citizens in a system where arguably the best government results from strong two-party competition. Using mobile units may be one way for parties to help themselves as well as the voters *and* to inject more competition into congressional politics. Granted, incumbent members of Congress will still have a decided advantage in service delivery and reelection, given their large staffs and their unmatched ability to get the attention of bureaucrats and the press. But some added competition is surely better than none at all, and there are subsidiary benefits to the party in terms of voter involvement and mobilization. The attractiveness of both the ombudsman scheme and the mobile units stems from the opportunities they give to build the parties in the only way likely to prove enduring: person to person, from the bottom up.

SERVICES TO PARTY MEMBERS

Strengthen solidarity between the party organization and its activists and adherents by providing nonpolitical services and other rewards. Strong-party attributes:

PARTICIPATION AND EDUCATION INCENTIVES

E. E. Schattschneider was among the first to recognize that party organizations do not own the allegiance of their partisans. Since there is no enrolled party membership in America, he understood that, much as individual politicians, interest groups, and even commercial institutions do, the voter must be "courted" by a political party.[15] Other scholars have long acknowledged the importance of nonpolitical social and personal motivations for party involvement.[16] That, combined with the regrettable but unavoidable fact that most Americans are not vitally concerned with politics, leads to another suggestion for party renewal: why not offer party-sponsored services and preferments to party activists, contributors, and identifiers?

The AFL-CIO and several other interest groups have already shown the way. The labor organization has recently launched a program to offer low-dues "associate membership" to millions of nonunion workers, providing discount credit cards, low-cost insurance, and cut-rate legal and financial services as incentives.[17] The "Union Privilege" MasterCard has interest rates a half dozen percentage points below average, with no annual fee and occasional "free payment" months with no interest charges. The other services boast similar advantages, using the labor federation's group strength and clout to benefit current members and attract others to join. "The bottom line of all this is to make the associate members [participatory] members of the union movement," explained one labor leader.[18] A number of other interest groups, including the Sierra Club, the National Organization for Women (NOW), and the National Lawyers Guild have gone the AFL-CIO one better, pushing reduced-rate credit cards that also pay several cents per card use to the sponsoring organization.[19]

Whether the parties make a profit or not on the transactions — and they should be encouraged to do so as long as the party members also benefit from discounted interest charges — there is no reason why the political parties should not undertake innovative service arrangements that help their partisans while strengthening party-voter ties. People join and stay active in organizations for many different reasons, and it is a fiction to believe that party membership can be enhanced and expanded by issues and ideology alone. In a culture that devalues politics as ours does, parties should employ every reasonable incentive to interest citizens in their groups. Before a congregation can be inspired and uplifted, it must be enticed to enter the church doors.

EXPANSION OF PARTY FUNDRAISING, CAMPAIGN SERVICES, AND VOLUNTEER AND CANDIDATE RECRUITMENT

Continue and expand both parties' fundraising capacities, services to the political campaigns of their nominees, and party efforts to recruit candidates and volunteer workers. Strong-party attributes:

EQUITY AND LEGITIMACY
ELECTORAL APPEAL
PARTICIPATION AND EDUCATION
ACCOUNTABILITY
RESOURCES
INCENTIVES
CANDIDATE ASSISTANCE

As Chapter Three reviewed, there has been no more substantial change in the political parties than their newfound role as provider of campaign funds and services. Candidates now depend on the parties (particularly the GOP, but increasingly so among Democrats too) for useful advice, training, and technologies. As the link between party and nominee grows, so too does the connection between party and elected officeholder. To the extent possible each party can and must further expand its capabilities to recruit candidates who share its basic philosophy, to train and instruct them and their staffs in the art of campaigning, and to make available the maximum allowable financial assistance, expertise, and campaign technology. The more outstanding the party's candidates, staffs, and campaigns, the more appealing the party will appear in the eyes of voters. (Unavoidably, the party's shine will always be in part reflected glory from its successful nominees.) Moreover, Martin Wattenberg has found evidence to suggest that party organizations strengthened by the new campaign technologies feed themselves, in essence, by encouraging candidates to spend less on media and more on party-building activities (such as canvassing) because the nominees realize the party will do them considerable electoral good.[20]

Of necessity, each of America's broad-based parties must follow a different path to raise the necessary resources. The Republicans already have a "critical mass" of direct mail contributors, large donors, and centralized technologies sufficient to sustain a steady growth in party offerings, even when an adverse political climate settles in. The promise of future Democratic advances is much more fragile, and will depend heavily on the fortunes of its presidential nominees and the ingenuity of national and state party staff. The Democrats have traditionally fared better in fundraising when they have been able to reach key constituency groups through a personalized (rather than a direct mail) approach. The national and state organizations could learn much from the successes registered by Massachusetts Democratic Governor Michael Dukakis. Instead of mass mailings Dukakis has painstakingly built up a dependable base of 40,000 $10 and $20 donors using small-scale events and receptions.[21] These individuals frequently are not just contributors but campaign workers, and Dukakis sends them periodic missives and newsletters that do not always have a fundraising pitch.

While both parties deserve praise for expanding their portfolio of campaign services to candidates, neither party has earned many kudos for volunteer recruitment. It has been as though the party leaders preferred to let efficient campaign technologies substitute for less efficient people the way automation has displaced factory workers. A corporation's decision to automate may be justified since profit is its goal, but parties need people to win. Voters respond best to a personal contact; television, direct mail, and literature, for all their advantages, are poor cousins. The more that citizens can be attracted to participate in a party's activities, the more the party's candidates will gain and the more that the party itself will benefit from the expansion of its cadre.

There is enormous untapped potential for party volunteer recruitment in the United States. When we asked, "How much interest would you have in becoming active with a political party at the local or state level?" 13 percent of the respondents replied, "a great deal of interest" and 41 percent had "some interest."[22] Given the minuscule level of current participation — a few percent of the population at best — these survey figures are heartening even after discounting for "good intentions." If only half of those who expressed great interest could truly be mobilized by the parties, politics could be revolutionized. Here again, precinct "ombudsmen" could act as intermediaries, identifying and involving volunteers. More traditional methods of telephone and neighborhood canvassing can also be employed, and the modern technique of "instant organization" — whereby a candidate's precinct walkers are recruited and selected by telephone solicitation[23] — could just as easily be applied to the party search for volunteers. In order to keep volunteers interested once they are signed up, the parties must also offer incentives and rewards. Patronage and honorary appointments (discussed in the next chapter) are certainly useful here, but the value of regular communication and social meetings should not be underestimated either. Periodic newsletters (sans fundraising pitch), issue forums, and relatively nonpolitical entertainment functions all build the solidarity of which real, lasting commitment is made. One thing is certain: the parties' current preferred vehicle for "voter contact," direct mail, is a one-way channel. It may provide for mass financial contributions but it is not the basis for mass action. Grassroots loyalty and two-way communications must be produced by other means.

Table 6.2 fleshes out the party activity interests of our poll's respondents. Not surprisingly, the most passive action requiring the least commitment (receiving literature) garners the greatest interest

TABLE 6.2 Public Interest in Party Involvement

QUESTION: "How interested would you be in having the following types of involvement with a political party in your area — would you be very interested, somewhat interested, not too interested or not interested at all in ____________ ?"

	PERCENT INTERESTED[a]			
ACTIVITY	VERY	SOMEWHAT	NOT TOO	NOT AT ALL
Receiving literature about the party's candidates	45	35	9	9
Going to party meetings	9	46	21	23
Contributing money to political parties that is tax deductible	8	42	19	28
Volunteering time to work on party projects	7	38	21	31
Getting involved in planning campaign strategies	8	28	26	36
Running for political office yourself	4	12	14	69

SOURCE: Poll 1 (see Appendix).

[a]Totals do not add to 100 percent since "don't know" responses are not listed in table.

level. But half or more are somewhat willing to attend party meetings or contribute money — and close to a tenth of the population is very interested in doing so. Volunteering time to the party is attractive to nearly half as well. Of all the activities, only "running for office" is clearly unpopular, and only 16 percent admit to any desire to throw a hat into the ring. (Given the awful gamut candidates are forced to run today, one can hardly blame citizens for keeping their headgear!)

PARTY INSTITUTIONAL ADVERTISING

Make party institutional advertising a permanent component of campaigns AND air it during noncampaign seasons as circumstances warrant. Strong-party attributes:

ELECTORAL APPEAL
PARTICIPATION AND EDUCATION
ACCOUNTABILITY
RESOURCES
POLICY CAPACITY
CANDIDATE ASSISTANCE

The party institutional advertisements described in Chapter Three[24] — such as the GOP's 1980 "Vote Republican for a Change" series or the Democrats' 1982 "It Isn't Fair — It's Republican" commercials — are noteworthy innovations in party politics. This kind of advertising permits the party to participate in setting the campaign or governmental agenda; it nationalizes key themes, thus making politics a bit more comprehensible for the voters while drawing its candidates and officeholders together (willing or not)[25] around common ideas and the party label itself. Survey research on the effects of party institutional advertising demonstrates that it can have a salutary impact on both the party and its nominees: recognition and understanding by the voters of a party's approach and philosophy increases, and (depending on the quality and context of the advertising) substantial gains can be registered for a party's ticket.[26]

Both parties ought to make institutional advertising a permanent aspect of the political landscape, and not just at campaign time. Why not air party commercials during the intervals between campaigns in support or opposition to a president's initiatives or mistakes, or Congress's actions (assuming Congress is controlled by one party)? State and local parties should also produce institutional advertising for campaigns at their level, or in support or opposition to governors, mayors, state legislatures, and city councils.[27]

Of course air time is notoriously expensive, though radio is a relatively cheap and often overlooked alternative.[28] Ideally, free time should be provided to the parties each year — campaign years and noncampaign years alike — by all television and radio stations, as proposed in more detail in Chapter Seven. But the parties should also take note of the successful tactics of the National Conservative Political Action Committee (NCPAC) and several other ideological PACs, who often have produced clever advertisements they never paid to air widely. Instead, they simply called timely, well-attended press conferences and released the spots to the delighted media, who promptly broadcast them gratis on all major evening and local news shows. The Democratic party, in fact, employed this technique in 1982 for its institutional advertisements.[29]

BIPARTISAN EDUCATIONAL CAMPAIGN

Undertake a bipartisan educational campaign aimed at both voters and the news media to explain the party system and its advantages, and to advocate party-strengthening changes in law. Strong-party attributes:

EQUITY AND LEGITIMACY
ELECTORAL APPEAL
PARTICIPATION AND EDUCATION
POLICY CAPACITY

Institutional advertising is one form of voter education about the parties, but much more is needed. Despite the encouraging potential for volunteer commitment to the parties cited earlier, fewer people seem to regard partisan activity as a civic virtue in recent times, as Jack Dennis has demonstrated.[30] It is not that citizens view the parties harshly; rather, says Martin Wattenberg, "people feel neutral rather than negative."[31] In other words, Americans do not particularly care about the parties or appreciate their central position in the nation's political constellation. So apathetic is the public that it is for the most part unaware of the stresses parties have been under. A December 1985 *New York Times* poll asked a representative sample of Americans: "Think about how much influence political parties have today. Do they have more influence than they had twenty years ago, less influence, or about the same . . . ?" Fully half responded "more influence," compared to 24 percent who said "less" and 18 percent who believed there had been no change.[32]

It will not be easy to counteract this indifference, though the task is considerably easier than it would be if public attitudes were openly hostile to political parties. As Wattenberg explains the work to be done:

> In order to reinvigorate political partisanship in the future, then, the public must be convinced that political parties perform a useful function in the American political process. The challenge that the parties face is not merely to espouse programs with popular appeal, but also to demonstrate that they play a crucial political role — from the recruitment of leaders to the implementation of policies.[33]

Many of the changes advocated in this chapter and the next one, including the ombudsman program, certain campaign finance reforms, and the free provision of broadcast time, can further the parties' demonstration of political service and clout. But it would also be useful for the two parties, preferably in concert and through an appropriate bipartisan foundation or commission, to undertake an educational campaign about the theory, operation, and advantages of the party system. The schools and universities are a logical place to begin the campaign, which would surely have the cooperation of most teachers and academics, who in the main need no convincing about the importance of parties. Using free public service spots on commercial radio and television, as well as more abundant time on citizen access and other cable channels, the parties can also aim their message at a postgraduate public that might prove surprisingly receptive to it, if it is properly couched in rational argument with patriotic overtones. Not only information but advocacy should be the goal of this educational campaign. The parties, working together where possible, ought to be more visible in urging adoption of party-strengthening reforms in Congress and the state legislatures.

Finally, the parties must direct their message at the news media as well as the general public. There is a thinly disguised distaste for political parties among many individuals in the media. Many television journalists, in particular, either ignore the parties as much as possible — viewing them as anachronisms opposed to the "public interest" — or they openly deride them, characterizing them with Tammany Hall terminology. NBC's "Nightly News" anchor Tom Brokaw expressed this prejudice perfectly when he wrote a magazine piece "in defense of TV news." "Because of television," penned Brokaw, ". . . the people standing for public office . . . no longer can hide behind party machinery or in smoke-filled rooms."[34] On behalf of the real "public interest," journalists ought to be encouraged to recognize and correct their antiparty bias.

PARTY POLICY FORMULATION

Increase the parties' capacities for policy formulation by empowering policy commissions for presidential interregnums. Strong-party attributes:

ELECTORAL APPEAL
PARTICIPATION AND EDUCATION
POLICY CAPACITY

American parties exist primarily to win, not to represent ideas. And yet one of their most crucial responsibilities is to prepare candidates to govern and citizens to be governed. The need to win does not eliminate the duty to propose policy. As the most broadly based political institutions in the United States, the parties must constantly develop and refine at least a generalized philosophy of government that differentiates one party from the other and presents voters with a rational choice.

Political scientists for decades have urged the parties to present well-publicized, specific, and comprehensive policy programs devised in representative fashion. In the late 1940s a blue-ribbon committee of the American Political Science Association urged not only that clear policies be developed, but that only candidates who supported the policies be nominated and that parties insure that the pledges were enacted after the election.[35] To a very limited extent, the APSA's conditions have been met. The party platform, after all, is drawn up every four years after platform committee members — who are usually broadly representative of the party's key constituencies — hold dozens of hearings and take thousands of pages of testimony. As we saw in Chapter One, the platforms are not just the pablum they are frequently presented as being, and they do sharply differentiate the parties on many vital issues. Occasionally, as in 1936, the platforms contrast dramatically and set forth sharply defined alternatives.

And yet American parties are fundamentally pragmatic and not strongly ideological (exactly as a large majority of American voters are). The European model of ideological parties simply does not and cannot fit the American experience, any more than a rigid, unitary parliamentary system could comfortably replace our nation's fluid separation-of-powers arrangement. Why? At base, it is because the American people do not favor centralized, ideologically narrow parties.[36] Survey respondents have consistently rejected proposals to realign the parties ideologically so that one party is unmistakably "liberal" and the other "conservative."[37] When given a choice between the policy coherence of ideologically distinct parties and the fuzzier centrism of the current more decentralized, ideologically diffuse parties, Americans unhesitatingly choose the latter.

At the same time, there is a public yearning for the parties to have between them "more than a dime's worth of difference" — to use George Wallace's 1968 indictment of the two-party system. The public certainly wants the parties to represent a choice,[38] though not an extreme one. And while voters hardly want to see officeholders become puppets of their parties, strictly bound to every nuance contained in the platform, there is a desire that officials be somewhat accountable to the parties that nominated them. When we asked our respondents whether they favored or opposed "having candidates be more accountable to their political party and its policies or issues," people approved by the sizeable margin of 67 percent to 26 percent.[39]

A useful possibility may be for the parties to offer more policy guidance to officeholders on a regular basis. As the brief history presented in Chapter Two suggested, such efforts must be carefully designed to avoid offending congressional sensibilities (as permanent policy councils have sometimes done) or producing ideologically extreme results that could damage a party's electoral chances (as midterm mini-conventions always threaten to do). Instead, the national Democratic party has recently provided a worthwhile model in its Democratic Policy Commission, chaired by former Utah Governor Scott Matheson. After more than a year's hearings and deliberations, the Policy Commission in 1986 issued a thoughtful and well-conceived report[40] that appealingly and perceptively presented Democratic ideas and alternatives to Reagan administration policies. The commission achieved a rare consensus for Democrats without losing all substance, and it suggested worthwhile proposals for the party's congressional leadership and presidential contenders to consider. If free television time or institutional advertising had been available, the report could have done much more to communicate to a broader audience the Democratic party's policy goals at midterm. It is unlikely that the party controlling the White House would undertake such an exercise, since the administration, in effect, articulates the policies of the president's party. But it would be a productive innovation if the party not holding the White House formed such a policy commission during each four-year cycle, and effectively used free and paid media to disseminate the product. To avoid the unpleasant side effects mentioned earlier, the commission's membership should always include a wide sampling of elected leaders from Congress, the statehouses, and the local level; should be temporary and appointed for a fixed period after the midpoint of a presidential term; should try to produce issue research useful to gestating presidential campaigns; and should have a clear mandate to arrive, where possible, at a party consensus on the most critical areas of concern.

PARTY-SPONSORED PRESIDENTIAL DEBATES

Have the parties sponsor and organize major presidential debates during both the prenomination period and the general election. Strong-party attributes:

EQUITY AND LEGITIMACY
PARTICIPATION AND EDUCATION
AUTONOMY
POLICY CAPACITY

Few electoral occasions rivet public attention as much as presidential candidate debates. The drama and excitement of such events attracts enormous media coverage, too. What better time to demonstrate the parties' legitimacy and to feature the parties in highly visible roles? The party profiles will be raised, and they will be placed in the center of the action in the public's mind while performing an invaluable public service.

Each party ought to organize separately a series of prenomination debates among its various candidates beginning prior to the first important delegate selection contest (currently the Iowa caucuses in January of the presidential election year). At the same time, in the prenomination period the parties ought to secure commitments from all contenders that they will participate in a series of party-sponsored debates during the general election. The national party chairs or their designates can make the basic arrangements (number of debates, place, time, topics, etc.) before the nominating conventions, though inevitably the nominees and their staffs will have to negotiate other debating details (such as the exact format and the identity of the questioners) in the late summer. For the first time ever, the parties have undertaken to sponsor jointly a series of general election (though not preconvention) debates in 1988.[41]

By no means should the party-orchestrated debates exclude other agents, such as the League of Women Voters (which deserves great credit for institutionalizing presidential debates since 1976), from organizing other debating forums. In the event that the parties deadlock on debate arrangements and cannot successfully manage them in any given year, the League or other groups could certainly undertake the burden. But no organization is as vital to our system as the political parties, and they ought to be given the chance to assume this great responsibility and to exploit the accompanying opportunity for enhancement in the eyes of the citizenry.

One final note: The charge can reasonably be made that the parties would seek to exclude major Independent candidates (such as John Anderson in 1980) from the debates. That may well be true, but one can argue that the public's broader interests are best served by preserving and buttressing the two-party system and the stability it has produced for our nation. This principle aside, the pressure of public and news media opinion might well force the parties to open their debates to significant Independent contenders, or an alternative forum hosted by the League might be unavoidable in such instances.

MORE UNPLEDGED, UNBOUND DELEGATES

Increase the number of unpledged and unbound delegates to the presidential nominating conventions of both parties. Strong-party attributes:

ELECTORAL APPEAL
CONFLICT CONTROL

The presidential nominating conventions of both parties need the leavening provided by the participation of large numbers of elected officials. Having stood for office, these individuals understand what it takes to satisfy an electoral majority, and most know that compromise is an essential ingredient of political success in a diverse democracy. Moreover, they frequently are well acquainted with the potential nominees and can share this experience and knowledge with the other delegates. Besides the benefit of "peer review," elected officials — generally having the respect accorded their positions — are in a position to broker a tumultuous conclave and smooth over conflict in some circumstances. Their presence at a nominating convention, given sufficient numbers, may increase the legitimacy of the convention as the electorate observes it, improve the public image of the party, and assist in the nomination of more moderate, electable candidates. In keeping the party's most crucial political decision out of the hands of ideologically extreme firebrands, the elected officials will help the party maintain credibility with "mainstream America," just as their participation draws them closer to their own political party.

All of this is widely acknowledged, yet for years — particularly in the Democratic party — the proportion of key elected officials attending the presidential convention was permitted to decline.[42] By 1980 only 14 percent of the Democratic United States senators and 15 percent of the Democratic United States representatives participated in the party's presidential convention. More appallingly, 38 percent of the Democratic National Convention delegates held no public or even party office. While the Republicans have done a much better job of recruiting elected officials for their conventions, more than a quarter (27 percent) of their 1980 delegates also held no public or party position.[43] Such figures are a sure sign of the increased representation of issue or interest-group ideologues. They also signify the reluctance of Democratic officials to become too closely identified with their national party, or to declare early preferences in the presidential contest and to compete against their party constituents for delegate slots, as the party rules then required.

Fortunately, the Democrats have taken steps to remedy this deplorable situation.[44] In 1984 a prestigious bloc of 566 delegates was created specifically for party and elected officials. By and large, these "superdelegates" were permitted to be free agents and to vote for the candidate of their choice, regardless of the results of their state's primary or caucus. This new contingent was in addition to a 1980-mandated bloc of 10 percent of each state delegation that was set aside for state and local Democratic politicians; unlike the superdelegates, however, these individuals were obligated to reflect the results of primary or caucus voting. For 1988, the Democrats expanded both categories of official representation. Seats at the convention were reserved for an additional 75 "superdelegates" and about 150 more "pledged" leaders in each state delegation. Now included among the superdelegates are all 362 members of the Democratic National Committee, 80 percent of the Democratic members of Congress, and all the Democratic governors.

Just as a result of the changes made for 1984, 62 percent of the Democratic United States senators and 66 percent of the Democrats in the House of Representatives became voting delegates or alternates — an enormous gain over 1980.[45] But more can reasonably be done. The "superdelegate" proportion of the convention total ought to be expanded from the current 15 percent to about a quarter of all delegates, perhaps by including the rest of the party's Democratic members of Congress as well as all Democratic statewide elected officials and big-city mayors. As for the Republicans, who have been more successful in attracting elected officials even without a "superdelegate" mandate,[46] it would still benefit them to broaden their convention base of public and party leaders, if only to minimize the influence of the fiercely conservative fundamentalist Christian element. And both parties would certainly gain from encouraging the states not to bind permanently any delegate (public official or otherwise) to the results of the state primary or caucus.[47] Political conditions, like the weather, can change drastically from a winter primary season to a summer convention, and delegates ought to be able to shift allegiances as circumstances warrant. Small *d* democrats have no reason for alarm at such a proposal, for it would hardly result in a return to the "smoke-filled room." A candidacy christened by party hacks in a back room at today's nationally televised conventions would be doomed from the start. Or as Leon Epstein observed in reference to the "superdelegates": "Only a most astonishingly bold group of politicians would in our time nominate someone other than the already acclaimed popular preconvention choice."[48] Rational delegates could be expected to select the popular choice save for a startling shift in the political winds after the conclusion of the primary process. All delegates should be free to shift with those winds in the interest of their party's electoral fortunes.

The eight party-initiated actions set forth in this chapter comprise an ambitious internal agenda for the American political parties to tackle, and the implementation of most or all of these proposals would go a long way toward generating the kind of partisan renewal that this study has advocated. Yet successful adoption of all these measures may prove insufficient to achieve the desired goal. The laws and practices of states and nation can and should be altered to supplement the efforts of the parties themselves, and the final chapter of this volume suggests how.

Notes

1. Frank Sorauf, *Party Politics in America* (5th ed.) (Boston: Little, Brown & Co., 1984), 427, 429, 446.
2. Leon Epstein, *Political Parties in the American Mold* (Madison: University of Wisconsin Press, 1986), 262.
3. Martin Wattenberg, *The Decline of American Political Parties, 1952–1980* (Cambridge: Harvard University Press, 1984), 51.
4. Advisory Commission on Intergovernmental Relations, *The Transformation in American Politics* (Washington, D.C.: ACIR, 1986), 232.
5. See Walter Roeltger and Hugh Winebrenner, "Politics and Political Scientists," *Public Opinion* 8 (October 1986): 41–43. Of 770 teaching faculty surveyed in the fall of 1984, just 22 percent rated the parties as "very" or "moderately" effective, compared to (for example) the 65 percent who gave high marks to the Supreme Court.
6. This list of ten is not exclusive, but certainly contains the most important items. For a somewhat different accounting of strong-party attributes, see David E. Price, *Bringing Back the Parties* (Washington, D.C.: Congressional Quarterly Press, 1984), 123.
7. Poll 1 (see Appendix).
8. Ibid. Sixty-seven percent named "an elected official," 12 percent responded "someone else" (usually a civic organization or church), and 7 percent had no opinion.
9. See, for example, Jack Dennis, "Public Support for the American Party System," in William J. Crotty, ed., *Paths to Political Reform* (Lexington, Mass.: D.C. Heath, 1980), 43.
10. See Working Partners pamphlet (Washington, D.C.: Republican National Committee, July 1986).
11. See, for example, William L. Riordon, ed., *Plunkitt of Tammany Hall* (New York: E.P. Dutton, 1963).
12. Poll 1 (see Appendix).
13. For example, suburbanites report the lowest rate (for location subgroups) of ever being "helped with a problem by a member of a political party."
14. The rates cited are for House members who actually ran for reelection; retiring congressmen are excluded from the calculation. The average reelection rate of House members who sought another term has been 92 percent since World War II. This figure takes into account both primary and general election defeats of incumbents.
15. E. E. Schattschneider, *Party Government* (New York: Rinehart, 1942), 61.

16. See Sorauf, *Party Politics in America,* 92–95.
17. Lee Byrd, "AFL-CIO to Offer Credit Cards," *Washington Post,* July 2, 1986, G10.
18. John J. Sweeney, president of the Service Employees International Union, quoted in an Associated Press dispatch, August 9, 1986.
19. See *Common Cause Magazine* 12 (October 11, 1986): 8–9.
20. Wattenberg, *The Decline of American Political Parties,* 103–105.
21. See Robert Kuttner, "Building a mass base for the party: The Dukakis Method," *Boston Globe,* September 15, 1986, 19.
22. Forty-four percent responded "not much interest"; 1 percent volunteered that they were already active; and 1 percent had no answer — Poll 1 (see Appendix). Blacks, white males, young people, and the currently divorced (perhaps looking for social rewards) were particularly inclined toward party volunteer work.
23. See Larry Sabato, *The Rise of Political Consultants: New Ways of Winning Elections* (New York: Basic Books, 1981), 200–201.
24. See also ibid., 292–294; and Sabato, "Parties, PACs, and Independent Groups" in Thomas E. Mann and Norman J. Ornstein, eds., *The American Elections of 1982* (Washington, D.C.: American Enterprise Institute, 1983), 76–86.
25. Some Republican candidates were reluctant to be tied to a then-unpopular President Reagan in 1982, when the GOP aired its "Stay the Course with Reagan" and "Give the Guy a Chance" ads in the midst of a severe recession. See Sabato, "Parties, PACs, and Independent Groups," 78–79.
26. Sabato, *The Rise of Political Consultants,* 293, 300–301 n 73.
27. See ibid., 157–158, for a Michigan State Republican party example.
28. Ibid., 195–197.
29. Sabato, "Parties, PACs, and Independent Groups," 85.
30. Dennis, "Public Support for the American Party System," 49–51.
31. Wattenberg, *The Decline of American Political Parties,* 50–51.
32. Cited in Martin Wattenberg, "Do Voters Really Care About Political Parties Anymore? A Response to Craig," a paper delivered at the annual meeting of the American Political Science Association, Washington, D.C., August 30–September 2, 1986, 21. Eight percent had no opinion.
33. Wattenberg, *The Decline of American Political Parties,* 126–127.
34. Tom Brokaw, "In Defense of TV News," *U.S. News & World Report,* January 13, 1986, 79.
35. Committee on Political Parties of the American Political Science Association, *Toward a More Responsible Two-Party System* (New York: Rinehart, 1950).
36. Dennis, "Public Support for the American Party System," 55–57.
37. Ibid.
38. Ibid., 44.
39. Poll 1 (see Appendix). Seven percent had no opinion. Women, blacks, and Democrats were heavily in favor, while white men and Independents were less enthusiastic (though still approving).
40. See the Democratic Policy Commission, "New Choices in a Changing

America" (Washington, D.C.: Democratic National Committee, September 1986).

41. In preparation for the 1988 general election, the two parties set up a joint tax-exempt foundation to make arrangements for party-sponsored presidential and vice-presidential debates in the autumn. See David S. Broder, "Party Run Debates," *Washington Post,* January 25, 1987, B7. See also Robert E. Hunter, ed., "Electing the President: A Program for Reform," report of the Commission on National Elections (Washington, D.C.: CSIS, Georgetown University, April 1986) 6–7, 12. This Commission made a similar recommendation to my own.
42. Nelson Polsby, *Consequences of Party Reform* (New York: Oxford University Press, 1983), 114.
43. Price, *Bringing Back the Parties,* 201–202.
44. See *Congressional Quarterly Weekly* 44 (November 29, 1986): 2987.
45. Also, 83 percent of the Democratic governors took part in the 1984 Democratic National Convention, compared to 76 percent in 1980.
46. The GOP rules expressly forbid automatic delegates by virtue of holding public office.
47. There is now no national party rule binding delegates to the primary/caucus choice (though the Republicans had one in 1976 and the Democrats did so in 1980). But most primary states still bind their delegates to the election outcome. See Price, *Bringing Back the Parties,* 217–218. On the general subject of presidential nomination reforms, see James W. Ceaser, *Reforming the Reforms: A Critical Analysis of the Presidential Selection Process* (Cambridge, Mass.: Ballinger, 1982).
48. Epstein, *Political Parties in the American Mold,* 107.

CHAPTER SEVEN

Toward Party Renewal, American Style Part II

Parties are *the* central intermediate and intermediary structure between society and government. — *Giovanni Sartori*[1]

THERE ARE FEW SOCIETIES ON EARTH whose diversity and complexity rival that of the United States. If political parties serve as the "central intermediary" wherever they exist, then their job is both more requisite and more exacting in an unbridled democracy such as the United States that teems with different peoples and beliefs. As the introductory chapter explained, the American people and their government have a stake in well-functioning strong parties, therefore, the people, acting through their government, should assist the parties in the effort to reform, renew, and advance.

Undoubtedly, the party-initiated actions set forth in Chapter Six comprise the most hopeful part of my agenda for party renewal since the political parties need nothing but their own resolve to accomplish them. But there are other changes that require the cooperation of government, and occasionally private enterprise and the public directly. It is to this more difficult yet still essential part of the agenda that I now turn.

An Agenda for Party Renewal: Government-Assisted Reforms

DEREGULATION OF PARTIES

Deregulate the parties and permit them to devise their own rules of operation to the greatest extent possible. Strong-party attributes:

EQUITY AND LEGITIMACY
CONFLICT CONTROL
AUTONOMY
INCENTIVES

Leon Epstein uses the phrase "public utilities" to describe the treatment of parties under state law since the state exercises governmental regulatory control without ownership and management of the organization — much as telephone and electric companies are treated in the United States.[2] Granted, some state control of parties is both necessary and desirable; for example, as Gerald Pomper points out, state statutes on ballot access help to assure the minority party continuity and legitimacy even in the face of minimal electoral success.[3] And as Malcolm Jewell has noted, only judicial regulation and congressional intervention eliminated some of the odious discriminatory practices of Democratic parties in the South.[4] Still, under the American system, political parties are primarily private associations, and despite their public responsibilities they should be accorded unbegrudgingly their right of free association as guaranteed by the First and Fourteenth Amendments to the Constitution. Within the broadest possible state legal framework — designed only to insure that equality and other fundamental democratic values are not violated — the parties ought to be permitted to set up their own structures and rules of operation as they see fit. After all, extensive state regulation of parties began mainly as a reaction to the excesses of America's post-Civil War, boss-controlled parties.[5] Conditions today are completely changed, and in the post-Tammany media age, parties will design open, fair, and inclusive procedures because it is in their own interests to do so; any significant moves that smack of bossism are sure to draw ire from the news media and retribution from the voters.

In this era when "less government" is the premiere political man-

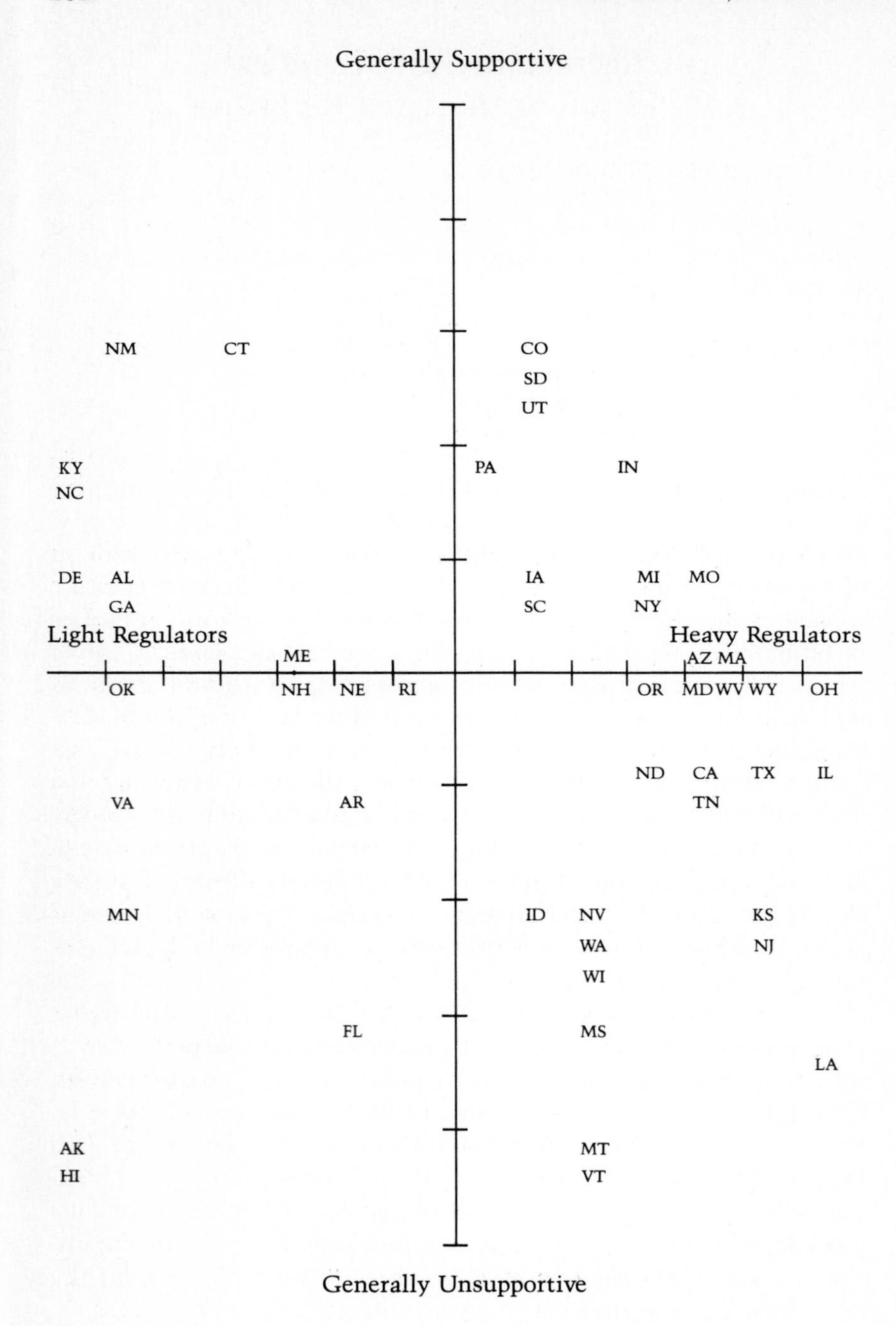

FIGURE 7.1 Party Regulation and Support in the States

SUMMARY STATE REGULATION INDEX

	LIGHT REGULATORS	MODERATE REGULATORS	HEAVY REGULATORS	TOTALS
GENERALLY SUPPORTIVE	28% (4)	23% (4)	5% (1)	(9)
MODERATELY SUPPORTIVE	50% (7)	30% (5)	79% (15)	(27)
GENERALLY UNSUPPORTIVE	22% (3)	47% (8)	16% (3)	(14)
TOTALS	(14)	(17)	(19)	100% (50)

SOURCE: Advisory Commission on Intergovernmental Relations, *The Transformation in American Politics* (Washington, D.C.: ACIR, 1986), 158–159.

tra, it is appalling to discover how overregulated the parties are in most states. In fact, the United States has the dubious distinction of hosting the most governmentally fettered parties in the democratic world.[6] Sometimes, the parties are treated little better, or worse, than any garden-variety political action committee or special interest group. Consider, for instance, that only five of the fifty states (Alaska, Delaware, Hawaii, Kentucky, and North Carolina) do not dictate crucial aspects of the parties' internal organizational structure, composition, or operating procedures. Most states tell the parties how to elect their governmental bodies, who may or may not serve on them, where and when they must hold meetings, and/or precisely how the meetings are to be conducted. A large majority of the states also regulate all local party committees as extensively as the statewide groups.[7]

Figure 7.1, compiled by the Advisory Commission on Intergovernmental Relations, indicates how mistrustful and unsupportive of the parties most states are. States are rated on two scales: a "support" index, based on whether states have enacted certain laws (such as voter registration by party and provision of a "straight-party ticket" lever in the voting booth) that are regarded as helpful to the development of strong parties, and a "regulation" index, based on the degree to which states regulate their parties' structures and operation. Only fourteen states can be classified as light party regulators, and only nine as having created a supportive legal environment for their parties. Just four states (Connecticut, Kentucky, New Mexico, and North Carolina) can be regarded as both supportive and light regulators of political parties. Regrettably, as the graph indicates, the largest grouping of states (in the lower right quadrant) not only regulates state and local party organizations heavily but simultaneously fails to create a legal environment that nurtures healthy parties.

States in a mood to clear statutory deadwood ought to start with their political party laws. The parties ought to be left completely free to organize and conduct themselves in any reasonable manner without state interference. In addition to deregulating the parties, the states ought to pass a number of measures (to be discussed in subsequent sections) to assist parties. Even simple allowances can be of enormous help. A number of states currently restrict the parties' access to voter registration lists.[8] This nonsensical regulation inhibits the parties' mobilization of supporters, raising of revenue, and communication with the voters. Finally, Congress should resist all impulses to federalize party rule-making in the presidential nominating process. Proposals for mandated national and regional presidential primaries, for instance, represent an unwarranted invasion and usurpation of state party prerogatives in this vital arena.

There would normally be little cause for optimism that states would suddenly cede regulatory authority back to the parties, save for a potentially momentous Supreme Court decision in late 1986.[9] By a 5-to-4 vote, the Court ruled in *Tashjian v. Republican Party of Connecticut* that states may not require political parties to hold "closed" primary elections (where only registered party members may vote). Such laws,[10] said the Court, unconstitutionally burden the parties' First Amendment freedom of association rights. Justice Thurgood Marshall, writing for the majority, explained that while the Constitution grants states the power to prescribe the "times, places, and manner" of holding elections, "This authority does not extinguish the state's responsibility to observe the limits established by the First Amendment rights of the state's citizens." Connecticut's badly outnumbered Republican party had wanted to allow registered Independents to vote in its primary in an attempt to broaden its base, but the GOP had been stymied by a Democratic legislature and governor intent on denying them that opportunity.

Other recent decisions regarding California and Massachusetts laws,[11] while not as significant as *Tashjian*, have clearly put the states on the defensive in justifying regulation of political parties. Indeed, Jerome Mileur believes the judicial balance, once weighted heavily in favor of state authority in disputes with parties, has now shifted decidedly in favor of the parties.[12] States are now being required both to show a compelling need anytime a party's associational rights are restricted and to prove that any restrictions are narrowly drawn. Such a substantial burden may well help parties to regain the prerogatives they have lost over the past one hundred years, and the parties should be aggressive in seeking to apply *Tashjian* to other situations.

Incidentally, the Connecticut case is a double-edged sword for party advocates. While they joyously welcome the judicial recognition of party rights, they note with dismay that Connecticut Republicans are using their newfound grant of authority to open a "closed" primary, diluting their own partisans' control over the nominating process. The dilemma of this case was best captured by Gerald Benjamin: "Should parties be allowed to do as they wish, or should they be required to do what's good for them?"[13] The danger in deregulation is that the political equivalent of Gresham's law might hold true, with "bad" nominating practices (e.g., open primaries) driving out "good" ones (e.g., closed primaries). There are risks involved, certainly, but they are probably worth taking. Connecticut Republicans may not be acting in the best interests of their party, but that is properly their determination. On the whole, if deregulated, I believe that parties will make the right decisions most of the time, will learn and adjust from their mistakes, and will be much the stronger for it all.

MORE CONVENTIONS AND CAUCUSES, FEWER PRIMARIES

Leave the choice of nominating method to the parties, which should choose to hold more caucuses and conventions and fewer primaries. If primaries must be held, preprimary endorsing conventions should be convened, and the preference should be for "closed" party primaries, not "open," "blanket," or "nonpartisan" ones. In states that conduct presidential primaries, select convention delegates in separate party caucuses following "beauty contest" primaries. Strong-party attributes:

ELECTORAL APPEAL
PARTICIPATION
ACCOUNTABILITY
CONFLICT CONTROL
AUTONOMY

A political scientist favoring stronger parties finds it easy to criticize popular primaries and to wax eloquent about the merits of caucuses and conventions as a preferred nominating method. Primaries may attract far more participants, but this quantity is more than matched by the quality of caucus participation. Compared to unenlightening minutes spent at the primary polls, caucus attendees spend several hours or more learning about politics and the party, listening to speeches by candidates or their representatives, and taking cues from party leaders and elected officials. While primaries measure only "first choices," conventions and caucuses permit brokering and compromise that can result in the nomination of a "second choice" acceptable to most; thus conventions can often dampen factionalism and promote party unity where primaries can exacerbate the divisions.[14] Similarly, a convention can engineer the nomination of a "balanced slate" of candidates representing all the party's major constituency groups; such a slate can emerge only by fortunate accident in a primary. Conventions and caucuses also provide for a "peer review" of candidates by other elected officials; are useful for party recruiting of volunteers and funds; generally cost less for the candidates than primary elections; and keep candidates and officeholders tied more closely to their party by requiring them first to woo party regulars before paying their attentions to the general electorate. If these advantages are not enough, caucuses and conventions offer an important incentive for involvement in the party: a major voice in the selection of potential governors, senators, and presidents. And by generally limiting participation to party loyalists, they greatly reduce cross-party voter raiding (voters of one party participating in the primary of the other party, presumably in some cases to choose the weakest nominee, but meddling, whatever the motive), a problem that frequently plagues primaries. Finally, one could also contend that caucuses and conventions, since they are normally limited to relatively informed partisans with a keen interest in politics, limit the power of the news media and of wealthy candidates whose money and advertising can sometimes sway the votes of the less involved.

With all of these wonderful arguments to recommend caucuses and conventions, why is it that the vast majority of nominations are made by primary? The amusing explanation may be that no one in authority listens to political scientists, but the more immediate cause is the popular affection for pure democracy. As the late Tom McCall, former governor of Oregon, once put it: "The people, if you gave them their choice, would like to elect everything clear down to dogcatcher."[15] The polls conducted for this study certainly confirm his observation. I frankly tried to construct a survey question that might attract a sizeable number of voters to the caucus standard. Since the terms *caucus* and *convention* are associated with *boss control* in the public's mind, I substituted "open meetings of party activists." (The word *open* in itself usually prompts higher approval from a "freedom of information"–conscious electorate.) And I emphasized that *party* candidates were being nominated, in the hope that respondents might make the connection between purpose and power. But it was for naught. To the question, "Would you favor or oppose having a party's candidates for office chosen in open meetings of party activists rather than by primary elections?" the population sample gave a resounding no, 67 percent to 27 percent.[16] (Only blacks indicated anything close to approval,[17] perhaps because of their group's recent successes in packing some Democratic presidential caucuses and securing disproportionate influence over the choice of the party nominee.) Other polls show support for primaries is even more lopsided. Recent surveys in Arkansas and Oklahoma, two presidential caucus states, indicated that by margins of 67 percent to 14 percent in Oklahoma and 70 percent to 13 percent in Arkansas, citizens wanted the parties to switch to primaries.[18] Some national surveys have even shown that a large majority want to eliminate the party presidential nominating conventions in favor of a national primary election to select presidential and vice-presidential nominees.[19]

There are a couple of supplementary reasons for the predominance of primaries today. In the Democratic party complicated new party rules on the choice of presidential convention delegates led many party leaders to push for primaries as the simplest method of selection and the one least open to challenge. Primaries also offered a way to separate the tumultuous presidential process from the conduct of other party business.[20] Then, too, the news media played a role by giving inordinate coverage to primaries and all but ignoring many state presidential caucuses.[21] Implicit in the news media's coverage was their view of primaries as open, democratic, and conflict oriented, and caucuses as closed, suspiciously party dominated, and sometimes consensual in nature.[22] For both the news media and the people, therefore, the primary is "an institutionalized means for pursuing [candidate-centered] politics in a civic culture that is broadly hostile to party organizational control."[23]

The state legislatures have, by and large, given the people what they wanted, though there are important variations. Not a single state relies completely on the convention system of nomination, though Virginia comes closest.[24] Even states such as Connecticut, Indiana, and New York that held out for many years against the primary tide have now been swept along. A few states (Alabama, Georgia, South Carolina, and Virginia) at least permit each state party to choose the method of nomination every year, though primaries, regrettably, are usually selected by the party leaders in all the states except Virginia. In four states (Colorado, Connecticut, New York, and Utah) party conventions are held for some offices but pick the nominee only if a candidate achieves a predetermined, extraordinary proportion of the delegate votes (of which more later). In Indiana, Iowa, Michigan, and South Dakota, at least a few statewide officials can be selected by convention, sometimes under special circumstances (such as a primary vote where no candidate secured 40 percent). In the remaining thirty-eight states all statewide offices are nominated by primary.[25]

Not only do most states nominate almost all offices by primary, but the type of primary frequently employed is not conducive to building strong parties. Twenty-four states use "open" primaries,[26] whereby voters may participate in either party's primary, regardless of their partisan affiliation. In nine of these states, the voter is not even forced to divulge in which party's primary he or she is choosing to cast a ballot; the selection is made in secret. In three other states the antiparty conditions of primary voting are still worse. Alaska and Washington have established a "blanket" or "free-love" primary where people can simultaneously vote in both Democratic and Republican primaries for different offices. Worst of all is Louisiana whose primary is completely "nonpartisan"; all Democratic and Republican candidates are listed together on the same ballot, with the general election "runoff" (assuming no primary candidate secures an outright majority) sometimes being held between candidates of the *same* party (usually, both Democrats). Unfortunately, the national Democratic party, in an attempt to accommodate Wisconsin's open presidential primary, has recently relaxed its rule limiting primary and caucus participation to Democrats only.[27] (Now "all those who wish to participate as Democrats" are included.) "Closed" primaries limited to registered party voters are obviously preferable, if strong parties are the goal, since there is greater incentive and reward for a voter's identification with a party, and the party itself is guaranteed that its nominees truly represent its constituency. Evidence has also been offered by Malcolm Jewell to suggest that states requiring closed primaries have higher party identification levels among the public.[28] In other words, voters who are encouraged to make a real choice between parties in the registration and primary voting processes are more inclined to admit allegiance to a party.

There is one bright spot on the presidential nominating front. The Democratic party's 1982–1983 Commission on Presidential Nomination, chaired by then-Governor Jim Hunt of North Carolina, encouraged states and territories to employ caucuses instead of primaries where possible. Partly in response, the number of Democratic primaries in 1984 fell to 24 from 33 in 1980, and the caucus total rose from 18 to 27. (Similar changes occurred on the GOP side.)[29] This was a dramatic reversal of the trend toward presidential primaries that had been observed since 1968 (when only 17 Democratic and 16 Republican primaries had been held). The gain in caucus states recorded in 1984 was expected to hold steady in 1988.

In the best of all party worlds, presidential primaries would either be eliminated in favor of caucuses or would be reduced to "beauty contests," nonbinding affairs held before separate caucuses as an indication of popular sentiment for caucus participants to consider. The idea of eliminating primaries or making them purely advisory is, of course, a pipe dream. Though the United States is almost alone among the world's democracies in insisting upon mass participation in party nominations as well as general elections, Americans prefer it that way. They have never accepted E. E. Schattschneider's assertion that "democracy is not to be found *in* the parties but *between* the parties."[30] They have not cared that, as Austin Ranney writes, "the direct primary has not only eliminated boss control of nominations but party control as well."[31] Recognizing popular sentiment, party leaders often have not exercised their right to hold a caucus even where the state properly cedes to the party committees at each level (statewide, congressional district, and local) the option of selecting the nominating method they desire each year.

So, reluctantly conceding the inevitable, if primaries must be the preferred method of nomination, then at least they should be closed party affairs; open primaries are inimical to strong parties, and blanket and nonpartisan arrangements are particularly offensive. And if primaries are to select all the individuals who will bear the party standard, then the parties ought to be allowed, and encouraged, to bestow preprimary endorsements at state, district, and local conventions. Ideally, the endorsed candidates should be designated as such on the primary ballot as a useful guide to voters, and the candidates should be listed in order of finish at the convention since there is probably some slight electoral advantage to being first on the ballot. Further, candidates' access to the ballot should be restricted to those who can muster at least 20 percent support among the convention delegates. If any candidate is able to muster an extraordinary majority of delegates (say, 70 percent), he or she should be declared the nominee and no primary should be held.[32]

The advantages of this system are many, and similar in many respects to the enticing qualities of caucuses and conventions generally. Potential and incumbent officeholders must campaign first among party loyalists, thus forcing the candidates to develop a rationale for carrying the party standard as well as the office title. The party's power and legitimacy are augmented considerably as a result, and politically interested citizens are given a greater incentive to become involved in the party. All primary voters, involved or not, are handed a valuable voting cue — a kind of "personnel review" by the candidates' peers. Preprimary endorsements seem to help a party manage disputes and resolve conflicts in a more controlled environment than an open primary, thereby helping to reduce party fragmentation.[33] And those who are concerned about candidates "buying" elections should also favor this reform. Money is of less value in this setting because participants are normally well informed and less subject to easy manipulation by media advertisements; a candidate's qualifications, proposals, and general election chances tend to weigh more heavily with savvy party activists than with average voters.

At present, eight states (Colorado, Connecticut, Delaware, New Mexico, New York, North Dakota, Rhode Island, and Utah) require or formally allow parties to make preprimary endorsements. Only two states (California[34] and Florida) prohibit this sort of party activity. In the remaining forty states, no law recognizes, requires, or prohibits endorsements. Parties in eight of these states (Illinois, Indiana, Massachusetts, Michigan, Minnesota, Ohio, Pennsylvania, and Wisconsin) make informal preprimary endorsements at least some of the time. They ought to do it regularly and for all state and local offices, as should both parties in the other states not currently taking advantage of this permissive — and unusually favorable — regulatory stance on the part of state legislatures.

There are other ways primaries can be made more palatable for political parties. One ingenious state party chairman, the GOP's

E. Spencer Abraham of Michigan, devised one in preparation for the 1988 presidential contest.[35] Fully two years ahead of 1988, Abraham piggybacked the selection of presidential precinct delegates onto Michigan's August 1986 statewide office primary, and he did it in a most unusual fashion. Instead of the normal 3,000 or so precinct delegates to a Michigan presidential nominating convention, Abraham created about 13,500 slots, and decreed that all of them would be filled in the primary.[36] Each potential delegate was required to secure a petition signed by at least 15 of his precinct neighbors (a very useful list for the party to have), and the presidential candidates were forced to spend large amounts of time and money recruiting potential delegates (who not incidentally would also prove to be an invaluable resource for the party organization). Moreover, each congressional district in the state was apportioned the same number of delegates, so that winning a majority of delegates in the heavily black, lightly Republican Detroit First District was as crucial as a victory in any solidly GOP congressional district in suburban Detroit. Therefore, candidates were pushed into unfamiliar party territory to recruit supporters and thereby to broaden the base of the party as well as serve their own interests. No one wants to see the presidential nominating process extended this far in advance of the actual election, but Abraham's basic idea to make the presidential candidates work for the party is a clever one worthy of emulation in election-year contests.

Another attribute that highly recommends the Abraham scheme is its emphasis on increased participation. The danger today in both primaries and caucuses is that such a small proportion of eligible voters actually participate that the results easily can be skewed by disproportionate turnouts of one voting bloc or interest group. This occurrence is far from rare, and it happened even in the Michigan case, where fundamentalist Christians supporting television evangelist Pat Robertson boosted their candidate to a virtual tie with Vice President George Bush in a moderate state where Bush has always enjoyed broad support.[37] Such unrepresentative results may become more commonplace if voting turnout continues to drop. Already, only about 30 percent of voting-age adults cast a ballot in all the primary states and both parties taken together, and in caucus states turnout is usually well below 10 percent.[38] Interestingly, caucuses seem to attract the same types of voters to participate as primaries do and for the most part result in similar presidential candidate choices,[39] suggesting that the caucuses' much lower turnout rate makes them no more unrepresentative of partisan identifiers than primaries. Still, saying that caucuses are no worse than primaries is a weak defense, and no defense at all against the argument that declining voter turnout and diminishing party participation make both primaries and caucuses ripe for manipulation by emotionally charged, unrepresentative voting blocs and groups. Obviously, the solution is to increase voter participation in primaries and caucuses by attracting a more representative cross-section of voters to the parties themselves, using devices such as the proposals (precinct ombudsman, provision of party services, etc.) made earlier in this chapter.

PUBLIC FINANCING PROVISIONS

Ideally, reestablish at least a 50 percent federal tax credit for small contributions to parties, and preferably make it a 100 percent credit. If the federal government offers a 50 percent credit, states with an income tax should also offer a 50 percent credit to be applied toward state taxes. Alternatively, allow citizens to make small contributions to parties by means of an "add-on" deduction from tax refunds on annual federal and state income tax forms. Strong-party attributes:

PARTICIPATION AND EDUCATION
RESOURCES
CANDIDATE ASSISTANCE

Before landmark tax reform legislation was passed in 1986, federal taxpayers were granted a 50 percent tax credit for all contributions to candidates, PACs, parties, and political committees of up to $50 for an individual and $100 on a joint return. Unfortunately this credit was one of those eliminated in the tax revision, and currently there is no credit for political gifts. It will not come as a surprise to this volume's readers if I recommend the restoration of the credit not only to the 50 percent level, but all the way to 100 percent. Such a move would clearly encourage small donations that have few if any real strings attached; the parties not only would remain unencumbered by the perceived debts that come with large contributions, but both parties would have an exceptionally valuable tool to use in expanding their donor and membership base.[40] This would be all the more so if income-taxing states agreed to offer a similar 50 percent credit if the federal government refused to give more than

50 percent; taxpayers in these 43 states[41] would, in effect, get a 100 percent credit.[42]

Realistically, in an era when gigantic budget deficits threaten even essential existing programs, the prospects of securing either a 50 percent or 100 percent credit at the federal level do not appear promising. Perhaps a few of the wealthier states could establish a full or partial credit, but even there a gambling man might fear to tread. Similarly, grandiose schemes for full public financing of either parties or candidates are unlikely to win passage. There is considerable evidence of rather substantial public hostility to the idea of providing public officials with taxpayer-funded reelection treasuries to supplement their generous taxpayer-financed salaries and perquisites.[43] Beyond that, campaign financing is not a high priority for most voters concerned about economic conditions, health care, and other matters. In one of the surveys taken for this study, a series of spending alternatives was posed to respondents, forcing them to make the same choices often faced by policymakers. Table 7.1 presents four of these pairs of alternatives. Literally everything from bridge repairs and missile defense systems to health care and budget balancing was rated far more important than public financing of political campaigns. Notice that we attempted to "sweeten" the public financing alternative by including the public's most consistently favored campaign reform — a limit on candidate spending — but it had little apparent effect. Moreover, when we separately asked respondents whether they would favor or oppose "giving people a full tax credit for contributing money to a political party," a solid majority of 55 percent to 39 percent disapproved. (Five percent had no opinion.) This is somewhat surprising since the public is usually inclined to approve tax credits that might provide some benefit to it. Respondents' negative reactions might signify concern about the budget deficit or, more likely, estrangement from political parties.

Luckily, there is another option that could win both public and legislative favor: a tax "add-on" that permits a citizen to channel a few dollars of his income tax refund to the party of his or her choice. Both parties would clearly gain funds but the budget deficit would be none the worse for it. The voluntary nature of this self-imposed tax will appeal to conservatives and Republicans, while the ready cash will draw the assent of money-starved Democrats and liberals. According to our poll, the public sees the merits of the idea[44] and approves by a solid majority. In its ideal form, the federal 1040 (short and long form) and every annual income tax form on the state level

TABLE 7.1 Public Campaign Financing and Voter Spending Preferences

QUESTION: "As you may know, the federal government faces a large budget deficit. That means *choices* have to be made about where government money will be spent. If you had the choice, which of these would you prefer government spend its money on?"

SELECTED ALTERNATIVES[a]	FAVORING PERCENTAGE[b]
A. Making airports, airlines, roads, and bridges safer	18
— OR —	
Regulating hospitals, nursing homes, and the costs of health care	69
B. Making airports, airlines, roads, and bridges safer	32
— OR —	
Reducing the budget deficit to eventually balance the budget	56
C. Making airports, airlines, roads, and bridges safer	55
— OR —	
Building a new advanced missile system to stop enemy attacks	31
D. Making airports, airlines, roads, and bridges safer	67
— OR —	
Public financing of political campaigns for federal offices — and limiting total spending by candidates	25

SOURCE: Poll 3 (see Appendix).

[a]These four alternatives were selected from eight pairings asked in the survey. They were chosen because all four contained the "making airports, airlines, roads, and bridges safer" alternative, and thus could be viewed comparatively. Note that in alternatives A and D above, the "making airports, etc. safer" alternative was actually asked second; it is listed first in this table for easy comparison.

[b]Totals for each pair of alternatives do not add to 100 percent since "don't know" and two volunteered responses ("both," "neither") are not listed in the table.

should include an add-on provision that gives a taxpayer the opportunity to check off a gift of $2, $5, $10, $25, $50, or $100 to the party he or she designates.

Will any significant number of taxpayers give money using this device? Five states (California, Maine, Massachusetts, Montana, and Virginia) currently have some form of add-on. The Virginia experience is somewhat typical, with only about 2.2 percent of all eligible taxpayers contributing in recent years, though even this tiny proportion has provided several hundred thousand dollars cumulatively to the parties. (Actually, Virginia is a little on the low side compared to other states; participation rates in all add-on plans combined have averaged about 4 percent.)[45] While giving even small amounts to the political parties will doubtless never become the rage among beleaguered taxpayers anticipating a refund, it is likely that the presently miniscule percentage of participation could be substantially augmented by a joint two-party educational advertising campaign undertaken at tax time. The campaign might profitably be keyed to patriotic themes, urging citizens to demonstrate their civic commitment in this small but crucial way. If afforded the add-on's superb opportunity for financial advancement by the federal and state governments, the parties certainly must take full advantage and capitalize on this golden entry on the tax forms. Such a cost-free reform should be among the highest priorities of both national parties and all state parties where an add-on does not now exist.

It ought to be mentioned here that the universe of potential contributors to the parties, while not enormous, is often underestimated. As the RNC and now the DNC have demonstrated with direct mail, millions of Americans are willing to give small and medium-size amounts to parties, if the right stimulus is applied. In one of our surveys, nearly half of the respondents (48 percent) indicated they had contributed money at least once to a political campaign, and 19 percent of these contributors claimed to have donated more than $100 in a single year.[46] Undoubtedly there is some "good citizen" overreporting in these figures, or perhaps some are counting their $1 check-off to the presidential Federal Election Campaign Fund on the 1040 form, but even halving these figures leaves a surprisingly substantial total. In any given year, of course, the proportion of people making a contribution is much less; during presidential years, it has been measured at between 8 and 13.5 percent; though only about 4 percent gave to the parties rather than (or as well as) candidates or PACs.[47] The more parties can develop closer personal contact with their partisans, and the more they can promote the funding options at their disposal, the higher will be their yield. The fundraising potential is great for creative and energetic parties with the ability to cultivate grassroots loyalty. An "add-on" provision — possibly the only campaign finance reform to which no one can have serious objection and thus the most feasible proposal on the table — would be one way for parties to fulfill their financial potential.

A PARTY ROLE IN PUBLIC FINANCING

Channel money raised in public financing schemes through the parties, permitting them to keep a portion for party building and administrative expenses. Annually allocate a portion of the Federal Election Campaign Fund to the national parties. Strong-party attributes:

PARTICIPATION AND EDUCATION
ACCOUNTABILITY
RESOURCES
INCENTIVES
CANDIDATE ASSISTANCE

It may be that one day, despite public financing's unpopularity, a Democratic Congress and a Democratic president will enact and sign a bill establishing publicly funded congressional elections. Solid Democratic control does not guarantee such an occurrence; President Carter and the heavily Democratic Congress of his term failed to produce public financing in the late 1970s. But Democratic control is probably a precondition of reform given the nearly solid conservative GOP opposition to public financing and the current Republican fundraising edge that would be partially neutralized by public funding. If public financing does come to pass, the taxpayer dollars should be channeled through the state parties, with some reasonable proportion of the funds (perhaps 10–20 percent) retained by the parties for their own administrative expenses and party-building tasks.[48] For instance, the party might want to spend the public money by undertaking a voter contact (canvassing) program that would strengthen the party's base while benefiting all party candidates. A get-out-the-vote effort on election day would be another sensible choice, as would the ombudsman, mobile unit, and institutional advertising programs described earlier.

From the standpoint of the party, it would also be advantageous if parties were given some discretion in allocating the public monies to their congressional candidates. Obviously, safe incumbents in one-party districts need far less than candidates in two-party marginal districts. Every party candidate should be guaranteed a "floor" amount, certainly, but the parties should have the authority, within reason, to concentrate resources where they can do the most good. Of course, it is difficult to imagine that an incumbent member of Congress — who must pass any public financing plan — would ever permit this degree of discretion to be enjoyed by the parties. After all, the parties conceivably could use this power to discipline a recalcitrant lawmaker or to transfer elsewhere some of the money he or she expected to get. Also, this extra increment of cash would be far more useful to the money-starved Democrats than to the well heeled Republicans, a fact that may make GOP legislators unreceptive to the idea.

Moreover, there are real risks for both parties in public financing schemes. It is at least as likely that Congress will choose to bypass the parties entirely, giving the money directly to candidates. Thus infused with a new source of money unconnected to the parties, nominees will be even more independent of their parties than they are now; moreover, the parties will receive no financial bonus for their own programs. At the other extreme, if the parties themselves were generously funded, it is possible that some state parties would lazily permit themselves to become overly dependent on an effortless source of funds, allowing their own grassroots fundraising apparatus to atrophy. There have been occasional reports of this distressing phenomenon at the state level when public subsidies were provided to the parties.[49]

On the whole, though, the states' experiences in public financing offer some hope.[50] Twenty-one states have established public financing schemes, and slightly more than half funnel the money through the parties.[51] Almost all of the public-finance states that utilize the parties as conduits allow them to use portions for their own administrative expenses. In North Carolina, about a quarter of the operating revenue of both major parties is provided by public funds, for example, and in a number of states the money has been well spent by parties on in-kind services to candidates modeled after the national parties' successful programs.[52] Iowa gives its parties more leeway than perhaps any other state, with the state central committees permitted to spend funds on any legitimate campaign purpose, from media advertising to staff salaries and expenses for candidates and their aides. Further, Iowa and a majority of the party-financing states allow the state central committees at least some discretion in distributing tax dollars to their nominees — an arrangement that magnifies the influence that party leaders can exert over their candidates.

Any public financing scheme at the federal level would certainly do well to follow the example set by some of the states. The Congress could make a useful start by providing the national parties with an untapped source of revenue requiring no enlargement of the deficit or new taxes. The Federal Election Campaign Fund — the repository for the federal $1 income tax check-off contributions — annually receives somewhere between $30 million and $40 million.[53] The only major disbursements presently made are to qualifying presidential candidates and the parties to pay for their presidential nominating conventions, and this regularly leaves the Fund with a sizeable surplus. Even after the bills from the 1984 presidential contest substantially drained the Fund, for example, there was a surplus of almost $93 million.[54] (Just a year later at the end of 1985 the surplus had grown to almost $126 million.)[55] It would not greatly tax the fund if $5 million per year (plus an annual cost-of-living adjustment) were provided to each of the national party committees to use for party-building purposes and administrative expenses.

FREE TELEVISION AND RADIO TIME

Require all television and radio stations to make available to each major state and national political party an hour of free time every calendar year, in five-minute, sixty-second, and thirty-second advertising segments with at least half the allocations in prime time. In the absence of such a mandate, at least require stations to charge parties their lowest unit rates and to guarantee that at least some substantial, choice time will be made available for purchase. Strong-party attributes:

PARTICIPATION AND EDUCATION
RESOURCES
POLICY CAPACITY
INCENTIVES
CANDIDATE ASSISTANCE

It is easy to become outraged when reviewing the political time policies of America's broadcast industry. No network and virtually no television and radio station offer any free advertising time to political candidates or parties. Media advertising costs are consuming an increasing portion of all candidates' budgets, and the commercial spot charges have risen far more quickly than the rate of inflation.[56] Yet consider that the public, not the stations, owns the airwaves; we merely lease those airwaves for limited durations to the station proprietors. Second, it is hardly that the station owners cannot afford the sacrifice of an hour or two of advertising revenue. American commercial television and radio stations had gross revenues in 1986 of about $27 billion. One industry executive noted recently that commercial television stations are among the most lucrative enterprises in the free world with collective profits exceeding even the oil companies; as he put it, "Having a license to operate a commercial TV station in this country is like receiving the government's permission to print money."[57] In light of these two facts, the broadcasting industry's attitude is nothing short of galling. As a regular practice, they charge political parties full, undiscounted rates — no free time and not even the lowest unit rate (the lowest charge for the same class and amount of time given the station's best customers) that Congress required the stations to make available to political candidates. Moreover, both political parties have reported great difficulty in getting many stations to sell them time at all, especially during peak, prime-time periods.[58] The stations are far more interested in pleasing their preferred business customers who regularly fill their schedule and coffers with hamburger, toilet paper, and deodorant spots. Congress in 1970 mandated not only the lowest unit rate rule for candidates but also forced stations to guarantee reasonable advertising time access to all candidates for federal office as a condition of license renewal. Given the need for increased emphasis on party institutional advertising, Congress needs to apply these mandates to the political parties as well.

Despite the understandable (if cowardly) fear of 535 media-addicted politicians to offend the owners of television and radio stations, Congress ought to go much further. Presently, the United States is the only major democracy in the industrialized world that does not allow the public to reclaim a little of its own air time for the most vital rituals (elections) and instruments (the parties) of democracy. As a condition of license renewal, and without providing any tax credits or other taxpayer-financed subsidies to an already wealthy industry, every television and radio station should be required to make available an hour of free time every year to each of the two major national parties *and* each of the state party organizations in the station's primary viewing or listening area. The time should be granted in five-minute, sixty-second, and thirty-second spots. (Like it or not, Americans prefer their political advertisements to be short and sweet; the "tune-out" factor, i.e., channel switching, is devastating for political commercials that are lengthier than five minutes.)[59] The parties should also be offered a wide variety of time slots, with at least half the allocations in weekday evening prime time. (It would be very much in character for television stations to attempt to bury the spots in all-night movies and Sunday afternoon garden shows.)

The broadcasting industry ferociously fights proposals such as this one, of course. One of their favorite arguments is that many metropolitan stations' media markets stretch over dozens of congressional districts, while others incorporate only one or a few. A free time requirement, they insist, would unfairly deluge the metropolitan stations with demands for free time, that, if met, would virtually eliminate other commercial spots from the air during election seasons. Their claim is valid if time is given to individual candidates, but a free time grant to parties rather than candidates neatly solves the problem since all stations would be accommodating just two entities. Generally, we might expect the parties to air generic, institutional advertising in the large media markets — crowding all candidates under the party umbrella without special attention to any one. But party leaders should have wide discretion in determining the uses to which the time is put. For instance, they may choose to focus some spots on one or a few specific candidates, probably those in marginal races. (Discretion of this powerful sort can only reinforce the party's efforts to draw its nominees more closely to it.) Party officials may wish to conserve all the time for the general election, or they may allocate a few spots to the party's primary or convention candidates to assist their efforts to become better known before the party nominees are selected. In any event, every candidate should still be free to make whatever additional purchases are necessary and available to promote his or her own individual candidacy. One would hope, however, that substantial free party advertising would reduce the need and demand for individual candidate advertising, thus relieving some of the fundraising pressure on politicians. This may well be a forlorn hope, given competitive campaign pressures, but even if candidate expenditures on media advertising are not appreciably reduced, this reform is nonetheless worthwhile because parties will so clearly benefit and voters will gain much useful campaign information presented in a party context. While both major parties have reason to welcome any free time offering, the Democrats obviously would be especially grateful since currently their party is rarely able to air a considerable amount of party institutional advertising.

No mention has been made here of third parties. Two-party advocates such as this author see nothing wrong in discriminating against third parties in the provision of privileges such as free media availability and public financing. It is in our country's interest to support and gird the two-party system that provides such stability and continuity to American democracy, and we would be foolish to encourage fragmentation by building in incentives for third-party formation and promotion. If a thoughtless impulse for unnecessary equity should triumph over rational self-interest, and third parties be thus included in the free time provision, then lesser parties should be allotted slots based on the percentage of the vote they received in the prior election (with 5 percent of the vote a minimum threshold).[60] New parties without electoral track records would simply have to wait until the next round for free time. (In the meantime, they could try to purchase some.)

While awaiting congressional action on free media time — possibly a lengthy biding — the parties should aggressively pursue opportunities for free broadcasts on the nation's 5,500 cable television operations and 800 public access channels.[61] Audience ratings are surprisingly high for many of these community-based stations, and any channel that can televise live the entire proceedings of the local city council and school board — as up to 2,000 of them apparently do[62] — can obviously afford to make significant amounts of time available to the parties.

CHANGES IN FEDERAL ELECTION LAW

Unshackle the political parties by raising the limits on the party's direct contributions to and coordinated expenditures on behalf of its federal nominees. Permit the national parties to spend unlimited sums on volunteer-oriented activities that benefit their candidates. Allow unlimited donations to underwrite the administrative fundraising, legal, and accounting costs incurred by the parties, and create a special contribution limit of $20,000 — separate from the current overall ceiling of $25,000 per year — for gifts by individuals to parties. Strong-party attributes:

PARTICIPATION AND EDUCATION
RESOURCES
INCENTIVES
CANDIDATE ASSISTANCE

The revisions in campaign finance law that followed the Watergate scandals in the 1970s did not always benefit the parties, and sometimes treated them as the functional equivalent of political action committees.[63] But as Chapter Three suggested, other provisions of the new statutes were very helpful in expanding party influence, particularly the allowance of substantial "coordinated expenditures" by the parties on behalf of their candidates, and of unlimited volunteer-oriented activities by state and local party committees.[64]

More can and should be done to tailor the federal campaign finance statutes to suit the needs of strong parties. First, the current limits on direct party contributions to, and coordinated expenditures on behalf of, House and Senate candidates should be raised somewhat. For example, the national party committee, the national congressional campaign committee, and the state party can each give a House contender $10,000 directly; that should be raised to $15,000 or $20,000, and the amount should be adjusted annually for inflation. The $17,500 that can be directly donated by the national party to each Senate candidate should rise to $25,000[65] or $30,000. Second, the national parties should be extended the same privilege now enjoyed by state and local parties to spend unlimited sums on activities carried out primarily by volunteers (such as voter registration and get-out-the-vote programs).[66] This change would undoubtedly encourage the national parties to direct more of their resources to party-building organizational efforts. Third, unlimited donations to parties from corporations, unions, and PACs should be allowed specifically for the purpose of underwriting the parties' substantial administrative, fundraising, legal, and accounting costs.[67] All such gifts, which would free up party funds for other, more crucial uses, should be reported to the Federal Election Commission and fully disclosed, of course.[68] Finally, individuals should be able to give $20,000 to all party committees combined each year without the amount counting against the overall annual ceiling on an individual's political giving ($25,000). Since most individuals who reach the $25,000 contribution ceiling tend to give to PACs and candidates first, parties are left with whatever remains (if any) before the ceiling is reached. Creating a special, separate $20,000 category for individual gifts to parties would eliminate the competition and clearly aid national committee fundraising.

All of these legal alterations do not merely enrich, or potentially enrich, the parties. There are several wholesome side effects for party organizations, candidates, and the political system generally.

The less party money there is available, the more candidates will have to rely on PAC money; the more resources the parties can share with their nominees, the less officeholders will be indebted to special interest groups. One also suspects that wealthier parties would produce better-funded challengers. PACs have regularly given about two-thirds or more of their money to incumbents, leaving most challengers cash starved.[69] The parties are far more inclined than PACs (or, for that matter, individuals) to supply funds to incumbents' opponents. If only to inject more competition into our congressional politics, we should enable parties to raise more ample war chests. Further, greater resources will enable the parties (especially the Democrats) to expand their technological capabilities and campaign services so that candidates become less reliant on independent, frequently antiparty political consultants who feed all the worst aspects of our personality-centered politics.[70]

Some party advocates go beyond my recommendations, suggesting that all expenditure limitations on the parties be completely eliminated.[71] But there are problems with this more drastic reform. Elimination of party spending limits might well increase pressure on the parties to channel additional funds to powerful incumbents who hold sway over party leaders. Such a development would only drain dollars from needy and deserving challengers. With a maximum limit on party gifts, there is a built-in brake on greedy incumbents. Also, one cannot avoid the practical political ramifications of unlimited party expenditures. Only one party, the GOP, is presently in a position to exploit the removal of limits. Already there is a wide disparity in spending between the parties, as Chapter Three made clear. Eventually, perhaps, all limits should be greatly expanded or even abolished, but in the interest of preserving vigorous and balanced two-party competition, this desirable property change must be deferred or moderated until the Democratic party becomes better funded.

UNIVERSAL STRAIGHT-PARTY LEVER

Add a straight-party voting mechanism in all states, and list candidates of the same party in a column on every ballot. Strong-party attributes:

ELECTORAL APPEAL
ACCOUNTABILITY
INCENTIVES

Students are always surprised to learn that the form and structure of the ballot alone can influence the results of elections. Perhaps they prefer to believe that all voters are purely rational, well informed, and issue oriented, but for better or worse the truth is quite different. There is no doubt that the presence of a straight-party voting mechanism — a lever to pull or a box to check that casts the voter's ballot for all candidates of the same party simultaneously — can, in and of itself, increase straight-party voting.[72] Similarly, a *party-column* ballot, where all candidates of each party are listed together in a vertical column, results in more party voting than the *office-block* ballot that groups candidates separately according to the office they seek.[73]

The incidence of straight-party levers began to decline with the onset of the antiboss Progressive Era, and just twenty states retain it today.[74] The party-column ballot is somewhat more popular, currently used in thirty states. There is nearly complete overlap, with nineteen of the twenty states with a straight-party lever using the party-column ballot.[75] Both party aids are valuable cues to voters, particularly disinterested and unaware citizens. A straight-party lever actually reduces the tendency of these voters to skip most races further down on the ballot, a phenomenon called "ballot fatigue."[76] Besides increasing voter participation for lesser offices, a straight-party mechanism and the party-column ballot increase the value of the party label by lengthening "coattails" and encouraging unity among the party's candidates and officeholders.

The thirty states without a straight-party lever should add one, and the twenty states not using the party-column ballot should adopt it. Despite these reforms' advantages for the party, however, most voters apparently remain unconvinced of their usefulness. When our poll respondents were asked whether they favored "making it easier to vote for all the candidates of one party by pulling a single lever or making a single mark on the ballot," a 61-to-36 percent majority was opposed.[77] Even residents of states where the mechanism already exists were against it by a large margin![78] Progressivism lives on, to the detriment of the political parties.

UNIVERSAL PARTY REGISTRATION

Require in all states that voters express and enroll a party preference (Democrat, Republican, or Other/Independent) when registering to vote. Strong-party attributes:

EQUITY AND LEGITIMACY
ELECTORAL APPEAL
PARTICIPATION AND EDUCATION

Half of the states already require registration by party,[79] and the other half should do so, too. By linking the act of registering to vote with a choice of party,[80] this procedure encourages and reinforces partisanship, perpetuates the party system, and may actually increase the number of Americans who have a party identity (however weak).[81] Party registration (or enrollment, as it is sometimes called) is also a necessary precondition for holding the closed form of primary advocated earlier in this chapter.

Like the straight-party lever, this reform will not be easy to enact, due to a lack of public support. Perhaps resenting perceived invasion of privacy, a 68 percent majority of our poll respondents opposed requiring voters "to name a party affiliation when they register to vote."[82]

MORE PARTISAN ELECTIONS

Identify all candidates who are the nominees of a party by their party label, and reduce the number of nonpartisan elections. Strong-party attributes:

EQUITY AND LEGITIMACY
ELECTORAL APPEAL
PARTICIPATION AND EDUCATION
ACCOUNTABILITY

The modern decline of American political parties should be traced not from the advent of television in the 1950s but from the adoption of the Australian (or secret) ballot from 1880 to 1900.[83] Prior to the secret ballot, voters selected a *party* ballot at the polling places to mark and place in boxes.[84] Since the parties or candidates printed these ballots and they were usually distinctively colored, a voter essentially made this party preference publicly known simply by choosing a ballot. Furthermore, under these conditions, casting a split ticket was impossible.

The Australian ballot radically changed the act of voting, because it listed candidates from all parties on a single government-printed ballot form, thus guaranteeing the voter privacy of choice but also permitting ticket-splitting for the first time and eliminating an important public display of partisanship.

No one seriously advocates a return to party balloting. Voter intimidation was widespread with its practice, and outright vote-buying was facilitated since a voter could publicly fulfill his part of the bargain. Employers, landlords, and creditors were sometimes able to control the votes of their employees, tenants, and debtors as well.[85]

But a secret ballot need not result in a nonparty ballot. In Virginia no party labels are included on the ballot except for presidential Electoral College slates; voters are thus denied the most revealing voting cue of all, and the candidates are separated from their party identity. The same is true in Nebraska where the state legislature is technically "nonpartisan," though almost all legislators' party affiliations are informally known by the press and political activists.[86] (Only the voters are left in the dark.) Moreover, a large majority of local municipal elections are officially nonpartisan, and regrettably the proportion is growing. While in the 1960s 65 percent of all municipalities used nonpartisan ballots, by the 1970s the percentage had grown to 76 percent.[87] Yet another lingering aspect of antiboss Progressivism, nonpartisan elections make parties irrelevant at the expense of responsible politics. Voters are denied a vital piece of information that brings order out of the chaos of personality politics. Elected officials lose a crucial link with their peers, a tie that helps them to work together on a common agenda. And the power taken from party elites is simply transferred to other entities. Wealthy candidates, the news media, and incumbents all gain power because they can buy or confer or possess "name identification" to substitute as a voting cue for lost party identification. Are any of these agents more worthy of our trust than the parties?

Ingrained political habits stubbornly persist, and it will be exceedingly difficult to convince states or localities to convert from nonpartisan to partisan elections. Yet the attempt should be made wherever possible. While the antiparty spirit of the Progressive age has endured in the popular mind, it is at least somewhat encouraging that our poll respondents favored "having all candidates for political office identified by party label on the ballot" by a margin of 76 percent to 19 percent.[88] Even 62 percent of the self-identified Independents were approving.[89]

CONSOLIDATION OF ELECTIONS AND GOVERNMENTAL STRUCTURE

In order to strengthen party unity and foster responsible party government, consolidate elections to increase the potential coattail effect and restructure state governments to favor the governorship. Strong-party attributes:

ACCOUNTABILITY
CONFLICT CONTROL
INCENTIVES

As was pointed out in the discussion on straight-party levers, the *coattail effect* — whereby candidates at the top of the party ticket can attract votes to those at the bottom — draws all of the party standard-bearers together since their fates are intertwined. It gives party officeholders a strong incentive to push for the strongest possible party nominees for president and governor, since these top-of-the-ballot candidates can sink or save their electoral chances. Similarly, all the party's legislators have a stake in seeing the executives succeed, once in office, so that at reelection time the party can boast a successful record.[90] Given these political ground rules, it makes sense to consolidate elections so that the coattail effect is magnified. Gubernatorial and state legislative elections should be held simultaneously with presidential elections, for example, and both houses of the state legislature should be elected at the same time as the governor.

Of course, what seems sensible to a party builder seems ludicrous to an elected official bound and determined to preserve his public office in a bad year for his party. Officeholders prefer to control their own fates, and as a consequence events have been moving in precisely the opposite direction to the course desirable for the good of the parties. In 1952, 30 states elected their governors in presidential years, but by 1988 the number had declined to 11.[91] Five states (Kentucky, Louisiana, Mississippi, New Jersey, and Virginia) insulate gubernatorial and state legislature elections even further than most by setting them in odd-numbered years when neither the presidency nor Congress is contested. Additionally, some states elect only half of their state Senate in the gubernatorial year, and in five states (Kansas, Kentucky, New Mexico, South Carolina, and Virginia) the entire upper house is permanently immune from gubernatorial coattail influence since it is always elected at the midpoint of the governor's term. North Carolina is the only state that permits maximum coattail influence by electing president, governor, and both houses of the state legislature simultaneously.

On the other hand, conditions in state governments have improved dramatically, empowering the governors and enabling them to exert strong party leadership in most of the states.[92] In 1950 twenty-one states had a short two-year gubernatorial term that often prevented bold executive action and long-range planning. By 1988 only three states (New Hampshire, Rhode Island, and Vermont) retained the outmoded short term; all other states had lengthened the tenure to four years. In like fashion, thirteen states (most of them in the South) restricted their governor to a single consecutive term in 1950, but by 1988 just three did so (Kentucky, New Mexico, and Virginia). More than a dozen state governments have been extensively reorganized or had their constitutions revised and modernized, creating state governments that were more rationally structured and easier for governors to lead. "Team election" of the governor and lieutenant governor, similar to the way the nation's top team is elected as a unit, has become the practice in twenty-two states — an ultimate form of coattail that potentially gives the chief executive much more influence over the second-in-command. Unfortunately for the governor and the parties, there are still more than two hundred other offices separately elected statewide, from attorneys general to boards of education, a situation that promotes factionalism within the governing party, occasionally split-party rule (with both parties controlling some executive offices), and diluted gubernatorial authority.[93] Despite this glaring omission in the otherwise impressive cavalcade of reform, state governments have generally increased the chances for successful gubernatorial administrations, and thereby boosted the strength of party leadership exercised by governors. There is room for improvement but much progress has already been made in this area.

"SORE LOSER" AND "DISAFFILIATION" PROVISIONS

Enact statutes in all states prohibiting losing party primary or convention candidates from launching Independent general election bids, and in states that register by party, prohibit persons who have been registered with a party from running as Independents. Strong-party attributes:

ACCOUNTABILITY
CONFLICT CONTROL
INCENTIVES

One of the oldest and most revered rules of good sportsmanship demands grace in defeat. This attractive, gentlemanly standard of human conduct should apply to all candidacies for party nomination. A candidate who loses a bid for nomination should not be able to file as an Independent in the general election. So-called sore loser laws are already in effect in twenty-six states,[94] and all states ought to have them. To the extent possible, the laws also should be applied to presidential candidates, so that an individual such as John Anderson would be prevented from running in a party's primaries and caucuses and then launching an autumn Independent candidacy.[95] (Anderson did just this after losing a number of GOP preliminaries.) Furthermore, all states with party registration should pass a law similar to California's "disaffiliation" statute, which prohibits any individual from running as an Independent if he or she had been affiliated with a party in the year preceding the primary.

Not just good sportsmanship but the prevention of electoral chaos and anarchy warrants these reforms. Without them, the party nomination potentially becomes round one preceding a free-for-all in the fall. In these circumstances, candidates can use the primary merely as a warm-up exercise, building up name identification in the process. A party can sponsor an "Independent" in the general election drawn from the other party's ranks in order to split the opposition vote. As a result, voters can be faced with a confusing welter of candidates on the general election ballot, and election winners can be denied the clear mandates and majorities necessary to govern effectively.

As with so many other proparty reforms, this one is distasteful to pure democrats and populists whose siren call for easy ballot access is so superficially alluring. Far better that we should protect the integrity of the parties and preserve a rational electoral process by universally enacting sore loser and disaffiliation provisions.

MORE PATRONAGE

Expand the number of patronage positions available to reward party workers, with appropriate safeguards to guarantee competence in public service. Strong-party attributes:

EQUITY AND LEGITIMACY
ELECTORAL APPEAL
PARTICIPATION AND EDUCATION
ACCOUNTABILITY
CONFLICT CONTROL
RESOURCES
INCENTIVES
CANDIDATE ASSISTANCE

Patronage — the use of appointive government jobs as a reward for party work — is one of the dirty words of American politics, thanks to the efforts of a century's worth of reformers.[96] The mere mention of the term is enough to raise the eyebrows of an enormous majority of the American public. Citizens are simply unpersuaded by the central party-building argument used by patronage's advocates, as the results of one of our survey questions indicate:[97]

> Some people say more jobs in government should be filled by people from the winning candidate's political party. They say this helps a leader govern better and get programs enacted. Others disagree. They say the current civil service process fills government jobs with qualified people regardless of who wins an election. In your opinion, should more government jobs be filled by workers and leaders of the winning candidate's party or not?
> Yes 13%
> No 79%
> Don't know 8%

It was not always this grim for patronage. In the last century, patronage was an accepted part of the party system and the electoral process. Beginning with the era of Presidents Andrew Jackson and Martin van Buren in the 1830s, the operating premise of politics became, "to the victors belong the spoils." Not until the Pendleton Act, establishing the first professional civil service system, was passed by the federal government in 1883 did the theory of "neutral competence" and the practice of competitive, standardized civil service examinations begin to supplant patronage. The Progressive movement accelerated the pace of change, and the big-city political machines began to suffer the consequences — though not silently. George Washington Plunkitt of New York's Tammany Hall machine well expressed the fighting spirit of his party contemporaries:

> This civil service law is the biggest fraud of the age. It is the curse of the nation. There can't be no real patriotism while it lasts. How are

> you goin' to interest our young men in their country if you have no offices to give them when they work for their party? . . . I have good reason for sayin' that most of the Anarchists in this city today are men who ran up against civil service examinations. . . .
>
> I see a vision. I see the civil service monster lyin' flat on the ground. I see the Democratic party standin' over it with foot on its neck and wearin' the crown of victory. I see Thomas Jefferson lookin' out from a cloud and sayin' "Give him another sockdologer; finish him." And I see millions of men wavin' their hats and singin' "Glory Hallelujah!"[98]

Plunkitt's vision was not to be, and gradually civil service came to dominate government at all levels. While there remain a few exceptions to the rule (such as Chicago, which still has thousands of local government jobs filled by patronage),[99] patronage has been reduced to a mere shadow of its former self. At the national level, less than one percent of federal jobs can still be classified as patronage (such as United States marshals and attorneys, and the collectors of customs).[100] More than three-quarters of all state employees are covered by merit systems, too, and in many states the proportion exceeds 90 percent.[101] What few patronage plums remain are often used by public officials to reward their own personal followers and staff members rather than longtime party workers. Thus, these patronage appointees serve an individual officeholder, not the needs of the party, and they reinforce the advantages of incumbency, not the exigencies of party organization. In the postpatronage age American political parties have become more structurally skeletal in character than before.[102]

The Supreme Court can take some credit — I would say blame — for the modern continued decline of patronage. First in *Elrod v. Burns* (1976)[103] and then in *Branti v. Finkel* (1980)[104] the Court used the First and Fourteenth Amendments to rule against the dismissals of patronage employees. In the first case, a majority of the justices said that a newly elected Democratic sheriff in Cook County, Illinois, could not fire the Republican appointees of his GOP predecessor just because they were not of his party. Political tests for employment, decreed the Court, would only be valid for policymaking positions, not lesser posts. In the second case, the Court added that patronage firings were only valid when partisan affiliation was a necessary condition for satisfactory job performance.

Given these judicial decisions, there would seem to be little hope of broadening the patronage base for bottom-level jobs, even if the public would acquiesce in an expansion of patronage. Where there is room for legitimate maneuver is at the top, in the policymaking posts recognized by the Court. Presidents, governors, and mayors should be given appointive powers for policymakers as broad as court rulings and public opinion will allow. There has already been movement in this direction in some states, and the public and press response, while cautious, has not been unfavorable.[105] Another way to increase patronage is through executive-initiated creation of more honorific posts (blue-ribbon commissions, watchdog committees, advisory boards, etc.). While nonpaying, these positions bring prestige and public recognition — not insignificant prizes, especially for middle-class party workers who already enjoy full-time employment elsewhere. The point here is not that we should return to bygone days of governments run by rank amateurs whose sole qualifications were party work and a willingness to kick back a portion of their public salaries to the party treasury. Rather, there is a serious need to involve more people in the party organizations. This can be accomplished by delivering help and service (ombudsman assistance, credit cards at reduced rates, and so on), but also by offering rewards of patronage employment and honors.

Concluding Remarks

To recapitulate, my agenda for party renewal consists of eight party-initiated actions and twelve government-assisted reforms:

Party-Initiated Actions

1. Designate ombudsmen and establish mobile offices.
2. Provide nonpolitical services to party members.
3. Expand fundraising, campaign services, and recruitment of candidates and volunteers.
4. Air more party institutional advertising.
5. Undertake a bipartisan educational campaign.
6. Increase the parties' capacities for policy formulation.
7. Organize and sponsor presidential debates.
8. Increase unpledged and unbound delegates to the presidential conventions.

Government-Assisted Reforms

1. Deregulate the parties.

2. Leave nominating method to the parties; hold more caucuses, closed primaries, and preprimary endorsing conventions.
3. Enact add-on tax refund deduction or a 50 percent or 100 percent tax credit for small gifts to parties.
4. Channel public financing money through parties; allocate part of Federal Election Campaign Fund to parties.
5. Grant annual hour of free time (in short segments and half in prime time) on television and radio to each national and state party.
6. Raise limits on party contributions to and expenditures for candidates; permit unlimited expenditures on national volunteer activities; allow unlimited donations to party administrative costs; create separate party contribution limit for individuals.
7. Make straight-party lever and party-column ballot universal.
8. Require party registration in all states.
9. Always use party labels on ballot, and reduce number of nonpartisan elections.
10. Increase potential for coattails and strengthen executive party leadership in government.
11. Add "sore loser" and "disaffiliation" provisions.
12. Expand patronage and other rewards for party work.

While all of these proposals would be helpful to the parties, they obviously cannot be accomplished at once. The party-initiated actions, especially the ombudsman idea, services to members, institutional advertising, and the bipartisan educational campaign, should be undertaken first (and can be started more easily since parties need no outside stamp of approval for them). Of all the government-assisted suggestions, perhaps none is both more feasible and potentially beneficial than the add-on contribution to federal and state income tax forms. And no proposal has more merit than the allocation of substantial free time on television and radio; perhaps an energetic bipartisan push for this reform can persuade or shame the broadcasting industry into acquiescence.

That this is an ambitious agenda is readily acknowledged, but I believe that all items are well within the realm of acceptable reform — change that does no injury and some good for American political life. As Leon Epstein wisely warned, "[P]arties can be maintained and strengthened but only within a well-established political culture that is hostile to both the revival of older American party organizational forms and the emergence of European-style parties."[106] There may well be some misguided suggestions in these two chapters, but none quite as silly as those regularly proposed by blue-ribbon groups of "wise men" urging us to move to some semblance of a parliamentary system — a reform completely out of the American mainstream and wholly inappropriate to our nation's culture and preferences.[107] These groups have forgotten what I have earnestly endeavored to remember — the sage advice of Austin Ranney on political reform:

> There is a part of the Hippocratic oath that doctors have to swear that says the first obligation of the physician is to do no harm. Then after that, if he is sure he is doing no harm, he can start seeing if he can do a little good. Maybe not a bad rule for political reformers, too.[108]

In this book I have attempted to avoid adding luster to the destructive myths that engulf the political parties in the United States: that parties were once all-powerful; that they are now headed straight for oblivion; and that their precipitous and continuing decline is irreversible. None of these myths is true. Except perhaps in some urban centers, few Americans have ever given fealty to a party in the manner of many Europeans; individualism runs too deep in our national character.[109] And if we are anywhere near a postparty age, that fact has escaped the millions of Americans who maintain an identity with the major parties as well as the thousands of candidates who greatly benefit each election year from the money, services, and people the parties provide.

One cannot dispute that some deterioration in party volunteer strength and voter identification has taken place, but my central assertion is that *the decline can be reversed.* Precisely as Martin Wattenberg has claimed, Americans are not hostile to the parties; they are increasingly neutral toward them, and await evidence that the parties are relevant to their lives.[110] This evidence the political parties must provide themselves. They must demonstrate that parties can accomplish more for an individual and an electorate than any PAC or candidate or officeholder. They must provide sufficient services and rewards to attract the participation of a broad cross-section of Americans, not only to produce partisan victory but to prevent takeover by ideological extremists and to preserve their own representative and diverse nature. And they must make political parties an integral contributing element of community life the year round, not just at election time. The goal ought not to be the restoration of what never was, but the shaping of effective, vibrant political parties for America's future using the technological tools and fundraising techniques unavailable to the parties of old. Because the parties' roots in the nation's political culture are so extensive, they will probably survive even if nothing is done. But the parties can prosper — and the people can benefit as a consequence — if words become actions. The party is not over, but there is not as much life to it as there ought to be. The party can begin anew if the will to rejuvenate and the desire to renovate are strong enough.

Notes

1. Giovanni Sartori, *Parties and Party Systems: A Framework for Analysis* (Vol. I) (New York: Cambridge University Press, 1976), ix.
2. Leon Epstein, *Political Parties in the American Mold* (Madison: University of Wisconsin Press, 1986), 156–157.
3. Gerald M. Pomper, ed., *Party Organizations in American Politics* (New York: Praeger, 1984), 149.
4. Malcolm Jewell, "Political Parties and the Nominating Process," *Comparative State Politics Newsletter* 7 (February 1986): 14.
5. Epstein, *Political Parties in the American Mold,* 158.
6. Ibid.
7. Advisory Commission on Intergovernmental Relations, *The Transformation in American Politics* (Washington, D.C.: ACIR, 1986), 128–132, 135–136.
8. Ibid., 367.
9. 107 S.Ct. 544 (1986). See Elder Witt and Jeremy Gaunt, " 'Closed' Primary Laws Barred by 5–4 Supreme Court Ruling," *Congressional Quarterly Weekly* 16 (December 13, 1986): 3064–3065; *Campaign Practices Reports* 13 (December 15, 1986): 2–3; and *Washington Post,* December 11, 1986, A12.
10. Twenty other states have closed primary laws similar to Connecticut's.
11. For a full discussion of these cases and others, see Jerome Mileur, "Federal Constitutional Challenges to State Party Regulation," a paper prepared for the annual meeting of the American Political Science Association, Washington, D.C., August 30–September 2, 1986.
12. Ibid. See also Charles Gardner Geyh, " 'It's My Party and I'll Cry If I Want To': State Intrusions Upon the Associational Freedoms of Political Parties," *Wisconsin Law Review* 1983:1 (1983), 220ff.
13. Correspondence with the author dated February 18, 1986.
14. Virginia provides an excellent example of this. Fratricide encouraged by primaries helped to cost Democrats twelve years (1969–1981) of control of the statehouse. A switch to the convention method of nomination in 1981 and 1985 did much to restore party unity and assist

Democratic statewide sweeps. See Larry Sabato, *Virginia Votes, 1979–1982* (Charlottesville: U. Va. Institute of Government, 1983) and *Virginia Votes, 1983–1986* (Charlottesville: U. Va. Institute of Government, 1987).

15. Personal interview with the author as quoted in Sabato, *Goodbye to Good-Time Charlie: The American Governorship Transformed* (Washington, D.C.: Congressional Quarterly Press, 1983), 66.
16. Seven percent were undecided.
17. Even blacks disapproved, 49 percent to 46 percent, with 5 percent undecided.
18. Both polls, taken by the Bailey survey organization, asked the following question to 655 adults in each state from December 11–18, 1985: "Thinking about presidential elections, some states select their delegates for presidential candidates by statewide party primary elections; other states, like Oklahoma/Arkansas, use the party caucus system to select delegates. Do you support the party caucus system, or would you prefer statewide party primary elections here in Oklahoma/Arkansas?"
19. See, for example, Jack Dennis, "Public Support for the American Party System," in William J. Crotty, ed., *Paths to Political Reform* (Lexington, Mass.: D. C. Heath, 1980), 55–56.
20. David E. Price, *Bringing Back the Parties* (Washington, D.C.: Congressional Quarterly Press, 1984), 207.
21. Michael Robinson, "Television and American Politics: 1956–1976," *Public Interest* 48 (Summer 1977): 21.
22. Richard Rubin, *Press, Party, and Presidency* (New York: W. W. Norton, 1981), 195.
23. Leon Epstein, *Political Parties in the American Mold,* 155–156.
24. Since 1978 both parties in Virginia have chosen to nominate all statewide offices in convention. However, the primary is still used in some regions by both parties to nominate candidates for United States House, the state legislature, and some local offices.
25. Illinois selects the trustees of the University of Illinois in a convention, but otherwise the primary produces all nominations.
26. These states are: Alabama, Alaska, Arkansas, Georgia, Hawaii, Idaho, Illinois, Indiana, Louisiana, Michigan, Minnesota, Mississippi, Missouri, Montana, North Dakota, Rhode Island, South Carolina, Tennessee, Texas, Utah, Vermont, Virginia, Washington, and Wisconsin.
27. See *Congressional Quarterly Weekly* 43 (October 26, 1985):2158. The Democrats' reason — to broaden their base — was similar to that of the Connecticut Republicans cited earlier in this chapter.
28. Malcolm E. Jewell, "Democratic or Republican?: Voters' Choice of a Primary," a paper prepared for delivery at the annual meeting of the Southern Political Science Association, Birmingham, Alabama, November 3–5, 1983.
29. The number of Republican primaries declined from 35 to 24; GOP caucuses increased from 16 to 27.

30. E. E. Schattschneider, *Party Government* (New York: Rinehart, 1942), 59–60.
31. Austin Ranney, *Curing the Mischiefs of Faction* (Berkeley: University of California Press, 1975), 129.
32. This plan is similar to the one existing in Connecticut and several other states.
33. See Sarah McCally Morehouse, "The Effect of Preprimary Endorsements on State Party Strength," a paper delivered at the annual meeting of the American Political Science Association, Washington, D.C., August 30–September 2, 1980.
34. California's prohibition is currently under legal assault. A ruling striking the prohibition is currently on appeal to the Supreme Court. See ACIR, *The Transformation in American Politics,* 133–134.
35. See Paul Taylor, "Michigan GOP Set to Begin Presidential Nominating Marathon," *Washington Post,* May 26, 1986, A3.
36. The actual nominating process was three-tiered under Abraham's plan. In early 1988 the precinct delegates were to meet in county or district conventions to choose delegates to a state convention held a few weeks later, which in turn would choose delegates to the national convention. Most precinct delegates ran unopposed, of course, so the contest was in recruiting large numbers of people to run. Another expensive challenge for the candidates occurred in those districts where more people filed than there were delegate slots to fill: delegates were not identified on the ballot by presidential preference, so each campaign had to undertake an expensive communications and turnout operation for election day.
37. Bush won the Michigan GOP presidential primary over Ronald Reagan in 1980, for instance. See *National Journal* 19 (August 8, 1987): 2041. On the unrepresentative nature of primaries and caucuses generally, see Austin Ranney, "Turnout and Representation in Presidential Primary Elections," *American Political Science Review* 66 (March 1972): 26–27; James I. Lengle *Representation and Presidential Primaries* (Westport, Conn.: Greenwood Press, 1981), chaps. 2, 5. Lengle concluded (p. 62): "Had the 1973 California Democratic primary electorate been demographically representative of the party rank and file, Hubert Humphrey, not George McGovern, almost surely would have won the primary and captured all of California's delegates . . . Undoubtedly, had Hubert Humphrey won the California primary, he would have been the presidential nominee in 1972."

    Not all research has supported the conclusion that primary electorates are unrepresentative (in ideology or candidate preference) of all partisan identifiers. See, for instance, Herbert Kritzer, "The Representativeness of the 1972 Presidential Primaries," *Polity* 10 (Fall 1977): 121–129. Still, there is little doubt that frequently, primary (and caucus) electorates are different in some important ways from general electorate populations, and that these differences can affect the identity of the party nominees.

38. Frank Sorauf, *Party Politics in America* (5th ed.) (Boston: Little, Brown & Co., 1984), 284.
39. See Thomas R. Marshall, "Caucuses and Primaries: Measuring Reform in the Presidential Nomination Process," *American Politics Quarterly* 7 (1979): 155–174; and Marshall, *Presidential Nominations in a Reform Age* (New York: Praeger, 1981). See also Everett Carll Ladd, "The Proper Role of Parties in Presidential Nominee Selection," *Commonsense* 4 (1981): 33–39.
40. A 100 percent tax credit would almost certainly increase party giving. The California Commission on Campaign Financing found that 35 percent of state residents would either increase their political gifts or give for the first time if there were a 100 percent credit. See California Commission on Campaign Financing, "The New Gold Rush: Financing California's Legislative Campaigns" (Sacramento: State of California, 1985), 15.
41. Only the states of Alaska, Florida, Nevada, South Dakota, Texas, Washington, and Wyoming have no income tax.
42. Minnesota and the District of Columbia already provide a 50 percent tax credit for political contributions.
43. See the polls cited in Larry Sabato, *PAC Power: Inside the World of Political Action Committees* (New York: W. W. Norton, 1984), 160–163.
44. By a margin of 54 percent to 40 percent (with 6 percent undecided), the public favored "allowing people to contribute money to political parties by means of a check-off on their income tax return" (Poll 1.) For clarity and brevity's sake, the term "check-off" was used instead of "add-on," an unfamiliar term that would have required explanation. Given the voluntary nature of this proposal, however, it is highly doubtful that the public would disapprove; after all, people are generally willing to let others spend their own money in any lawful way — even if they regard the spending as foolish. If we had also noted that no individual's tax burden would be increased without his or her consent, and had stressed that no public money was being used, I would wager that a much higher proportion than 54 percent would have approved.
45. See Holly Wagner, "Costly campaigns attract special interest dollars," *State Government News* 29 (October 1986): 20.
46. In other words, 9 percent of the total sample (Poll 1) claimed to have given more than $100 in any given year. Most likely to contribute are white men, executives and professionals, and those aged 35–49. Least likely to give are Independents, women, blue-collar workers, and young people aged 18–34.
47. See David Adamany, "The New Faces of American Politics," The Annals, *AAPSS* 486 (July 1986): 23–24; Herbert E. Alexander, *Financing the 1980 Election* (Lexington, Mass: D.C. Heath, 1983), 422; John C. Green and James L. Guth, "Partisans and Ideologues: A Profile of Contributors to Party and Ideological PACs," a paper prepared for the annual meeting of the Southern Political Science Association, Birming-

ham, Alabama, November 3–6, 1983, 11–15; and Ruth S. Jones and Warren E. Miller, "Financing Campaigns: Macro Level Innovation and Micro Level Response," *Western Political Quarterly* 38 (June 1985):187–210.

It is also worth noting that between 23 and 29 percent of the eligible taxpayers have regularly checked the $1 federal Presidential Election Campaign Fund box. Similar check-offs in the thirteen states that have them have garnered an average 22 percent participation rate (Wagner, "Costly campaigns attract special interest dollars," 20). Finally, about 7 percent of the federal taxpayers annually took advantage of the 50 percent tax credit when it was available (California Commission on Campaign Financing, "The Gold Rush," 15–16).

48. This proposal has also been made by, among others, David Price, *Bringing Back the Parties,* 255, and Herbert E. Alexander, "Public Funding of Congressional Campaigns," *Regulation* 4 (January/February 1980): 31–32.
49. See political scientist John Bibby's comments quoted in ACIR, *The Transformation in American Politics,* 306–307.
50. Ibid., 298–326. See also Herbert E. Alexander and Mike Eberts, *Public Financing of State Elections: A Data Book and Election Guide to Public Funding of Political Parties and Candidates in Twenty States* (Los Angeles: Citizen's Research Foundation, 1987).
51. States with public funding provisions that channel money through the parties are: California, Idaho, Indiana, Iowa, Kentucky, Maine, North Carolina, Oklahoma, Oregon, Rhode Island, Utah, and Virginia. States that allocate funds directly to candidates are: Alaska, Hawaii, Maryland, Massachusetts. Michigan, Minnesota, Montana, New Jersey, Oklahoma (included in both lists because its statute provides for both disbursements), and Wisconsin. Maryland and Oklahoma's public funding schemes are now defunct. See ACIR, *The Transformation in American Politics,* 300–301.
52. Epstein, *Political Parties in the American Mold,* 328–329.
53. Figures provided by the Federal Election Commission. The percentage of taxpayers using the check-off varies annually, and thus the amount of money deposited in the Fund also varies.
54. Ibid. The surplus declined from $177 million in December 1983 to $93 million the next year.
55. Ibid.
56. See Larry Sabato, *The Rise of Political Consultants: New Ways of Winning Elections* (New York: Basic Books, 1981), 179–182, 321–328. At least a third and sometimes half or more of all dollars spent on United States Senate campaigns in the mid-1980s are devoted to media advertising and related expenditures.
57. Fred Flaxman, a vice president of public station WTTW-TV, Chicago, writing in the *Washington Post,* January 4, 1987, C5.
58. See ACIR, *The Transformation in American Politics,* 377–379, and Sabato, *The Rise of Political Consultants,* 186–192, 326–328.
59. Sabato, *The Rise of Political Consultants,* 123–126.

60. This is not unlike the arrangement that exists in Great Britain.
61. ACIR, *The Transformation in American Politics,* 380–381.
62. Ibid.
63. For background discussion of the new campaign finance laws, see Sabato, *PAC Power,* 3–27, 141–159.
64. See Chapter Three.
65. Coordinated expenditures should also increase. National and state parties can each currently spend $10,000 in 1975 dollars adjusted for inflation on House candidates; the base figure of $10,000 should rise to $15,000 or $20,000. For Senate candidates (and House candidates in states with only one United States representative), national and state parties can each now spend $20,000 in 1975 dollars adjusted for inflation, or two cents times the state's voting age population, whichever is greater. This amount should rise to perhaps $30,000 in base dollars, or three cents times the voting age population.
66. Under the 1979 Amendments to the Federal Election Campaign Act, state and local parties were permitted to do this, but not the national parties.
67. Currently PACs are limited to $15,000 in contributions to all parties each calendar year. Direct corporate and union treasury donations to the parties are forbidden except to special "building funds" maintained by the national parties that are not disclosed or reported to the FEC. See Jean Cobb, "Party Favors," *Common Cause Magazine* 13 (January/February 1987): 23–29.
68. So should the "building funds" noted in Cobb, "Party Favors."
69. Sabato, *PAC Power,* 75, 188.
70. Sabato, *The Rise of Political Consultants,* especially 302–337.
71. See, for example, Joel L. Fleishman, ed., *The Future of American Political Parties: The Challenge of Governance,* final report of the 62nd American Assembly (Englewood Cliffs, N.J.: Prentice-Hall, 1982), 71.
72. ACIR, *The Transformation in American Politics,* 152–153; Sorauf, *Party Politics in America,* 236; Price, *Bringing Back the Parties,* 134–136; Angus Campbell et al., *The American Voter* (New York: Wiley, 1960), 276.
73. Ibid.
74. States with a straight-party voting mechanism are: Alabama, Georgia, Illinois, Indiana, Iowa, Kentucky, Michigan, Missouri, New Hampshire, New Mexico, North Carolina, Oklahoma, Pennsylvania, Rhode Island, South Carolina, South Dakota, Texas, Utah, West Virginia, and Wisconsin. Connecticut had a party lever until 1986 when voters narrowly passed a constitutional amendment eliminating it.
75. Only Pennsylvania has a straight-party lever combined with the office-block ballot.
76. See Jack L. Walker, "Ballot Forms and Voter Fatigue: An Analysis of the Office Block and Party Column Ballots," *Midwest Journal of Political Science* 10 (August 1966): 460.
77. Poll 1. Three percent were undecided.
78. Blacks were the only significant group favoring the straight-party le-

ver, and by only a narrow 51 percent to 46 percent margin.

79. Party registration is required in Arizona, California, Colorado, Connecticut, Delaware, Florida, Iowa, Kansas, Kentucky, Maine, Maryland, Massachusetts, Nebraska, Nevada, New Mexico, New Hampshire, New Jersey, New York, North Carolina, Oklahoma, Oregon, Pennsylvania, South Dakota, West Virginia, and Wyoming.
80. Granted, citizens can also register as Independents, but there is evidence that some Independent-leaning voters may be induced to register with a party anyway, if only to vote in the primary of the locally dominant party. See Epstein, *Political Parties in the American Mold,* 246.
81. Jewell, "Democrat or Republican? Voters' Choice of a Primary," 13; and Steven E. Finkel and Howard A. Scarrow, "Party Identification and Party Enrollment: The Difference and the Consequence," *Journal of Politics* 47 (May 1985): 620–642.
82. Twenty-eight percent supported party registration, and 4 percent were undecided. Once again, even respondents from states currently having a system of party registration opposed the practice. And again, blacks were the only group in favor, by a statistically insignificant margin of 49 percent to 48 percent.
83. ACIR, *The Transformation in American Politics,* 124–126.
84. In the colonial period, a voter simply appeared before election officials and told them his preferences. But by the mid-1800s party ballots were standard.
85. V. O. Key, Jr., *Politics, Parties, and Pressure Groups* (5th ed.) (New York: Thomas Y. Crowell Company, 1964), 639.
86. Nebraska has had a "nonpartisan" legislature since 1935; Minnesota had one from 1913 until 1974.
87. Epstein, *Political Parties in the American Mold,* 126–127.
88. Poll 1. Five percent were undecided.
89. Thirty-two percent were opposed, and 7 percent had no opinion.
90. See Sarah McCally Morehouse, "Legislatures and Political Parties," *State Government* 59:1 (1976): 21.
91. The eleven states are: Delaware, Indiana, Missouri, Montana, New Hampshire, North Carolina, North Dakota, Utah, Vermont, Washington, and West Virginia.
92. Larry Sabato, *Goodbye to Good-Time Charlie: The American Governorship Transformed* (2nd ed.) (Washington, D.C.: Congressional Quarterly Press, 1983), 57–96.
93. Ibid. 63–66.
94. Sore loser laws are on the statute books in Arizona, Arkansas, California, Colorado, Delaware, Idaho, Indiana, Kentucky, Maine, Maryland, Massachusetts, Michigan, Minnesota, Missouri, Nebraska, New Mexico, North Carolina, North Dakota, Ohio, Oregon, Pennsylvania, South Carolina, Tennessee, Utah, Washington, and Wyoming.
95. In his 1980 campaign, Anderson was able to work around the sore loser laws using a court suit contesting the early deadline for filing as an Independent. (See Price, *Bringing Back the Parties,* 131–134.) There

is surely a constitutionally sound way to word the sore loser provision and set the Independent candidacy deadline to avoid this difficulty in the future.

96. Parallels occur to this author between the ruination of patronage in the public mind and the campaign waged by a new set of reformers against political action committees today. See Sabato, *PAC Power,* xi–xiv.
97. Poll 1. Not even a fifth of any significant population subgroup could be found in favor of patronage.
98. William L. Riordon (ed.), *Plunkitt of Tammany Hall* (New York: E.P. Dutton, 1963), 11, 89.
99. See, for example, Milton Rakove, *Don't Make No Waves — Don't Back No Losers* (Bloomington: Indiana University Press, 1975).
100. Sorauf, *Party Politics in America,* 88–89.
101. Sabato, *Goodbye to Good-Time Charlie,* 67–68.
102. Epstein, *Political Parties in the American Mold,* 144.
103. 427 U.S. 347 (1976).
104. 445 U.S. 507 (1980).
105. Virginia, for example, recently moved about 450 positions from its merit system to gubernatorial control. While some concern about "spoils" was expressed in the media, there was no uproar and the bill, with then-Governor Charles Robb's strong support, passed easily. See Deborah D. Roberts, "State Civil Servants Who Serve at the Will and Pleasure of Political Superiors," *University of Virginia Newsletter* 63 (March 1987): 37–42.
106. Epstein, *Political Parties in the American Mold,* 343.
107. For the latest example of this nonsense, see the discussion of the report of the "Committee on the Constitutional System" in Stuart Taylor, Jr., "Citing Chronic Deadlock, Panel Urges Political Restructure," *The New York Times,* January 11, 1987, 1, 18.
108. Quoted in Herbert E. Alexander and Brian A. Haggerty, *The Federal Election Campaign Act: After a Decade of Political Reform* (Washington, D.C.: Citizens' Research Foundation, 1981), 124.
109. See, for example, Philip M. Williams, "Power and the Parties: The United States," in Vernon Bogdanor, ed., *Parties and Democracy in Britain and America* (New York: Praeger, 1984), 7–37.
110. Martin Wattenberg, *The Decline of American Political Parties, 1952–1980* (Cambridge: Harvard University Press, 1984).

A P P E N D I X

• ☆ • ☆ •

Public Opinion Survey Data

THREE NATIONAL RANDOM-SAMPLE, telephone surveys of adult Americans were conducted for this study of political parties:

- *Poll 1.* Sample size 1,400; taken from May 30 to June 16, 1986, with a margin of error of approximately ± 2.5 percent. (Of 1,400 respondents, 1,070 claimed to be registered voters.) Total items asked: 122.
- *Poll 2.* Sample size 506, a panelback of Poll 1; taken immediately following the 1986 midterm elections from November 7–13, with a margin of error of approximately ± 5 percent. Total new items asked: 29.
- *Poll 3.* Sample size 1,399; taken from November 10–19, 1986, with a margin of error of approximately ± 2.5 percent. Total items asked: 140.

Data taken from these surveys are referred to in the text and chapter notes by the poll numbers (1, 2, or 3) listed here.

Sample subgroup breakdowns are tabulated on the following pages.

SAMPLE SUBGROUP BREAKDOWNS[a] OF EACH POLL

POLL 1 (N = 1,400)

SUBGROUP	N	% OF SAMPLE
Male	676	48
Female	724	52
Black	122	9
White	1,195	85
Other	55	4
18–34	462	33
35–49	406	29
50 +	532	38
Under $12,000	182	13
$12,000–$23,999	350	25
$24,000–$34,999	364	26
$35,000–$41,999	140	10
$42,000 +	280	20
Refuse	84	6
Married	840	60
Never married	303	22
Widowed	93	8
Divorced/separated	118	8
Don't know/refuse	46	4
Northeast	319	23
Midwest	369	26
South	505	36
West	207	15
Democrat	452	32
Independent[b]	531	38
Republican	386	28
City dweller	323	23
Suburban	382	27
Small town	399	28
Rural	266	19
Protestant	814	58
Catholic	341	24
Jewish	33	2
Other	58	4
None/refuse	153	11
Born-again[c]	337	24

SAMPLE SUBGROUP BREAKDOWNS[a] *(continued)*

POLL 1 (N = 1400)

SUBGROUP	N	% OF SAMPLE
Executive/professional[d]	158	11
Other white-collar[d]	355	25
Blue-collar[d]	330	24
Unemployed	76	5
Retired	222	16
Student	61	4
Homemaker	150	11
Refuse	48	3

POLL 1 (N = 1,070 REGISTERED VOTERS)[c]

SUBGROUP	N	% OF SAMPLE
Male	520	49
Female	551	51
Black	72	7
White	955	89
Other	22	4
18–34	246	23
35–49	334	31
50+	490	46
Under $12,000	105	10
$12,000–$23,999	246	23
$24,000–$34,999	268	25
$35,000–$41,999	130	12
$42,000+	246	23
Refuse	76	6
Married	686	64
Never married	194	18
Widowed	81	8
Divorced/separated	85	8
Don't know/refuse	25	2
Northeast	227	21
Midwest	298	28
South	389	36
West	156	15

(continued)

SAMPLE SUBGROUP BREAKDOWNS[a] *(continued)*

POLL 1 (N = 1,070 REGISTERED VOTERS)[c]

SUBGROUP	N	% OF SAMPLE
Democrat	356	33
Independent[b]	393	37
Republican	303	28
City dweller	244	23
Suburban	274	26
Small town	312	29
Rural	217	20
Protestant	653	61
Catholic	253	24
Jewish	25	2
Other	36	3
None/refuse	104	10
Born-again[c]	272	25
Executive/professional[d]	121	11
Other white-collar[d]	271	25
Blue-collar[d]	252	23
Unemployed	56	5
Retired	194	18
Student	37	3
Homemaker	129	12
Refuse	10	2

POLL 2 (N = 506 PANELBACK OF POLL 1)

SUBGROUP	N	% OF SAMPLE
Male	243	48
Female	263	52
Black	46	9
White	442	88
Other	14	1
18–34	142	28
35–49	152	30
50+	212	42

SAMPLE SUBGROUP BREAKDOWNS[a] *(continued)*

POLL 2 (N = 506 PANELBACK OF POLL 1)

SUBGROUP	N	% OF SAMPLE
Under $12,000	66	13
$12,000–$23,999	126	25
$24,000–$34,999	130	26
$35,000–$41,999	51	10
$42,000+	101	20
Refuse	32	6
Married	344	68
Never married	71	14
Widowed	39	8
Divorced/separated	41	8
Don't know/refuse	5	1
Northeast	99	20
Midwest	133	26
South	191	38
West	77	15
Democrat	187	34
Independent[b]	174	36
Republican	136	28
City dweller	106	22
Suburban	146	29
Small town	151	29
Rural	103	21
Protestant	314	62
Catholic	127	25
Jewish	10	2
Other	16	3
None/refuse	40	8
Born-again[c]	137	27
Executive/professional[d]	53	10
Other white-collar[d]	121	24
Blue-collar[d]	116	23
Unemployed	25	5
Retired	106	21
Student	11	2
Homemaker	70	14
Refuse	4	1

(continued)

SAMPLE SUBGROUP BREAKDOWNS[a] *(continued)*

POLL 3 (N = 1,399)

SUBGROUP	N	% OF SAMPLE
Male	695	50
Female	704	50
Black	121	9
White	1,228	87
Other	27	2
18–34	434	31
35–49	391	28
50+	573	41
Under $12,000	168	12
$12,000–$23,999	364	26
$24,000–$34,999	336	24
$35,000–$41,999	112	8
$42,000+	305	22
Refuse	122	9
Married	924	66
Never married	224	16
Widowed	126	9
Divorced/separated	42	3
Don't know/refuse	26	2
Northeast	304	22
Midwest	374	27
South	491	35
West	230	16
Democrat	517	37
Independent[b]	467	33
Republican	375	27
City dweller	321	23
Suburban	378	27
Small town	434	31
Rural	252	18
Protestant	810	58
Catholic	364	26
Jewish	29	2
Other	70	5
None/refuse	112	8
Born-again[c]	390	28

SAMPLE SUBGROUP BREAKDOWNS[a] *(continued)*

POLL 3 (N = 1,399)

SUBGROUP	N	% OF SAMPLE
Executive/professional[d]	151	11
Other white-collar[d]	364	26
Blue-collar[d]	322	23
Unemployed	56	4
Retired	294	21
Student	55	4
Homemaker	125	9
Refuse	15	1

[a]Many other demographic questions were asked in this survey, and thus other subgroups were constructed or generated. This represents only a sampling. Also, for space reasons, categories shown here have been collapsed for age, income, party, religion, and occupation. Totals do not always equal 100% due both to rounding and to respondents who refused to answer.

[b]Independent total before party leaners were extracted.

[c]The following separate question was asked only of those who gave "Protestant" as their religious preference: "Do you consider yourself a born-again Christian resulting from a personal experience with Jesus Christ?"

[d]Categorized based on open-ended responses to an "occupation" question.

[e]The 330 self-reported unregistered voters have been subtracted from the total N of 1400 to produce this listing. It is included here since the text occasionally cites data from these registered respondents only. In all cases the use of registered voter data is made clear in text or endnotes, and unless otherwise noted, all data from Poll 1 cited in the text is taken from the total N of 1400.

• ☆ • ☆ •

Index